Power Places
and the
Master Builders
of Antiquity

"For decades, Frank Joseph has unraveled with compelling evidence the vast hidden and complicated history of Earth and the rise and fall of advanced civilizations across every continent. In his latest book, *Power Places and the Master Builders of Antiquity*, he unwinds the mystery of mysterious ancient sites left here by these advanced cultures whose knowledge of the multidimensional universe empowered them with expanded consciousness and otherworldly science. Break free from the old paradigms that lock you into a fixed illusion of hopeless reality by unleashing the unbridled beliefs, told brilliantly in Frank Joseph's writings, that shift us into immortal sovereignty. A courageous warrior of truth, Frank leaves you with the deepest yearning for the truth of where we came from and why we are here."

DEBBIE WEST, PRODUCER AND HOST OF
LOST KNOWLEDGE RADIO SHOW

Power Places
and the
Master Builders
of Antiquity

UNEXPLAINED MYSTERIES
OF THE PAST

Frank Joseph

Bear & Company
Rochester, Vermont

Bear & Company
One Park Street
Rochester, Vermont 05767
www.BearandCompanyBooks.com

SUSTAINABLE FORESTRY INITIATIVE   Certified Sourcing
www.sfiprogram.org
SFI-00854

Text stock is SFI certified

Bear & Company is a division of Inner Traditions International

Library of Congress Cataloging-in-Publication Data
Names: Joseph, Frank, author.
Title: Power Places and the Master Builders of Antiquity : Unexplained Mysteries
  of the Past / Frank Joseph.
Description: Rochester, Vermont ; Toronto, Canada : Bear & Company, [2018] |
  Includes bibliographical references and index.
Identifiers: LCCN 2017046800 (print) | LCCN 2018013510 (e-book) |
  ISBN 9781591433132 (pbk.) | ISBN 9781591433149 (e-book)
Subjects: LCSH: Civilization, Ancient. | Civilization—Extraterrestrial influences. |
  Curiosities and wonders.
Classification: LCC CB311 .J637 2018 (print) | LCC CB311 (e-book) |
  DDC 930.1—dc23
LC record available at https://lccn.loc.gov/2017046800

Printed and bound in the United States by Lake Book Manufacturing, Inc.
The text stock is SFI certified. The Sustainable Forestry Initiative® program
promotes sustainable forest management.

10   9   8   7   6   5   4   3   2   1

Text design by Debbie Glogover and layout by Virginia Scott Bowman
This book was typeset in Garamond Premier Pro with Nocturne and Trade
Gothic used as display typefaces

To send correspondence to the author of this book, mail a first-class letter to the
author c/o Inner Traditions • Bear & Company, One Park Street, Rochester, VT
05767, and we will forward the communication, or contact the author directly at
www.ancientamerican.com.

Contents

SECTION I

Master Builders of Antiquity

SECTION II

Ancient Unsolved Mysteries

SECTION VI

Altered States and the Afterlife

SECTION VII

Numinous Nature

Foreword

I have known author Frank Joseph for a quarter century, dating back to his first book about sacred sites and power places. What people might not realize at first is how Frank personally explores and studies the places he writes about.

I happened to work at the publishing house that released Frank's first book and it was a personal joy and privilege for me to promote the book. I remember how Frank and I worked out a slide show for the national bookfair held that year at the Anaheim Convention Center in California. We rented a private room for Frank's slides of sacred sites and power places and pretty much packed the room. Frank narrated the picture show, something he continues to do today with much relish (although he's now updated his photo presentation to Power Point pictures from his laptop). Frank always speaks with great enthusiasm and knowledge about the places he has explored and studied as a journalist. He climbs hillsides, jumps into boats, and dons a diving suit to get a first-person perspective wherever possible.

Well, I always wanted Frank to write a big sequel to his first book on power places; somehow I believe Frank always did, too. Nonetheless, he moved along successfully as a writer with something like three dozen other books, all on parallel subjects. He has written about synchronicity, early American civilizations, runes, dolphins, and many other ancient mysteries around the world. All of these other books, of course, are fascinating and eye-opening, as he explores the mysteries of both the modern and ancient world.

Meanwhile, Frank's pent-up appetite for studies of power places and sacred sites of the Earth led to many magazine articles. Frank worked for a while at *FATE* magazine in marketing and as a writer and also served as an editor in chief at *Ancient American* magazine.

I am very familiar with *FATE* magazine. It was for several years a part of the same publishing house where I once worked on Frank's first book. To some small degree while there, I helped build the distribution of the magazine and managed the advertising department for *FATE*. It was at this publishing house where I also met the editor of the magazine, Phyllis Galde. She subsequently purchased the magazine and moved it down the road to her place.

Frank followed Phyllis to serve awhile on staff and also to write for *FATE*, contributing many articles. Many of his best articles from this long-revered magazine are now collected here in this wonderfully illustrated book.

There is something for everyone in this colorful collection. Are you interested in pyramids, UFOs, the Templars, Atlantis, the Bermuda Triangle, or the Ark of the Covenant? Then read this book. How about communicating with the dead or elemental beings? Read on.

One thing you can always be certain about when you read a Frank Joseph book. He puts his entire heart and soul into exploring and describing the ancient mysteries of our world. And he includes a lot of wonderful illustrations to bring it all home for you. What could be more interesting?

VON BRASCHLER

VON BRASCHLER, a former faculty member at Omega Institute for Holistic Studies, has led workshops through the United States and the United Kingdom in the areas of consciousness development, time, chakra healing, pet healing, and dream work. He is a trained massage therapist, pet therapist, energy healer, and Kirlian photographer. A lifetime member of the Theosophical Society, he is the author of several books, including *Seven Secrets of Time Travel* and *Confessions of a Reluctant Ghost Hunter.* Previously, Braschler worked at Llewellyn Publications, an independent publisher of books for body, mind, and spirit. He is a frequent magazine, television, and radio contributor.

Strange, but True

In an earlier century, as a twelve-year-old student, I was sternly warned by Dominican nuns at St. Joseph Catholic Grammar School in Homewood, Illinois, to avoid a neighborhood drugstore, where copies of the demonic monthly *FATE* magazine lured Christian souls into Satan's clutches. It would have horrified me at the time to know that someday, in an inconceivably distant future, my words would appear in the Devil's own journal. True, *FATE* has played fair with "pagan" and non-Christian concepts. But, because its writers and readers are nondenominationally interested in every manifestation of the other-worldly, extraordinary places like Father Dobberstein's Grotto of the Redemption and Bosnia's Virgin Mary apparitions at Medugorje are also favorably reviewed in *FATE*.

I've been working for the magazine since 1989, beginning with the "Visionary of Atlantis," included in this anthology of my *FATE* articles. Writing them has been a life-changing experience, because they opened up whole vistas of existence I knew little or nothing about, until forced to investigate. There was the incredible responsiveness of water to human interaction, both ancient and contemporary sacred sites across America and around the world, prehistoric pyramids in China, a lost city in the Pacific Ocean, the Bermuda Triangle, modern-day prophets, nature spirits, snake handlers, reincarnation, communicating with the dead, psychic viewing of the Great Sphinx with our readers—the variety and scope of these alternative realities was not only mind-altering, but also conscience-expanding.

FATE magazine has been in continual publication since 1948. As such, it is America's longest-running periodical devoted to expert opinions and personal experiences about every conceivable paranormal and metaphysical topic. "No product, especially a magazine, can stay around for so many years unless it meets a need,"[1] noted Carl Llewellyn Weschcke, who acquired *FATE* forty years later from its founders. The magazine's premier article was by a Minnesota-born aviator and businessman, describing his encounter with flying saucers near Mount Rainier, Washington. Kenneth Arnold's sighting is generally considered the first observation of its kind, triggering a popular interest in unidentified flying objects that continues to the present day. The report also propelled *FATE* magazine to national prominence overnight with its first issue, attracting more than 100,000 subscribers over the next seven years, with hundreds of thousands of additional rack sales in book stores, coffee shops, and a variety of public venues across the United States.

While our interest in reading magazines has faded, our curiosity about topics explored in *FATE* has not. In 2001, the magazine passed to its editor in chief, Phyllis Galde. She steered it through the economic typhoons of 2008 that sank many other and far larger publications. A report from the Brookings Institution five years later revealed that the number of newspapers per million people fell from more than eighteen hundred to less than four hundred. Going on seventy years of smooth sailing and rough waters, *FATE* is still afloat, thanks as much to tireless Phyllis as to her loyal readers, who continue to renew the lifelong treasures of intellectual and spiritual enrichment and enlightenment through the broad diversity of alternative thought offered for consideration. They have come to appreciate that the world is not entirely what consensus reality insists, as demonstrated by the mostly unconventional, occasionally suppressed or neglected, sometimes heretical information and conclusions presented in the following pages.

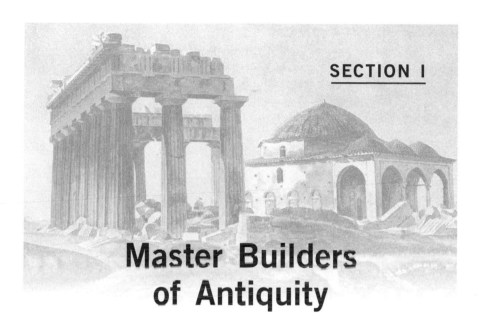

Master Builders of Antiquity

1

Old World Connections with New World Sacred Centers

"An author writes about the country he knows," observed Ernest Hemingway. "And the country he knows is in his heart."[1] Such a country transcends arbitrary map boundaries and political borders by which nations identify themselves. The places in question exist on every continent. They are the chakras of Mother Earth—points of focused, spiritual energies welling up from the bowels of the planet, or instilled in the site by concentrated human will. They are great energy sources from which we can replenish and empower ourselves, if only we knew their secrets.

So much has already been written about sacred sites overseas that Americans are left with the impression that their own country has few if any of its own and, in any case, that its sites are far less significant or impressive than foreign locations. They imagine that only a European countryside featuring a Stone Age megalith, or an antediluvian pyramid standing in the Egyptian desert are mystically endowed. While some prehistoric monuments may qualify as sacred sites, more recent, even modern structures may be no less charged with supernal energies. Their power emanates from placement within a particular Earth field, or derives from some special human impact they received.

Other spiritualized centers owe nothing of their greatness to external influences, because they are the pure outpouring of Nature's soul. To disabuse readers of the impression that America is devoid of such locations, they are included in our description of European sacred sites—foremost among them, Britain's Stonehenge. Today, visitors are kept beyond arms' length by an encircling cordon of staked ropes and an elaborate security system.

These were installed after some of the megaliths were badly damaged in the early 1990s by persons spray-painting the porous stones. Modern vandals were preceded by the Romans nearly two thousand years ago. They partially tore down the original circle of standing megaliths because native Druids were using the location as a base for Keltic resistance. First-century Druids were not the builders, but were merely following a tradition begun long before them in Neolithic times.

The masterminds who designed and set up this sophisticated astronomical computer around 3000 B.C.E. are lost to history. But the resonant power they established continues to attract visitors from around the world. Older than Stonehenge and no less potent is Ireland's Newgrange, the oldest intact building on Earth, predating the Egyptian pyramids by at least six centuries.

An hour's drive north of Dublin, Newgrange sits on top of a high hill overlooking the Boyne Valley. Built 5,200 years ago, it is a huge mound of earth covering a large, stone-lined chamber connected to the exterior by a narrow corridor. The entrance to the structure is a face with five hundred tons of white quartz and flanked by imposing monoliths emblazoned with spiral and lozenge designs. Once a year, during sunrise of the winter solstice, a shaft of golden light snakes along the floor of the corridor to illuminate a triple spiral on the far rear wall of the chamber. This annual occurrence exemplifies the Neolithic builders' belief that the human soul is linked eternally to cycles of birth, death, and rebirth, as paralleled by the yearly highlighted triple spiral. The number three is traditionally associated with eternity, while the spiral is a universal symbol of soul, mimicking its perpetual evolution.

Off the south coast of Scotland, among the Hebrides, is one of the strangest islands on Earth. Resembling some impossibly man-made mausoleum, Staffa is the result of a cataclysmic volcanic outburst that took place millions of years ago. Magma boiled to the surface and was frozen by sub-zero temperatures into great blocks of hardened lava. Its greatest feature is an immense cavern known as Fingal's Cave, which resembles a cathedral for Titans. Everywhere, huge square columns of basalt arch high overhead toward a monumental dome. When the tide surges into this massive interior space and hurtles itself against a wall at the far end, the resultant crash is deafening. Nothing and no one lives on barren Staffa, although visitors can reach its shores if the seas allow. Far more than a geologic curiosity, the island and its cavern have attracted religious worshippers for fifty centuries, from Stone Age sailors to Viking raiders who gave Staffa its name (literally, "staves," a reference to the columnar basalt), to modern pilgrims who sense the powerful accumulation of Earth and sea energies here.

Figure 1.1. Fingal's Cave on the Hebrides island of Staffa, photographed around 1900

On the European continent, Medugorje is a small town in the Croatian countryside famous for reported apparitions of the Blessed Virgin, beginning in the mid-1980s. These appearances are supposed to take place on a rock-strewn hill, its barren summit scorched black with the ashes of thousands of votive candles and littered with crucifixes. It still drew visitors from around the world, despite a murderous war that raged around the place the divine Queen of Peace chose for her modern manifestation. Catholics and non-Catholics alike tell of the strange appearance of the sun when viewed from atop the Hill of Apparitions. More commonly, pilgrims experience a powerful spiritual presence in its vicinity. In any case, Medugorje is a developing sacred site Christians and followers of the Blessed Virgin find inspiring.

One of the world's most overlooked centers of its kind lies on the northwest coast of Turkey. Here, more than three thousand years ago, the foremost city of the late Bronze Age encompassed palaces and temples unmatched for their splendor within a concentric series of immense walls. The crown of thirteenth-century B.C.E. civilization, Ilios was the legendary capital of Troy, lost after the fall of classical times, until a self-styled German archaeologist, Heinrich Schliemann, brought it back into the light. While the war that consumed the city around 1240 B.C.E. irrevocably imprinted the very stonework with energies of profound human drama, Ilios was a sacred center long before its fiery destruction. It was the seat of Apollo, the sun god, the patron of creativity and beauty.

Visitors to the archaeological zone are surprised to find the environs little changed from Homer's description in the *Iliad*. From the Trojan battlements, one can still see the unobstructed plain where the great conflict was fought, and beyond to the seashore, long ago crowded with a thousand ships of the Greek invasion fleet. Instances of clairaudience are known to occur at Ilios, together with other paranormal phenomena largely associated with past-life experiences. A focal point for these is located at the open-air theater, which is preserved in good condition. Here, the receptive visitor will find an opportunity for meditation.

Across the Aegean Sea on the south coast of Greece, the columns of Delphi still stand high up the slope of Mt. Parnassus, on the Gulf of Corinth. Where today's tourists gather year-round, in ancient times initiates into the mysteries of Apollo and Poseidon followed threads of destiny to the Pythia, a priestess who spoke of the future while in an altered state of consciousness. Delphi was the leading sacred site of the entire Classical World, and its attraction to people in our time proves it has not lost its deep, spiritual resonance. It was preceded in significance by Delos, a small island in the eastern Mediterranean Sea, birthplace of divine twins associated, respectively, with lunar and solar—feminine and masculine energies: Artemis and Apollo. Most temples on Delos were built in their honor.

The island's high ground is Mt. Cynthos, with a shrine to sky father Zeus at its summit. Some one hundred feet below, facing west, is the very ancient and megalithic Temple of Apollo, raised on the site of the god's birth. It was from here that he took the *omphalos,* the Navel Stone of power and prophecy, to Delphi. Delos shares the Aegean with Crete, where the groves of Knossos still flourish as they did when Minoan kings held sway over this part of the world nearly forty centuries ago. The colorful ruins of sacred architecture, including the bull-leaping arena, are all that stand of that splendid epoch.

Southward across the Mediterranean, Egypt is most famous for her Great Pyramid, but to walk down the monumental Avenue of Sphinxes toward the colossal pylons of Karnak in the Upper Nile Valley is to achieve a personal highlight in one's life. Here is the best preserved of Pharaonic civilization, a living house of grandeur inscribed with thousands of hieroglyphic texts and occupied by colossal representations of the gods and goddesses. Yet, for all its outsized stonework, visitors often speak of a lightness and buoyancy of spirit at Karnak.

On the other side of the world, Uxmal (pronounced "Ooshmahl") is an atmospheric ceremonial center set like a crystal in Mexico by its Maya builders more than a thousand years ago. Its Pyramid of the Magician is shaped like a gargantuan egg. A serpent writhes in stone on its walls, disgorging an egg from its jaws. Visitors stroll from the unusual pyramid to the Governor's Palace, gleaming like bleached bones in the Yucatán sun, its lofty, corbelled arches gracefully pointing toward the cobalt blue heavens. Behind it is the ceremonial ball court, where a ritual game imitated the daily struggle of the sun to cross the sky. A small, elaborately carved stone seat still stands alone before the Governor's Palace. To sit on that prehistoric throne with the measureless jungle at one's back is to conjure images of empires and spiritual powers sleeping among the silent ruins.

Far away to the north, in the Ohio Valley, Mound City consists of twenty-three prehistoric but skillfully constructed earthworks on thirteen acres, surrounded by a squarish embankment. This ancient site near the Scioto River is a necropolis, a city of the dead, but not only a cemetery. The departed here are part of a sacred ceremonial center, where this life and the next converge. Mound City's precisely constructed pyramids contain the cremated remains of several hundred persons from a lost civilization that flourished from the first to fifth centuries C.E. Archaeologists label that period of North American prehistory "Hopewell," after the farmer on whose adjacent property a turn-of-the-century excavation was made. They do not, however, know how this otherwise nameless, ancient people actually referred to themselves.

The Hopewell lived in numerous villages along the river valleys and were skilled in working stone, especially into the likenesses of birds, reptiles, and human heads. They operated a vast commercial trading network, importing copper from the Upper Great Lakes region, obsidian from what is today Yellowstone National Park, shark teeth from Chesapeake Bay, mica from the Smoky Mountains, seashells from the Gulf of Mexico, and silver from Ontario. These far-flung imports were not only used as luxury items, but also for ritual purposes. The archaeological zone known as Mound City was the shaman's special arena, where all the high magic of a spiritualized community was dramatized.

A holy man selected the location for the precinct by a geomancy,

Figure 1.2. Mound City

or ritual interpretation of the landscape, and directed the creation of the mounds according to the telluric forces in evidence at the site. The structures were methodically created to contain the dead, to memorialize them and, most importantly, to continue serving the descendants for generations thereafter as spiritual powerhouses for the soul's growth. At the center of a typical mound, the Hopewell raised a circular clay platform, upon which the cremated remains of a socially prominent person were laid, together with pottery shards, stone and copper tools, broken spear points of obsidian, flint, or garnet, and pebbles. Researchers from the Smithsonian Institution in Washington, D.C., scientifically investigated Mound City for the first time in 1848, but the site was requisitioned by the U.S. Army as a training camp during World War One, and many of the ceremonial structures were destroyed.

The ancient necropolis was finally rescued from total oblivion when it was declared a national monument in 1923. Since then, restoration has been proceeding under the auspices of the Ohio State Historical Society. The excavators retrieved artifacts from the earthworks as strange as they are beautiful. Some of the structures contained the bones of an extinct mastodon, a creature that vanished from the American plains

about ten thousand years ago. The Hopewell may have preserved shamanic paraphernalia of the last ice age. A Mound of pipes enfolded two
hundred stone bowls exquisitely carved to represent animals and men.

The most visually attractive of the earthworks has been cut open
to reveal the splendid entombment of four men who were laid out on a
floor entirely covered with oversized flakes of jewel-like mica. Imported
from as far away as Georgia for mortuary reasons, the glittering, pastel
wafers were joined by elk and bear teeth, metal ornaments, large obsidian points, a cache of five thousand polished mother-of-pearl beads, and
toad and raven effigy pipes. Copper armor was also found, including
two helmets or headdresses, one with three pairs of copper antlers, the
other in the likeness of a bear with hinged ears and legs attached by
tiny rivets. The workmanship was of a high quality. This grave signifies
a vast technological difference between the ancient Hopewell and the
historic Shawnee who occupied the region at the time of early European
settlement.

The Shawnee knew nothing of Mound City, made no claims to it,
and did not have the large-scale social organization that went into con-
structing the earthworks. Some fundamental connections with ancient
Egypt appear in the site's square embankment, which shares precisely
the same area—13.6 acres—with the base of the Nile Delta's Great
Pyramid. Moreover, the twenty-three burial earthworks at Ohio's prehistoric necropolis find their counterparts in the same, original number of tombs at the Giza Plateau. Ephraim George Squier (1821–1888)
and Edwin Hamilton Davis (1811–1888), surveyors who first mapped
the area in 1845, concluded that the Mound City structures were built
by immigrants from Yucatán, perhaps Maya culture bearers interested in Ohio Valley traded goods. Since Squier and Davis arrived at
their nineteenth-century supposition, material evidence supporting a
Mesoamerican connection has come to light in the form of an excavated Hopewell necklace made of parakeet bills. Also recovered from a
Mound City earthwork was a copper ornament fashioned to represent a
parrot. Neither bird is native to the Ohio Valley.

Moreover, Hopewell hunters and warriors were armed with the same kind of throwing stick used in the Valley of Mexico. Circumstances surrounding the sudden disappearance of Mound City's residents also suggests Mesoamerican influence. The Maya regulated their society by a sacred calendar, the largest division of which was the so-called Long Count, a four-hundred-year period opened and closed by massive, fundamental changes, including large-scale migrations. The history of Hopewell occupation at Mound City covered a four-century time span that may have started with Maya immigration to the Ohio Valley, two thousand years ago.

According to the same ceremonial calendar, the site was abandoned after four hundred years, its inhabitants returning to Yucatán. Whatever their origins or fate, they left behind an impressive, magical memorial to their vanished greatness. The number and arrangement of the mounds form a ritual pattern, the meaning of which has been lost. It is therefore impossible to identically reconstruct the Hopewell ceremonies that took place in Mound City. The squarish earthwork perimeter with rounded corners resembles the outline of a house, with gaps where doors should be at the north and south ends. In Native American tradition, north is the Spirit Direction; south, the Direction of Becoming.

Perhaps ritual enactments began when initiates entered through the northern portal of death, participated in shamanic ceremonies among the mortuary mounds, then departed through the southern exit of rebirth. Such an interpretation is suggested by the close proximity of the Scioto to the northern gap. Along the opposite banks, the live-in village of a Hopewell town was located. Crossing a river is a universal human archetype for death. Hence, traveling over the Scioto from their homes to the necropolis might have had the same significance as fording the River Styx did for ancient Greeks. Leaving Mound City through the southern Direction of Becoming implies that the rituals that took place within the sacred precinct dealt with death and transfiguration.

The existence of a reincarnation or rebirth cult at work here has been underscored by some of the physical evidence excavated over the past one hundred years. The Death Mask Mound, largest of the site's earthworks, contained fragments of a human skull that had been sawed and drilled for use as a mask, probably worn by a master of ceremonies more than sixteen centuries ago. The same mound was also a burial site for thirteen adult males accompanied by effigies shaped to resemble falcons or parrots wrought in copper. The bird is another universal symbol for the human soul, and copper is associated with the sun and immortality.

Of the hundreds of expertly carved stone pipes recovered from Mound City, most depict animals that clearly signify death and rebirth, such as the raven, serpent, and bear. Those carved into human heads may be portraits of the deceased; at least some of them were probably shamans. Tobacco was and is revered as the holiest herb. The mildly altered state of consciousness it produces was considered intimately connected with the spirit world. The pipes were not smoked for pleasure alone, but for purposes of communication with entities on the Other Side. Indeed, Mound City is a simulacrum of that parallel existence. Archaeologists believe it was valued as a visible representation of the Hopewell heaven for leading families of the power elite. While this speculation seems plausible, the overall implication of the site suggests it was far more than a political cemetery for the privileged dead. Rather, they were part of the spiritual empowerment generated within the sacred center by the entire community.

Eight hundred miles west, in the state of Kansas, stories of a splendid, ancient civilization with a mystical center at its heart may seem too farfetched for belief. But the first white men to hear those tales were Spanish conquistadors, who overthrew the Aztec Empire during the early sixteenth century. In the insatiable quest for gold, they were informed by subjected Mexicans about Quivira, the Seven Cities of Cibola, allegedly an old, powerful state of magnificent temples and high magic, where the gold of the sun god was allegedly preserved. Only a few aged advisors of Emperor Moctezuma III supposedly knew of Cibola-Quivira's whereabouts, and shared their knowledge with some younger followers of the rapidly declining Aztec religion. They acted as guides for the greedy Spaniards, who mounted an expedition in search of the legendary Seven Cities of Gold under the command of Francisco Vazquez de Coronado in 1541.

Along the way, he was encouraged by various tribal and pueblo peoples who had heard at least something of Cibola, and urged the foreigners ever northward. Finally, Coronado and his forty men reached what is now central Kansas. The Aztec guides had followed their instructions faithfully, and the landscape matched descriptions provided by their elders back in Mexico. But not one of the Seven Cities of Gold was to be found. Not even their ruins. All that the Spaniards saw were scattered, underpopulated villages of grass huts inhabited by hunter-gatherers. Coronado's disappointment was keenly felt.

"I arrived at the province they call Quivira, to which the guides were conducting me, and where they had described to me houses of stone with many stories, and not only are they not of stone, but of straw, but the people in them are as barbarous as all those whom I have ever seen and passed before this."[2]

Over the next 430 years, the lost Seven Cities of Gold were consigned to legend. But in the 1960s, Waldo R. Wedel of the Smithsonian Institution excavated the first of five unusual structures in Rice and McPherson Counties, in not only central Kansas, but the precise center of the North American continent. Referred to as "council circles," the ruins are circular mounds sixty to ninety feet wide, averaging about three feet high.[3] They are surrounded by shallow ditches and show evidence of intense burning covered over by numerous sandstone boulders. Pits contained the bones of children and adult skulls. The local Wichita Indians knew nothing of the council circles, but after a more than four-century lapse, stories of Cibola began to circulate again.

Nothing conclusive about the excavations was obtained until 1982, when archaeologist R. Clark Mallam identified a startling feature nearby. It was the image of a gigantic snake cut into the ground like a reverse image, or intaglio. From its gaping jaws emerged a huge, oval shape. Subsequent tests of the 160-foot-long effigy revealed that it was oriented not only to the three Rice County council circles, but more significantly, to the winter and summer solstices. The fires that long ago burned in the pitted mounds were lit when the sun's position was opposite the tail of the snake. Solar alignments of the serpent intaglio and council circles suggest that the lost Cibola-Quivira does indeed lie below the plains of central Kansas.

The "gold" of which the Aztecs spoke, however, may not have anything to do with the metal sought by Coronado. Rather, the gold of this vanished culture was far more precious: sunlight. Such an interpretation is supported by the Aztec description of the Seven Cities of Gold. Seven separate and distinct "cities" may have never existed in prehistoric Kansas. Instead, "seven" might be understood as a sacred number defining the essential, esoteric principles of Cibola. The number seven signified the completion of cycles for many cultures around the ancient world and was associated with the movement of the sun, together with serpent symbolism, which describes the Rice County effigy and its solar orientation.

The real mystery is: Who were the sophisticated astronomer-engineers that created the serpent intaglio and its council circles in the middle of Kansas, three thousand or more years ago? Why did they choose such a remote site, hundreds of miles from the nearest civilization, to fashion their solar observatory? The mystery is made all the more curious when we learn that there are only two other snake images of this kind anywhere. One is the Great Serpent Mound, a 1,200-foot-long earthworks atop a hill in Adams County, southern Ohio, and a 110-foot-long snake disgorging an egg-shaped cairn from its mouth, likewise on a hilltop, near Loch Nell, in western Scotland.

Both the Ohio and the Scottish effigies share a common construction date, circa 1200 B.C.E. This is the same date archaeo-astronomers assign to the near miss of a comet that bombarded the Earth with a barrage of meteoric material sufficient to cause the collapse of late Bronze Age civilizations across Europe, Asia Minor, and the Near and

Middle East, even as far as Shang-dynasty China. Could the American and Scottish snake mounds spitting out an egg shape have been originally designed to represent a sky serpent, or comet, disgorging an asteroid or large meteor? If so, the survivors of some European culture may have sought refuge in both the northern British Isles and North America, where they constructed uniquely identical earth effigies as memorials to the cataclysm.

While these are the only geoglyphs of their kind, the concept they express was familiar to dynastic Egyptians, preclassical and classical Greeks, and the Maya, where the serpent-and-egg theme appears in stone relief on the flanks of Uxmal's Pyramid of the Magician, itself an egg-shaped structure, in the Yucatán jungle. The snake-egg image was regarded everywhere as the symbol of healing, regeneration, and rebirth, attributes connected with the sun. The Kansas intaglio's relationship to the council circles may extend to the local environment, comprising an organic whole. As Mallam noticed during a flyover of the site, "the council circles, demarcated by dark-green patches, seemed to be located virtually in the center of this network. It was as if we were seeing an architectural order."[4]

The intaglio's resemblance to Ohio's Great Serpent Mound is even closer than its common design suggests. The Adams County earthwork, like its Kansas counterpart, is aligned to the solstices. Clearly, these two effigies were created by the same landscape engineers, whoever they may have been. And what does its resemblance to identical European and Mayan egg-disgorging snakes imply? Is the Rice County site the remains of a transatlantic visit during the remote past? Remarkably, its memory lived on in the traditions of the Aztecs long after they ceased to have any physical contact with the place they called Cibola.

Mallam was obviously enthusiastic about the strange site: "I believe that in this cosmological conviction the serpent intaglio functioned as a 'life metaphor.' It signified and expressed through its placement and orientation the natural and cyclical processes of death, rebirth, and the regenerative power of life. Inherent in this theme are certain basic

Native American concepts. Cross-culturally, the serpent represents primal chaos, disruption, disharmony and dissolution, and continual life renewal through annual shedding of its skin and hibernation. The theme of cyclical order and centrality became visibly evident at least twice each year as *hierophanies*—physical manifestations of something sacred. During the solstices, the sacredness of the headwaters defined, reaffirmed, and intensified the arrangement of cultural symbols: Cosmos emerges from chaos, summer out of winter, and life from death."[5] Astronomically related to the Rice County serpent, though seven hundred miles away, a lonely boulder stands atop a hill overlooking thousands of commuters daily speeding by on the expressway below, to and from the city of Chicago, about two hours' drive east. This part of northern Illinois is flat farmland, so the appearance of even the fifty-foot-high hill crowned with its solitary stone seems outstanding. Across from the hill is an adjacent hill, flatter, but of almost equal height, and in fact, both are referred together as "Indian Hills." The stone in question rests at the highest point, the apex, of the more pyramidal hill to the north. Despite its "Indian" attribution, Sauk tribes that inhabited the area until the mid-nineteenth century did not haul up the two-ton burden to its lofty position. They did, however, venerate it as a Manitou, or holy object, left behind by "shamans of the Moon," who set up the hilltop altar in thanks for their survival from the Great Flood.[6] Before moving on to the north, the shamans suffused the precinct with their potent energies.

The stone is probably a glacial remnant from the last ice age, but investigators believe at least some of it was worked to shape its pointy top. Centuries of continuous weathering have effaced all traces of human modification, however. Getting the massy monolith moved up the hill's steeply inclined slope self-evidently merited a major collective endeavor. Given the presumed technological limitations of pre-Columbian man, we can only speculate how it was achieved. It is the same dilemma we face when confronted by the creation of the sacred site with which this article began: Britain's Stonehenge. Nor does our comparison with the more famous site on the Salisbury Plain end there. In the Arthurian tradition of Stonehenge, Merlin the magician supposedly levitated the ponderous monoliths through the air and set them up in perfectly concentric circles.

A surviving legend among the Sauk recounts that the ancient shamans, through the power of their magic, floated the Indian Hills' Stone from its original location at the bottom of a river, and set it gently down to face and pay homage to the moon goddess at the summit of the hill where today it perches. And as the lunar alignments of Stonehenge are generally recognized today, so the Illinois monolith is oriented to the most northerly rising of the moon. The orientation is still observable from the nearby hill across the expressway. Judging from the precise position and the not insubstantial physical labor that went into erecting it, the Indian Hills' Stone apparently meant a great deal to whoever set it up.

While any connection between a Midwestern monolith and Britain's Stonehenge may seem farfetched to conventional archaeologists, Sauk traditions of moon-worshipping shamans and ancient European myths of a prehistoric, worldwide civilization should at least give us pause for reflection. Once each year, the moon still seems to rise from out of the Indian Hills' Stone itself, then balance for a minute or less at its pointy apex before resuming its journey across the night sky. At such an effective moment the monolith—intensely black because backlit and suffused by a temporary lunar radiance—does indeed resemble an altar to the Moon, as told by the Sauk.

The alignment must have been particularly important to prehistoric Americans, as suggested by the same orientation anciently observed 350 miles away in central Ohio at the sprawling Newark mound group at least two thousand years ago. The reappearance of the moon at its most northerly point undoubtedly heralded an annual, universal beginning of some kind related to the resurgence of feminine power. Lunar energies are especially associated with psychic phenomena—dreams, visions, telepathy, healing, clairvoyance, clairaudience—all elements that belong to the shamanic experience recalled by native Sauk.

When the moon rises to its most northerly point, it exerts its strongest tidal or gravitational pull on our planet and assumes its largest, brightest appearance in the night sky. While the latter visual manifestation generates a dramatic special effect each year at the Indian Hills' Stone, lunar influence on human behavior at that time reaches its optimum potency. Clearly, all this was understood and applied in forgotten ways by the stone's astronomer-shamans. They eventually migrated somewhere farther north, the Sauk remembered, perhaps to build Aztalan, a thirteenth-century C.E. celestial observatory on the banks of Wisconsin's Crawfish River, about one hundred miles to the north. Like the Indian Hills' Stone, Aztalan features a massive, roughly carved monolith originally aligned with the peak of nearby Christmas Hill in alignment with sunrise of the winter solstice.

These fragments of the deep past are all the pieces left to us from the grand mosaic of American prehistory. But if its builders and worshippers have long since vanished into time, the energies with which they imbued their creations resonate still in sacred sites across our continent and around the globe.

2

Ancient American Cities of the Sun

The most spectacular of all the ancient human-engineered sacred centers in North America lies just across the Mississippi River from the modern city of St. Louis. An earthen step pyramid rises in four gigantic terraces above the southern Illinois plain. Comprising 22 million cubic feet of soil, its base in excess of fourteen acres is larger than that of Egypt's Great Pyramid. Exceeded only by the Mexican pyramids at Teotihuacán and Cholula, it is the largest prehistoric structure north of the Rio Grande. Known as Monks Mound after the French Trappist monks who briefly occupied it in the early nineteenth century, the Illinois pyramid is so huge its flat top easily accommodated over four thousand persons during a Harmonic Convergence meeting in 1987.

During its hey-day nine hundred years earlier, the turf-covered colossus may have been entirely encased in clay decorated with fabulous geometric designs painted blue, red, and yellow. More certainly, a great, steeply gabled wooden temple then occupied the summit. The building was 48 feet wide and 105 feet long, bringing the original height of the pyramid to over 150 feet. From its lofty vantage point, the chief priest or regent would have looked out over a 224-acre ceremonial city completely surrounded by a twelve-foot-high wall more than two miles

Figure 2.1. Artist's re-creation of Monks Mound near Collinsville, Illinois

long. More than eighty thousand logs arranged in a stockade with regularly spaced watchtowers were plastered with a white limestone cement. The entire metropolitan area covered nearly six square miles over a 2,200-acre tract.

Behind the walls south of Monks Mound spread an open-air plaza where sporting events alternated with religious ceremonies and market activities. Beyond the plaza shimmered an artificial lake reflecting a trio of large pyramidal structures, a conical mound, and a platform mound, which contained the body of a forty-five-year-old man laid out on a grave of silver mica flecks imported from the Carolinas. Surrounding him were over twenty thousand polished marine shell disc beads from the Gulf Coast and three hundred sacrificed young girls. More than

120 mounds of various shapes and sizes adorned the area, though only sixty-eight still survive. More than fifty million cubic feet of earth went into their construction.

To the west, the observer atop Monks Mound would have been able to see a twenty-foot-high circle of cedar posts painted bright red and arranged in an astronomical position 410 feet in diameter. Known today as Woodhenge, it was an observatory to chart significant celestial events, such as the winter solstice sunrise aligned with the first platform level of the big pyramid itself. Woodhenge also computed the positions of the Pleiades and other constellations of religious and agricultural importance.

An estimated twenty thousand people resided within and beyond the walls of Cahokia, although no one knows the real name of the great city. Investigators do know, however, that it did not evolve slowly over the years, but was built suddenly, almost as though transported from some previous location, around 2500 B.C.E., just when Egypt's Great Pyramid was built. After 900 C.E., it was the dominant capital of the Mississippian culture. Then, about 1100 C.E., internal violence of some kind occurred, part of the wall was burned, the leaders fled, and Cahokia society rapidly deteriorated. By the time Monks Mound was seen by the first white explorers in the late seventeenth century, it was overgrown and long abandoned.

Who the great civilizers of southern Illinois may have been, where they came from, and what became of them are questions archaeologists cannot yet answer with material evidence. Links with Mesoamerica, however, seem obvious; connections made all the more suspicious by Cahokia's own foundation date in the early tenth century, the same period in which the Maya were evacuating their pyramidal cities in Yucatán.

Archaeologists speculatively call ancient Cahokia the City of the Sun, from Woodhenge's solar orientations. The sun has long been associated with ultimate power, an association implicit in the dominating aspect of Monks Mound itself. To be sure, that power was once commercial and political but it was also spiritual, if only in the sense that the enormous effort exerted by thousands of workers and artisans necessary to create the Cahokia megalopolis needed something transcending material and civic motives. Like the builders of Khufu's pyramid, they were not slaves. They were more likely inspired laborers and craftsmen motivated by a religious ideal whose priestly spokesmen convinced them they were doing God's work in building the City of the Sun.

Comparison with Egypt's Great Pyramid does not end with Monks Mound's relative size and the motivation of its builders. Both structures are aligned to true north and both are oriented to solar solstices. In fact, the Egyptians referred to Khufu's pyramid as the Mountain of Ra, their sun god. While Monks Mound may be only a little more than a thousand years old, the earliest settlement at Cahokia has been carbon dated to around 3000 B.C.E., the same era as Egypt's first dynasty. Hesiod and other early Greek historians wrote of an *ecumene*, a worldwide civilization that flourished in a prehistoric Age of Gold. Could that ecumene have once touched both America and Egypt, where their solar principles—religious, scientific, and political—were preserved for thousands of years, generation after generation?

Angel Mounds was founded at roughly the same time Cahokia began to decline, around 1100 C.E., although the southern Indiana ceremonial center was substantially smaller. Some believe that site was built by migrants fleeing social dislocation at Cahokia. An important cultural link with Cahokia is a common solar alignment. The doorway of Angel Mounds' chief temple was oriented to sunrise of the summer solstice, the same alignment occurring at Monks Mound. Cahokia is, in fact, physically linked to Angel Mounds by the Mississippi and Ohio Rivers.

About four thousand residents inhabited the 103-acre settlement, which included eleven earthen platform mounds surmounted by temples and palaces made of wooden posts and dried grass daubed over with white adobe. The mounds were interspersed with two hundred secular dwellings, some for winter, others for summer. Their walls were decorated with geometric themes colored red, yellow, and blue, lending

Figure 2.2. Photograph of Angel Mounds' reconstructed wall
by Heironymous Rowe

the site a cheerful aspect. Nearby were numerous gardens of corn, beans, pumpkin, gourds, and sunflowers. Pecans were gathered in a lovely grove beside a step pyramid forty-four feet high and four acres in area. There was an unusual plaza sunk like a great bowl into the ground. Ceremonial, athletic, and market activities took place within this broad depression.

Originally, the site was almost entirely surrounded by a river channel, practically rendering Angel Mounds an island. Whether or not this river channel was made by the ancient inhabitants is still a matter of professional debate. In any case, Angel Mounds was inexplicably abandoned by its leaders and most of its population about 1310 C.E. Why they left and where they went remain as mysteries still bedeviling scholars' best efforts to understand America's prehistory. The inhabitants left behind no signs of disease, war, social upheaval, crop failures, overfishing or hunting, earthquakes, or severe weather. For the next 140 years, the site was occupied off and on by diverse, small numbers of primitive wanderers who knew little or nothing of Angel Mounds' former glories. By 1450 the place was deserted and unoccupied.

Among the unusual items recovered by archaeologists are a mastodon's tooth from a shaman's grave, and burial urns—circular pots containing the bones of infants covered over with pebbles. The most outstanding feature at Angel Mounds is a faithful reconstruction of the large temple building. The Indiana ceremonial city and Cahokia, as mentioned above, shared an identical solar orientation. But the Indiana center has a markedly different ambiance, not only because it is smaller than its parent city near the banks of the Mississippi River but also because, unlike Cahokia, little or no human sacrifice took place, and there were no large-scale acts of social violence. As a result, the godhead here may be less dramatic.

The sacred aspect of Angel Mounds is underscored by its island-like configuration, either natural or man-made. Its origins are relatively unimportant because the inhabitants of this place either chose the location for its peculiar features, or they purposely altered it (terraformed it) to conform to their requirements. In many ancient cultures, water was perceived to be a boundary between this world and the next. Consequently, passing over the water from mundane existence outside the walls into the Otherworld of pyramid mounds constitutes an important ritual act in and of itself.

That the inhabitants of Angel Mounds regarded their city as something more than a commercial or political enterprise may also be surmised from the fragments of broken pottery decorated with cultic emblems. Among these are symbols delineating the sacred center. In every recovered example, the signs appear midpoint in representations of the sun. Angel Mounds was the leading sacred center of ancient America's solar cult after the fall of its former capital at Cahokia. Refugees from that collapse not only fled eastward into Indiana, but also northward into Wisconsin.

3

Riddles of the Pacific

On one of our planet's most remote corners, in the Caroline Islands of the Pacific Ocean, are gargantuan ruins half hidden under masses of tropical foliage. Here sprawl the vast towers, courtyards, boulevards, and canals of Nan Madol, among the most inscrutable places on Earth. As author David Hatcher Childress succinctly describes it in *Ancient Micronesia & the Lost City of Nan Madol,* "Over two hundred fifty million tons of prismatic basalt are stacked up in artificial islands and structures over an eleven square-mile area."[1]

Although discovered 160 years ago, archaeologists still do not know who built the vast ceremonial center or when. Local legends recount only that Nan Madol, or "Spaces-in-Between," as it is known to the natives, was raised by outsiders in the dim past. Incomplete radiocarbon dating reveals that the city was occupied perhaps two thousand years ago, but the actual period for its construction has not yet been determined. Outstanding is a square tower composed of basalt crystal beams that, notwithstanding their average weight of twenty tons each, are powerfully and precisely piled up like a massive log cabin to more than twenty feet.

Surrounding this imposing edifice, in the central area of the complex are some one hundred artificial islets connected by an intricate system of canals. The physical, intellectual, and organizational effort that went into realizing such a phenomenal public works project must

Figure 3.1. The ruins of Nan Madol.
Photograph by C. T. Snow.

have been staggering. Yet it belongs to no known people or culture in the Pacific or elsewhere. Childress not only visited Nan Madol several times but also led scuba-diving expeditions to the ocean bottom in the island's immediate vicinity. There, at depths of forty and fifty feet, he and his team members found twenty-five-foot-tall stone columns, some inscribed with enigmatic glyphs.

Beyond the Caroline Islands are the no less puzzling monuments of Guam and Tinian, where the Latte monoliths stand as mute testimony to some vanished genius of prehistory. Aligned in double rows to the shoreline, the Latte are fifty-ton, fifteen-foot-high basalt pillars surmounted by huge, spherical stone caps, and said by the islanders to have been set up by the *Taotaomona,* the "Spirits of the Before-Time People." Then there is Malden Island, an uninhabited speck in the ocean, yet covered with dozens of pyramidal stone platforms, some connected to paved roads that lead to the shore and actually into the sea. The island of Truk, famous for its lagoon of sunken Japanese warships, features an ancient tunnel excavated straight through a mountain.

These haunting ruins of what must once have been a powerful culture are spread across the Pacific. Are these atypical structures the remnants of sunken Lemuria, the legendary fountainhead of earthly civilization?

4

The Great Pyramid
of China

From an orbiting spacecraft, Earth seems uninhabited. New York, London, Paris—no cities appear. Only the effect produced by a single object may be seen to suggest that some advanced form of life has touched this planet. At dawn and again during evening, over Asia a long, thin, sinuous shadow snakes its way across the otherwise indistinguishable Chinese landscape to inform observers in outer space that, yes, Earth is a civilized place.

This twice-daily phenomenon is caused by the rising and setting of the sun as it casts lengthening shadows from the Great Wall of China. Although this colossal edifice ranks among the most famous sites in the world, not many people in the West know much about it. The Great Wall had its origins in the dire pronouncement of an oracle in 235 B.C.E. Having just been made emperor, Chin Shih-Huang, the son of an itinerant dancing girl, was informed by the royal soothsayer that the empire would be overrun, his dynasty collapse, and he himself slain by huge waves of savages, the Hu, unless he undertook building the single most powerful barrier ever erected by the hand of man.

"Fear not the tiger from the south," the oracle said, "but beware even the rooster from the north."[1] To the south lay the young emperor's docile subjects. But populous tribes of fierce Mongolian horsemen lay to the north. Thus warned, Chin Shih-Huang drafted all able-bodied men in his extensive realm. Every man from scholar to convicted criminal was herded into an army-size workforce. Schools and prisons alike were emptied of their residents, who were put to work year after year through every season. Under downpouring rains, in blistering summers and winter blizzards, they struggled with stone and mortar under the overseer's whip.

Shirkers were dragged off to the construction site and buried alive as examples to their fellow slaves. They were joined by anyone who died of other causes, which were numerous. Injuries, overwork, and disease took their toll. In time the project became not only the longest wall on Earth but also its biggest cemetery. The same high-quality workmanship that went into the imperial palace was applied to the Great Wall, with every inch superbly made. A miracle of ancient engineering, its ramparts stretched over mountain peaks and across deep valleys. Uniform dimensions were maintained over 2,500 miles—a twenty-five-foot height and nineteen-foot base width.

In its final form it ran from the Tibetan Plateau to the Bohai Sea. If the structure were reassembled eight feet high and three feet thick at the equator, it would encircle the entire Earth. In the late eighteenth century an English mathematician determined that it contained more stones than all the buildings in the British Isles combined. The blockhouses seen today spaced at regular intervals were watchtowers for archers. They were manned by numerous garrisons—enough infantry to stand a warrior every two hundred yards along the entire length of the unprecedented fortification. The imperial army numbered around three million men. The Great Wall was a military success.

It kept out the Mongols for nearly fifteen hundred years. It was only breached by the masses of Genghis Khan's Golden Horde. As the Chinese themselves used to say, referring to the numberless dead who perished in its construction, "The Great Wall destroyed a generation, but saved a hundred."[2] Building it had been a state-forming act as well and the previously disunited kingships were welded together in a single empire named after Emperor Chin—China. But he was the last ruler of his dynasty, the Chou. He received some compensation at his death, however, when his body was interred in the suitably immodest mausoleum he designed for himself years before his death in 210 B.C.E.

With walls of sheeted bronze and surrounded by subterranean rivers of mercury, the tomb's ceiling was covered with gold and silver representations of the night sky. Its floor represented the extent of Imperial China itself. Although its exterior resembled nothing more than a grassy hill, tomb robbers who learned about its true identity were greeted by numerous hidden booby traps. Automatic crossbows activated by trip wires were set to fire in the direction of strategic entrances. The emperor did not retire alone to his immense sepulcher. He was accompanied by hundreds of the very laborers and architects who built his mausoleum, together with a bevy of his favorite concubines.

A comparable Chinese achievement to the Great Wall is far less well known. It stands forty miles southwest of Xian and seems oddly out of place. The structure is the largest of no less than sixteen ancient pyramids located in an area designated a forbidden zone by the Communist authorities, so little information and fewer photographs of the site have made their way to the West.

Like everyone else, Childress was not allowed to go near the Great Pyramid of China, but the little he learned about it is revealing. In the 1930s, some aerial observers who flew over it claimed it was twice the height of Egypt's Great Pyramid, about a thousand feet, but that does not seem likely. It is said to have been built during the Hsia dynasty, from 2205 to 1767 B.C.E. The Hsia were the first historical monarchs of China, having been preceded by five semi-legendary rulers. They reigned from 2852 to 2206 B.C.E. This mythical time parameter includes official dates for the Egyptian pyramid age, but very few other points of comparison are apparent.

Unlike its counterparts on the other side of the world at the Giza Plateau, surviving traces of original pigments show that the Xian pyra-

Figure 4.1. Although largely unknown to the outside world, China has its own ancient pyramids, such as the Tomb of the General, circa 37 B.C.E., in Ji'an, Jilin. Photograph by Kevin Felt.

mid was painted different colors on each of its four flanks. The east was bluish grey, with white facing the west, black on the north, and red on the south. Perhaps mimicking Egypt's Great Pyramid, which was originally topped with a thirty-foot-tall apex of sheeted gold, the apex of China's Great Pyramid was painted bright yellow. What these colors meant to the pyramid builders is not known, but here, too, analogies can be found in other parts of the world.

The ancient Maya of Yucatán and, much later, the Aztecs in the Valley of Mexico, associated the four cardinal directions with different colors, as did many Native tribes of North America. Various colors likewise represented different directions for the Bön people of pre-Buddhist Tibet. But none of the colored directional schemes of the Maya, Aztecs, Indians, or Tibetan Bön match those associated with Xian's pyramid.

Yet another parallel is found with Mesoamerica in the numerous green stones—jade artifacts—recovered at the Chinese site. As part of burial practices for individuals of royal lineage, the Aztecs interred small jade objects they referred to as *chacalchuilatls*—literally, "green stones"—in sacred commemoration of the Great Flood that destroyed almost all mankind in the deeply ancient past, when only a few survivors landed on the eastern shores of Mexico to reestablish civilization. It is not known if the jade items had a similar significance for the builders of the Xian pyramid, but their occurrence in both pre-Spanish Mexico and legendary China gives one pause for consideration.

The Communist authorities denied that the Xian pyramid even existed until the late 1980s, when they issued a brief statement to the effect that the structure was not really a pyramid but rather a trapezoidal tomb of the Han dynasty, contemporary with the Roman Empire. How they arrived at such a conclusion was not explained, although they admitted that the site had never been excavated. The first Westerner to see the Xian pyramid was an American trader, Fred Meyer Schroeder, in 1912.

"We rode around it, looking for stairways or doors, but saw none," he reported.[3] He did see, however, that the entire structure was encased in common fieldstone, each block about three feet square. The next outsider to see the pyramid was another American, James Gaussman, during World War Two. He was the pilot of a C-47 transport plane flying supplies over the renowned Burma Hump from U.S. bases in India to Chiang Kai-shek's forces in Chungking. During a return flight to Assam, Gaussman experienced engine problems due to icing conditions, so he descended to warmer temperatures, hoping to unfreeze the fuel lines. It was a dangerous descent, because he was over a virtually unexplored area of the Himalayan range skirting the borders of Tibet, India, and China.

Even if he survived a crash there, no one would ever find him. Gaussman banked close around a snow-covered peak when a broad, flat valley suddenly appeared before him. In moments, he swooped over the

Xian pyramid. His engines fully restored to life, he circled the structure three times before resuming his return flight. "There was nothing around it," Gaussman wrote in his intelligence report, "just a big pyramid sitting out in the wilderness. I figure it was extremely old. Who built it? When was it built? Why was it built? What's on the inside?"[4] Although those questions, when applied to the Great Wall, are easily answered, Xian's Great Pyramid is still the most intriguing enigma of China.

5

Construction Wonders
of the Ancients

Some years ago compiler William R. Corliss set himself the daunting task of publishing a Catalog of Anomalies in no less than thirty-two volumes devoted to literally dozens of archaeological mysteries, all described and referenced in cogent detail.

The first section of *Ancient Infrastructure: Remarkable Roads, Mines, Walls, Mounds, Stone Circles* tells of the often-colossal irrigation works completed by prehistoric peoples.[1] Outstanding among these was the La Cumbre Canal, a fifty-mile-long system that brought water from Peru's Chicama River to the Pacific coastal city of Chan-Chan, built about one thousand years ago by a pre-Inca people, the Chimu. But even their achievement was dwarfed by the ancient Egyptians' nearly 250 mile Bahr Joussuf Canal, really more an aqueduct, constructed around 2000 B.C.E.

Perhaps the single most incredible construction feat of the ancient world predated the Bahr Joussuf Canal by at least a thousand years. This was *Le Grand Menhir Brise,* "The Great, Broken Menhir," or *Er Grah,* a 340-ton stone originally towering more than sixty feet over the shores of Brittany. Today, it lies shattered into four massive segments, perhaps toppled by an earthquake. Assigned by archaeologists to the enigmatic "megalith builders," Er Grah's intended function is unknown.

Figure 5.1. The Broken Menhir of Er Grah.
Photograph by Myrabella.

More perplexing yet was the means by which it was erected. No single machine in the world today is capable of erecting and setting a single stone of such weight and height.

In Corliss's section on Terrestrial Zodiacs he compares a group of prehistoric effigy mounds along the western banks of the Mississippi River, Iowa's Marching Bears, with Britain's Glastonbury Zodiac, terraformations in the English landscape representing the Twelve Signs in the Wheel of Life.

The ancient stone circles of the British Isles are world famous, but Corliss describes no less intriguing—though far less well-known—arrangements in North America, such as the Burnt Hill Site in western Massachusetts and Maryland's Polish Mountain stone circle. He does not neglect the stone spheres of Costa Rica. These are granite balls, sometimes eight feet in diameter, superbly crafted by an unknown people for unknown purposes. But the number and labor-intensive creation of these objects, discovered from the jungle to mountaintops, cry out for answers.

Around the world ancient constructions beckon us to explore their mysteries.

6

Ancient Acoustics

When we walk among great ruins, such as Britain's Stonehenge, Egypt's Karnak, or the Greek Parthenon, we usually fail to realize that an essential component is missing from them all: namely, sound. The music and chanting that went on at these places when they were in use must have been an integral part of the visitor's experience. In *Stone Age Soundtracks* Paul Devereux reports that recent acoustical experiments conducted with high-tech instruments at several ancient locations have revealed a sonic dimension to these sites never before suspected.[1]

An outstanding discovery was made at Ireland's Newgrange, the great mound and passage grave atop a high ridge overlooking the Boyne Valley some thirty miles north of Dublin. It is perhaps the oldest building in the world, radiocarbon dated to 3200 B.C.E., a century before the first Egyptian dynasty. At thirty-six feet high and three hundred feet in diameter, the structure is particularly impressive for its eastern face, covered in white quartz, and a tall entrance. The man-made hill features a long corridor that is so oriented to the winter solstice that each sunrise on that day focuses a ray of light down the length of the stone-lined passage on a triple spiral in the deepest recesses of the interior.

Newgrange is decorated inside and out with spiral and lozenge designs whose meaning seems irretrievably lost in time. No less enigmatic are large stone basins placed in a high-ceilinged chamber at the

Figure 6.1. Ireland's Newgrange.
Photograph by Tjp finn.

far end of the corridor. The significance of the vessels and symbols, however, appears to be related to sound. A team of acoustical technicians experimenting with various tones at Newgrange found that producing a 110 hertz sound inside the corridor, while facsimiles of the original basins were filled with hot water, generated vibration patterns that appeared in the rising steam duplicating the spiral and lozenge designs carved on stone throughout the site.

Implications of this experiment suggest that Neolithic celebrants used the mound's interior as a sweat bath, a common feature used by shamans of various cultures to help achieve altered states of consciousness. As sunrise on the winter solstice, with all its death-rebirth significance, shot a ray of light through the structure's interior, sound was made by chanting or by musical instruments at a particular frequency to produce spirals and lozenges floating dramatically in the steam-filled corridor.

Apparently, a relationship between sound and stone as part of a spiritual experience was understood and put to use thousands of years before Newgrange was built. Nearly fifty years ago French archaeologist Iegor Reznikoff wanted to determine whether there was any connection between acoustics and the painted masterpieces illustrating the walls of Old Stone Age caves found throughout his country. The most famous examples of the three hundred known subterranean sites are Lascaux and Les Trois Freres, which were originally occupied from roughly 32,000 to 10,000 years ago. Reznikoff and his colleagues brought their investigations to illustrated caves in the French Pyrenees. There, at Niaux, they found that almost 90 percent of the cave paintings occurred in key resonant locations.

There are a multitude of possible locations for paintings in this cavern system, yet most of the pictures were discovered in places with the most remarkable acoustics. Deep inside Le Portel, 80 percent of the paintings occurred in the chief resonant places. Ordinary sounds produced in front of a section depicting a herd of horses had the sonic quality of stampeding hooves. It would appear, then, that the cavemen chose to paint their pictures at precisely the optimum points for generating the most dramatic sounds.

Common in various parts of the world, spiritual dimensions at these ancient locations give us an expanded appreciation for ancient man in his enduring monuments.

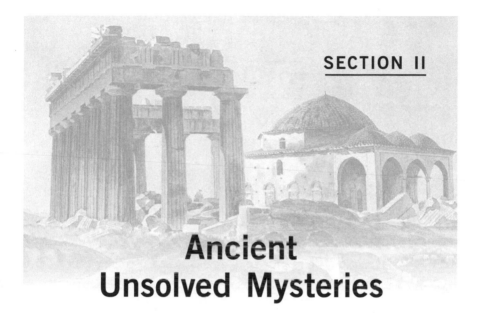

Ancient
Unsolved Mysteries

7

Is a Templar Treasure at the Bottom of the Money Pit?

Connected to the Canadian mainland by a 660-foot-long causeway, Nova Scotia's 140-acre Oak Island hides one of the most frustrating if enduring mysteries of all time. Over the past 221 years, six men died and millions of dollars were invested in search of a nameless secret that has attracted hundreds of miners, engineers, archaeologists, treasure hunters, and enthusiasts, including John Wayne, Errol Flynn, Admiral Richard Byrd, President Franklin Roosevelt, and England's King George VI.

The enigma first came to light in early fall, 1795, when three woodsmen walking through southeastern Oak Island's unexplored, uninhabited wilderness happened upon a badly weathered tackle block dangling from the end of a thick, frayed hawser—a ship's rope—attached to the outstretched branch of an old tree. The old pulley was suspended directly over a circular depression suggesting the disturbed earth of a large burial. Intrigued, the men put aside their muskets and began shoveling. At two feet, they uncovered neatly laid out flagstones, a surprise that encouraged them to excavate another twenty-eight feet. After encountering log platforms every ten feet, they abandoned their strenuous effort.

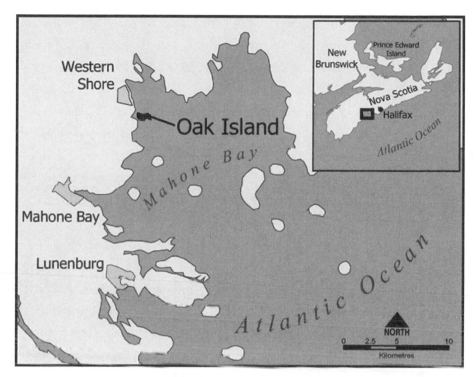

*Figure 7.1. Map showing the location of Oak Island,
where the Money Pit is allegedly located*

Subsequent digs at what became known as the Money Pit for its assumed riches came to nothing until 1803, when an expedition sailed three hundred miles from central Nova Scotia to Oak Island, where construction engineers dug farther down, finding log-made levels every ten feet, interspersed with mysterious layers of charcoal, putty, and coconut fiber at forty, fifty, and sixty feet. The nearest source for coconut is Georgia, seventeen hundred miles away. After a large stone bearing an inscription of unknown symbols was recovered at ninety feet, the pit was suddenly flooded with fifty-eight feet of water. Bailing efforts failed, and the excavation terminated.

Drilling forty-six years later passed through spruce and oak platforms at ninety-eight feet. Further excavations in 1866, 1893, and 1909 yielded no positive results due mostly to recurrent flooding. When a twelve-by-fourteen-foot shaft was sunk close to the Money Pit in 1931, a metal axe, pick, and an anchor fluke were removed at 127 feet. Subsequent excavation projects in 1935, 1936, and 1959 came to nothing. The only scientific study of the Money Pit was a two-week survey conducted in 1995 by researchers from Massachusetts's Woods Hole Oceanographic Institution. They concluded that its flooding was caused by natural interaction between Oak Island's freshwater fens and tidal pressures in the underlying geology, refuting the proposition of artificially constructed flood tunnels. Nothing else could be determined.

Current excavations are being undertaken by treasure hunters Rick and Marty Lagina, whose operations began airing in 2014 as *The Curse of Oak Island,* a documentary series on the History Channel. Among their most significant finds to date occurred when a sonar mapping device was lowered into a subterranean space over two hundred feet below the surface of the ground. The instrument revealed a rectangular room containing two moderately large rectangular objects. The chamber and possible chests appear to be man-made.

Until they are positively identified, however, wild speculation will continue to describe Oak Island as a repository for the Ark of the Covenant, Inca gold, King Solomon's mine, Marie Antoinette's jewels, Captain Kidd's treasure, Shakespeare's lost manuscripts, and a host of similarly implausible candidates. Of them all, one possibility stands out from the rest as being most likely responsible for the original creation of the Money Pit.

In the early twelfth century, Bernard de Clairvaux—better known after his death in 1153 as Saint Bernard—selected nine monks from his monastic order in France to serve as the Knights of the Poor Fellow Soldiers of Christ. He dispatched them to Palestine, where they were supposed to protect travelers on pilgrimage to the Holy Land. They were welcomed by the Latin king of Jerusalem, Baudoin II, and he allowed them to establish their headquarters at the site of Solomon's Temple, on the city's Temple Mount, from which the name *Templar* derived.

Figure 7.2. Excavating Oak Island's Money Pit, circa 1900

Over the next two hundred years their numbers and wealth grew to such prodigious political and economic influence that they emerged as a state within a state, with its own church buildings, armies, and banks spread throughout Christendom. Within a few decades the Knights Templar had become the first Pan-European organization, its members and officers drawn from all over the continent, regardless of nationality, but less devoted to any particular country than to their own theology, more gnostic than mainstream Christian. Gnosticism emphasizes direct experience of God through mystical experience, which does not require priestly mediation. This heretical concept combined with royal greed during the early fourteenth century to bring about the sudden demise of the Knights Templar.

In October 1307, King Philip IV of France issued warrants for their arrest and seized all their holdings, while Pope Clement V disbanded the Order throughout Europe. Warned in advance, Templar Jean de Châlon heard rumors that Gerard de Villiers, the Templar Master of France, had put to sea with eighteen galleys, and the brother Hugues de Châlon fled with the whole treasury of the brother Hugues de Pairaud, in charge of the Order's French assets. De Châlon's statement gave rise to modern theories that a Templar fleet loaded with riches escaped to somewhere in the Americas.

With papal proscription, the Knights Templar's Mediterranean fleet fled through the Straits of Gibraltar into the Atlantic Ocean for Portugal, where they were temporarily safe from the French king and Roman pope. Resupplied, ships and crews were joined by de Villiers's galleys, resuming their passage to Argyll, in Scotland. In just seven years they made themselves invaluable by turning the tide at 1314's Battle of Bannockburn, enabling Robert the Bruce to become the first king of an independent Scotland. Eighty-four years later, Henry Sinclair, Earl of Orkney, accompanied by fellow Templars, mounted a transatlantic expedition of twelve ships.

Fitchburg, Massachusetts, historian Michael Kaulback wondered why "Henry Sinclair set off with twelve ships and over three hundred men, a rather large force for an explorative mission, across the sea? The prince may have been looking for a place to start a colony far away from the suppression of the Templars that still raged in Europe."[1]

In any case, theirs was not entirely a voyage of discovery, because Henry had supposedly been informed by the survivor of four fishing boats blown across the sea to Newfoundland. From there, after twenty years, the lone castaway eventually fashioned his own makeshift craft that carried him back to Scotland, where he died just before the Earl's expedition was about to get underway.

"It is possible that Sinclair already knew of lands west of Greenland," writes researcher Steven Sora: "The Sinclair family had Norse connections through marriage, and they were aware of the Norse settlements in the western isles."[2] Years previous to his voyage, Henry conferred with Nicolo Zeno, who had been put in charge of designing and outfitting the Scottish vessels. Italy's foremost cartographer and navigator later penned a detailed account that left no doubt the expedition arrived at the appropriately named, Nova Scotia, "New Scotland."

In 1981 directors of Nova Scotia's Ministry of Culture asked Michael Bradley, an expert on the life of Henry Sinclair, to examine the ruins of a stone structure atop a hill at the middle of the peninsula. Bradley closed his two-year investigation of the site after concluding that the remains resembled rubblework construction consistent with Scottish fortifications as they appeared in the late fourteenth century.[3]

Kaulback described the early-twentieth-century discovery off Nova Scotia of "a cannon of the same kind displayed at the Naval Museum in Venice, and typical of the ordinance aboard Zeno's ships. The Nova Scotia cannon is presently housed in the fortress of Louisbourg, on Cape Breton Island. Such artillery was obsolete by the end of the fourteenth century, so the American find dates to the period of Prince Henry's expedition."[4]

Skeptics deny that he was a Templar, and assert that none existed by 1398, when the earl set sail for North America, because the Order had been officially abolished ninety years before. But they forget that Henry was also the Baron of Rosslyn, where his Chapel features an engraving portraying a Knight Templar holding his sword over the head of an initiate, to protect the secrets of the Order from being disclosed.

"Earl William St. Clair (Sinclair), the last Earl of Orkney," Kaulback writes, "was the Grand Master of Craftmasons in 1439. He was also the Grand Prior of the Scottish Knights Templar."[5]

Rosslyn Chapel is also adorned with the carved representations of aloe cacti and ears of corn—plants native only to the Americas at a time when the New World was as yet officially unknown. Speculation has been fueled by Templar artifacts "discovered in the Province of Quebec and elsewhere in the Maritime Provinces of Canada," writes Gerard Leduc in *Ancient American* magazine.[6]

A Templar breastplate "was found in the early 1950s by a farmer on the shores of Lake Memphremagog, which crosses into Vermont. It was purchased by Mr. Jacques Boisvert from Magog, Quebec. The surface of the metal appears free from corrosion, which suggests it was tin-plated. It has a reinforced rim all around its exterior, and the surface is incised with fine etchings illustrating various male and female figures," features characteristic of neo-Templar craftsmanship of the late fourteenth century.[7] This was the same period that Prince Henry Sinclair appears to have arrived in New England.

"A related discovery," Leduc continues, "was made during the early nineteenth century in Irasburg, Vermont, not far from Lake Memphremagog, when another farmer found chain armor under a large tree stump while plowing his field. The chain mail was made of rings about an eighth of an inch connecting a collar made of closely interwoven brass rings, all consistent with Templar armor. The object was given to surveying engineers, who happened to be in the area at that time. It was supposedly taken to New York City, as reported in an 1826 edition of the *Vermont Patriot*."[8]

On a midsummer's day in 2000, diver Nelson E. Jecas was hunting seashells along the Atlantic shores of New Jersey, near Bernardsville, where his attention was attracted by an unusual circular stone.[9] One side was embossed with a Knights Templar cross and a small hole had been drilled near the edge. The three-inch granite object impressed him as a kind of ornament or badge, its image partially water eroded by wave action over the course of what must have been a very long time. At least one such cross has been found engraved on a boulder at Oak Island, and some if not all glyphs on the stone dredged up from ninety feet beneath the surface of the ground in 1803 match mid-fifteenth-century mason marks from Scotland.

These mysteries coincide with the Knights Templar themselves, whose vast wealth—the real objective of King Phillip's hostility—disappeared before he could lay his hands on it. The treasure vanished with the Templar fleet to Henry Sinclair's kingdom, where the gold was partially used to buy protection from the Scottish prince, then spirited across the North Atlantic to a remote landfall at Nova Scotia, in 1398.

There, the Knights—long renowned for their genius as master

masons, the builders of cathedrals, irrigation systems, the strongest bridges and impregnable castles—excavated the complex shaft as a deep deposit vault only they knew how to access. At its bottom, still untouched after more than six hundred years, perhaps in the rectangular chests recently detected by sonar, lies a fortune of incalculable riches.

8
The Navel
of the World

The most beautiful, famous, and influential sacred site of the ancient world still exists. Perched on the side of a mountain high above the Gulf of Corinth, Delphi reaches up to the sun god to whom it was dedicated more than three thousand years ago. The name itself was mysterious even to the ancient Greeks who built their renowned sanctuary to Apollo. Some believed *Delphi* derived from *dolphin,* Poseidon's pet. One of them was said to have guided a Cretan ship to the new place for the solar deity's worship.

More likely, *Delphi* was a pre-Greek word for "womb," synonymous with "cave." Long before the magnificent temples were constructed there, a fundamentally similar oracle was sought out seven miles away in a cave on the steep slopes of a hill, today's Sarandauli. Known originally as Korykian, "the Maiden," after Kore, she is better remembered today as Persephone. She was the young daughter of Mother Earth, abducted by Hades who imprisoned her in the Underworld.

Kore was eventually allowed to live with her Mother half of each year, but had to spend the other six months with her subterranean husband. Ever since, her biannual disappearance causes fall and winter. Persephone's myth is cogent to Delphi, where its mysteries of death and rebirth were celebrated, the cave serving as a dramatic metaphor for the

Figure 8.1. Delphi. Photograph by Arian Zwegers.

womb and tomb of Mother Earth, into which all living things descend in death and from which they are reborn. But the chief function at Delphi for which it was far famed was the incomparable excellence of its oracle.

The kings and emperors of the ancient world crowded the sanctuary for information long respected for its validity, however difficult to correctly interpret. It was originally administered by a *hosioi,* or college of five men who could claim direct descent from Deucalion. In Greek myth, he and his wife, Pyrrha, were lone survivors of the Great Flood that destroyed a former civilization. With them aboard their vessel they carried the omphalos, or Navel Stone, a tall, white, egg-shaped boulder, the very umbilicus of Zeus, King of the Olympian Gods, and possessed of the powers of eternal life.

Arriving in the Eastern Mediterranean Sea, they installed the omphalos atop Mount Parnassus and instituted the hosioi for its administration. Henceforward, one of their number always spoke as the prophet responsible for interpreting Apollo's often obscure utterances that emanated from it. The mountain itself had been named for the inventor of augury, Parnassus.

Every spring a ceremony known as the Aigle, commemorating Deucalion's escape from the Deluge, was performed at Delphi. Historian Richard Hastings writes, "The Omphalos represents the in-coming of a new race with different and, on the whole, higher ideas of religion."[1] While the hosioi continued to serve at Delphi, its male prophet was replaced by the Pythia. This was a female virgin chosen by the five descendants of Deucalion, regardless of her background, high or low, for her extraordinary psychic abilities.

She performed her duties at Delphi's most sacred structure, the *adyton*. There, she drank once from a sacred spring, then poured a libation of holy water over the omphalos. After chewing a leaf from Apollo's sacred Tree of Life, the laurel, the Pythia seated herself on a tall, bronze tripod, from which she inhaled narcotic vapors issuing from either a cleft in the ground or a hole at the top of the omphalos itself. Shortly thereafter, she was seized by a divine frenzy, during which her utterances were interpreted by the priests as pronouncements from the sun god.

Modern historians attribute the accuracy and cogency of these oracular instructions to the clever college of hosioi, for whom the Pythia was only their mouthpiece. But French geologists studying Delphi's remains during the late 1990s found that a fissure at the base of the adyton emitted unusually high levels of ethylene dioxide, a relatively rare gas used today by anesthesiologists.

The scientists stated that anyone confined in a small chamber over the rising ethylene dioxide would be almost overwhelmed with euphoria. Long before their discovery, the narcotic properties of laurel leaves chewed by the Pythia were widely known. Together with the natural sensitivities for which she had been especially chosen, these external influences undoubtedly produced in her an altered state of consciousness that may very well have enabled the priestess to envision some higher awareness.

Figure 8.2. The Omphalos in the Delphi Archaeological Museum. Photograph by Sergey Prokudin-Gorsky.

Unlike generations of trance mediums who followed her, Herophile was not Greek, perhaps, as were the hosioi, a direct descendant of Deucalion. In any case, her prophecy of the coming Trojan War dates Herophile and the establishment of Apollo's oracle at Delphi to the first half of the thirteenth century B.C.E. The title she and those who came after her bore, Pythia, derived from the giant serpent, Python, slain by Apollo and rotting forever in the adyton cleft or perhaps inside the omphalos. The myth signified the eternal conquest of light over darkness, life over death. The Pythia's best-remembered prophecy was delivered to Croesus, the greedy Lydian monarch, who asked the Delphic oracle if he should attempt the military take-over of his prosperous neighboring kingdom.

"If you do so," the sun god assured him through her, "a great empire will surely fall."[2] Encouraged by what he assumed was a clear reference to his targeted victim, Croesus launched a full-scale invasion. But it miscarried. His own land was overrun and he himself overthrown. While the story is only a legend, like all myth it is not without its kernel of truth, as the Pythia was well known for speaking in language open to interpretation. Even so, many thousands of visitors, a great deal of them the leading personages of their times, made the steep trek up the flanks of Mount Parnassus to hear the prophetic words of the Pythia.

One king was so grateful for the crucial counsel she gave him, he commissioned a life-sized reproduction of a palm tree—also sacred to the sun god—in solid gold to be erected on the shores of Delos, a small island sanctuary in the middle of the Aegean. There it stood for many centuries, until a great storm, said to have been the wrath of the gods for their substitution by Christianity in the fifth century, blew it over and rolled it out into the sea, never to be seen again. Indeed, the triumph of the new religion demonized all other spiritual disciplines, including the Delphic oracle, which was closed in 390 C.E. Today, however, it is visited by tourists from around the world who leave with something of its ineffable mystical power.

9
The Atlantis Blueprint

Colin Wilson and Rand Flem-Ath posit an underlying link connecting most (all?) of the ancient world's monumental structures, from Britain's Stonehenge and Bolivia's Tiahuanaco to the statues of Easter Island and Egypt's Great Pyramid. While such ruins may be widely separated by time and distance, an Earth wide heritage is supposedly common to them all. The fount of that heritage may be surmised from the title of their book, *The Atlantis Blueprint: Unlocking the Ancient Mysteries of a Long-Lost Civilization*.[1]

Wilson and Flem-Ath base their speculations on the conclusions of Charles Hapgood. The New England anthropology professor concluded, before his death in 1982, that ice accumulating at the North Pole caused the entire planet to slip like an orange peel through "crustal displacement," suddenly dislodging continents and causing universal catastrophes. All this was supposed to have happened eleven thousand or twelve thousand years ago. Hapgood's ideas never went much further, but they still inspire writers who see in his theory an explanation for the lost civilization.

Hapgood additionally tried to show that someone allegedly made an accurate map of Antarctica about six thousand years ago, and from this his followers deduce the location of Atlantis. After all, both places are continental and they supposedly shared a common geologic fate at approximately the same time. On this supposition

Figure 9.1. The epic Atlantis, *by Danish poet Janus Djurhuus (1881–1948), is celebrated in this Faroe Islands postage stamp*

Wilson and Flem-Ath's argument is based. The most complete ancient source for the story of Atlantis is found in the fourth-century B.C.E. dialogues of the Greek philosopher Plato.

Never once does Plato describe it as a continent. The word he uses is *nessos,* an "island" about the size of "Libya and Asia Minor combined."

Plato's description sounds pretty big, until we realize that at most the "Libya" of his day was a thin strip of coastline from the western Egyptian border to today's eastern Algeria. So too, Plato's "Asia Minor" comprised only about a third of modern Turkey.

He did state that Atlantis was destroyed eleven thousand years ago, but the "years" Plato mentioned were lunar, not solar, which places Atlantis in the late Bronze Age (circa 1200 B.C.E.), not the last Ice Age. There can be little doubt about this chronological downshift, because the concentric city Plato describes is identifiably Bronze Age.

The authors of *The Atlantis Blueprint* choose to ignore these fundamental discrepancies, but that does not prevent them from giving us a useful addition to the estimated 2,500 other titles on the subject.

For example, Rand Flem-Ath writes that the Guanches (the original, pre-Spanish inhabitants of the Canary Islands off the coast of North Africa) were known to never leave their remote islands, not for any lack of maritime skill but because they believed the Canary Islands were located on a sacred alignment established by their Atlantean ancestors. Historians have always wondered why the Guanches, able pyramid builders in their own right, never made use of the seas all about them.

The mysterious stone spheres of Costa Rica are also described. The sometimes large (nine feet in diameter), always perfectly carved granite balls continue to mystify conventional and unconventional investigators alike, and *The Atlantis Blueprint* includes them as part of surviving clues to the lost civilization.

Another clue is that the Native American Ute, Kutenai, Okanagan, A'a'tam, Cahto, and Cherokee all share catastrophe myths with the Araucanian Indians of Peru. Their common oral heritage seems to describe the same kind of worldwide cataclysm Professor Hapgood was sure had destroyed a high civilization already tens of thousands of years old when it was obliterated. He believed the destruction was not an isolated disaster but a global event.

Perhaps a sophisticated network of cultural connections among the ancient world's foremost sacred sites was established millennia ago by the Atlanteans. Apparent similarities, sometimes superficial, sometimes more intimate, seem to link places like the Egyptian pyramids with Yucatán's Pyramid of the Feathered Serpent, showing Atlantis could have been the father of them all.

10

Closing in on
the Ark of the Covenant

The Ark of the Covenant is probably the most famous, sought after, and mysterious object ever described. It was supposed to have been a gold plated wooden box for storing the original Ten Commandments given by God to Moses atop Mount Sinai. According to the Old Testament, however, the Ark was no mere sacred repository, but was endowed with energies powerful enough to defeat all enemies of the sorely outnumbered Hebrews. They used it to demolish the otherwise impregnable walls of Jericho and spread panic among their Philistine opponents.

Wielding this biblical weapon of mass destruction, they blasted their way into Jerusalem, founding Israel on the ruins of that Gentile kingdom, henceforward ruled by Solomon. He built a special temple to house the precious vessel in a central holy-of-holies, where it was venerated for more than three centuries. During 597 B.C.E., as Jerusalem was about to fall to invading Babylonians, the Ark was hidden by Levite priests and vanished forever after. Ever since, people have been searching for its whereabouts. Undeterred by their consistent lack of success, author Graham Phillips believes he is close to solving the age-old enigma.

"We have not yet managed to find the Ark," he admits, "but we did

Figure 10.1. Moses and Joshua bowing before the Ark.
Painting by James Tissot, circa 1900.

discover a strangely inscribed stone slab which may have been one of the tablets it contained."[1] About an inch thick, a foot and a half long, and a foot wide, the tablet is inscribed with thirteen separate symbols cut into it at a depth of about a quarter of an inch. Epigraphers in the United States have so far failed to effect their translation, but the sandstone itself comes from a mountain Phillips identifies as Mount Sinai. No less remarkably, the inscribed tablet believed to have been originally housed in the Ark of the Covenant was found in the center of England, not under Jerusalem's Temple Mount where majority opinion locates it.

Phillips writes that the Ark was discovered in a cave near the ruins of the ancient city of Petra in southern Jordan by Knights Templar from

Temple Herdewyke in the English county of Warwickshire during the twelfth century. They brought it back to Britain after the crusaders went down in defeat. Two hundred years later, just before their descendants were wiped out by the Black Death, they left a series of strange paintings on the walls of a church in nearby Burton Dassett as clues to where they hid the Ark. Phillips traced the location revealed in these paintings to an old, holy well beside a road in the English village of Napton-on-the-Hill, in Warwickshire. It was during the course of these local investigations that the sandstone tablet was found.

"The Ark cannot be far behind," Phillips believes. And so the quest goes on.

11

The Mystery
of the Cathars

One of the most infamous yet least understood episodes in human history was the immolation of two hundred religious heretics outside their mountain fortress in the year 1244. Since then the man responsible for burning them alive, King Louis of France, has been canonized by the Catholic Church he served with such vigor, while his victims are still suspected as guardians of a secret dangerous enough to warrant their persecution by the most powerful monarch of the High Middle Ages.

Searching for the nature of that secret is the avowed goal of Jean Markale in his *Montségur and the Mystery of the Cathars*.[1] Though so many recent if not always accurate books about the contemporary Templars attempt to guide readers toward their impenetrable secret, Markale is needed to steer us on a more firmly reliable course through the intriguing if bewildering labyrinth of thirteenth-century Grail quests. Dispensing with all the imaginative nonsense still associated with the Cathars while uncovering the real causes behind their doom and the enigma they supposedly carried with them to the stake, Markale describes their still-controversial origins and surprisingly modern belief system.

Indeed, there is even controversy regarding the real meaning of

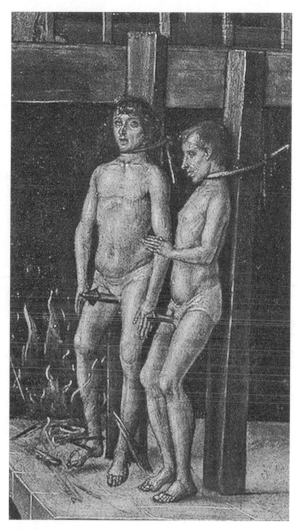

Figure 11.1. Cathars being burnt at the stake in an auto-da-fé,
or "act of faith"—the public penance of condemned heretics—as depicted by
Spanish painter Pedro Berruguete (circa 1450–1504)

this group's name. Interpretations run the gamut from esoteric classical origins in the Greek *catharsis,* or spiritual purging, to medieval
German slang for "cat's ass-kisser"—an allusion to the perverse initiation rites supposedly indulged in by the antiestablishment Cathars.
Less uncertain was their insistence that God required no priestly

middlemen. The original teaching of Christianity's founder, they declared, had been perverted and debased by church rulers to form a political tyranny masquerading as a spiritual authority.

It is thought that the Cathars condemned the Vatican as a Synagogue of Satan, the real creator of the world with all its pain and sin. Women rose to high positions in the Cathar hierarchy, abortion was decriminalized, tolerance of other faiths (including Islam) encouraged, vows of personal poverty taken, and killing, under any circumstances, was abhorred. Cathar leaders, known as *perfecti,* swore an oath to die rather than defend themselves, so the kindred Templars volunteered to fight for them. By the early thirteenth century, Cathar gnosticism had spread across western Europe like wildfire, presenting mainstream Christianity with the most serious challenge in its history.

At the urgent behest of their pope, France's Catholic royalty waged a war of extermination against the Cathars, eventually cornering the last of the perfecti atop the Pyrenees peak of Montségur, the "Mountain of Salvation." For several months, the lofty fortress lived up to its name, defying every attempt by Catholic forces. Through brilliant military strategy and incomparable courage, however, Montségur eventually fell, and with it the Cathar heresy.

In the midst of the siege four perfecti slipped through the king's lines. They carried "a great treasure" that vanished. Was it the Grail, as some authors insist, or documented proof that, if exposed, would bring down the whole edifice of post-Jesus Christianity? The answer is revealing, if not altogether disturbing.

12

Today's Megalith Builders

While many cannot explain why anyone would want to erect such ponderous stone structures, in Paleolithic times or now, some people today nonetheless feel compelled and delighted to exert back-breaking labor for the raising of colossal circles. Author Rob Roy tells how to move and align large stones for modern megalith-builders in his guide *Stone Circles: A Modern Builders Guide to the Megalithic Revival.*[1] Roy has himself participated in the design and construction of several such arrangements in Europe and North America and is part of a small but far-flung community, or fellowship of persons, determined to build their own megalithic sites simply because they love them.

He is the founder of the Earthwood Building School in West Chazy, New York, where he specializes in such unconventional building techniques as cordwood masonry and underground housing. The original megalith builders flourished in western Europe from four thousand to six thousand years ago. Although their most famous achievement was England's Stonehenge, many hundreds more stone constructions were set up throughout the British Isles and across the Channel to the Atlantic coast of France. The sites included not only circles, but stones arranged in lines or standing alone. The largest surviving example is a single upright, referred to as a menhir, near Plouarzel in Brittany.

How such massive construction could have been accomplished millennia before the Industrial Age is an enigma underscored by modern

*Figure 12.1. The infamous Georgia Guidestones represent
an example of modern-day megaliths.*

attempts to duplicate the ancient megaliths, albeit on a much smaller scale. Modern builders have to use backhoes, machine-driven chain pulleys, and cranes just to lift and fit stones weighing less than a thousand pounds.

Roy and his fellow enthusiasts do admit to the nameless, spiritual joy the structures impart, and try to incorporate both heaven- and earth-oriented alignments in the placement of the stones. In doing so, they appear to have instinctually hit upon the original intention of the megalithic forerunners, who appear to have been driven to harmonize man with the powers of Mother Earth and Father Sky.

Not surprisingly, modern stone sites are often celebrated with Neolithic-like dances and rituals. Appropriately dressed celebrants dance through hoops raised aloft by flower-garlanded ladies at the old Keltic *Beltane* festival, and a Wickerman is immolated during *Lugnasad* in the company of newly erected megaliths.

Clearly, some of the old magic seems to have been revived by the very placement of the stones themselves in imitation of ancient practices. Perhaps the loving intentions expressed are sufficient to conjure some of the old megalithic magic.

Pharaoh's Egypt

13

The Tutankhamun Prophecies

Maurice Cotterell, author of *The Tutankhamun Prophecies*,[1] is a professional mathematician, engineer, and scientist formerly with Britain's prestigious Cranfield Institute of Technology. In 1992 he was awarded the Voluntariado Cultural Medal for his contributions to Mexican culture. He claims that his scientific training made it possible for him to decipher the knowledge and wisdom of the ancient Maya encoded in their hieroglyphs and monumental artwork.

The Maya were a people living in the lowland and coastal areas of southern Mexico and Central America from around 200 B.C.E. to 900 C.E. During that time they reached heights of cultural greatness unsurpassed in the pre-Columbian world as the builders of numerous beautiful cities and as extraordinary astronomers. By the early tenth century their civilization simply stopped for no apparent reason. The causes of this abrupt cessation have been inconclusively debated for more than a hundred years.

Even more controversial are persistent claims, mostly by unconventional investigators, that the Maya were the inheritors of overseas influences, particularly from the Nile Valley. Cotterell was compelled by the evidence he found to come to similar conclusions. He found that the same techniques used for deciphering the Maya code could

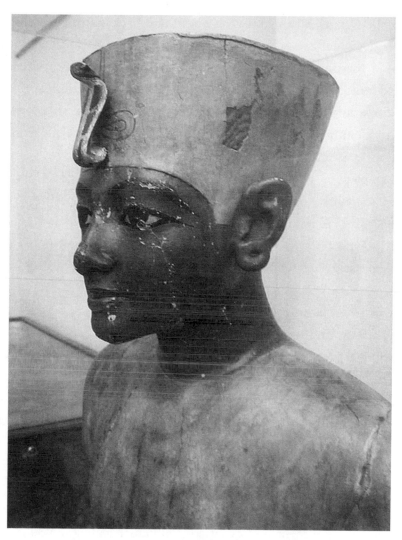

Figure 13.1. Tutankhamun's realistic, cedar-wood
portrait bust removed from his tomb.
Photograph by Jon Bodsworth.

be used with equal success when applied to the funerary details of
ancient Egypt's most famous monarch, Tutankhamun. The dramatic if
short and unaccomplished life of King Tut, as he is popularly known,
does not seem to lend itself to any direct comparisons with his Maya
counterpart, Lord Pacal, who was born about two thousand years

after the Egyptian boy-king was assassinated at eighteen years of age by a well-aimed axe blow to the base of his skull. Tutankhamun had the bad fortune to have lived at a transitional period between the end of a monotheist's unpopular reign and the restoration of the old gods. It would appear that someone was not taking any chances, and Tutankhamun was liquidated to prevent him from carrying on in his predecessor's heretical footsteps.

In any case, both the dynastic Egyptians and ancient Maya possessed a sophisticated understanding of sunspot activity and other astronomical phenomena. Amazingly, their comprehension of solar function was only rediscovered by European and American astronomers operating telescopes and infrared sensors during the twentieth century.

Cotterell claims that knowledge of the connections between sunspot patterns and human destiny allowed the Egyptians and Maya to harness the energy generated by our star to achieve spiritual illumination and growth of the soul. The link between reincarnation and solar energy encoded in the tombs of Tutankhamun and the Maya ruler Lord Pacal, discovered in the ruined ceremonial city of Palenque around 1950, is still a jealously guarded secret held by a select number of occult groups, including the higher orders of Freemasonry. Supposedly the most carefully guarded and important of these secrets hold that god-kings like Tutankhamun and Pacal incarnate on Earth to help mortals achieve enlightenment and eventual, individual realization as comparable "solar beings."

While this position is extreme, there are numerous parallels between the ancient Egyptian and Maya civilizations.

14

Remote Viewing
the Great Sphinx

In the ancient past, men and women who claimed to extend their conscious minds beyond space and time were known as sorcerers or sibyls. Even today, Native American shamans engage in controlled out-of-body vision quests, traversing all limitations of the physical world to bring back information valuable for the spiritual growth of their tribe. After the fall of classical civilization fifteen centuries ago, such experiences were condemned first as witchcraft, then as superstition, throughout the Western world.

But nearly fifty years ago, Ingo Swann coined the term *remote viewing* to describe an ability to perceive hidden or remote information by anomalous psychic means. Since childhood Swann believed that his spirit was not permanently confined to his body. As an adult, this feeling matured into a conviction that projecting our consciousness through space and time is not a special gift or mental aberration but a natural function of the human mind. Together with fellow researcher Janet Mitchell, Swann made a presentation at the American Society for Psychical Research in New York and at California's Stanford Research Institute, where his conclusions were favorably received.

While he was putting his case for remote viewing, American surveillance learned that Soviet scientists were seriously attempting to develop psychic powers for espionage. In a counter move the U.S. Army launched its own psi research at a special facility in Fort Meade, Maryland. Project Star Gate was designed to determine the military feasibility of remote viewing and, if possible, create America's first psychic spies. According to Paul H. Smith of the International Remote Viewing Association (IRVA), a nonprofit organization located in Palo Alto, California, "remote viewing is a mental facility that allows a perceiver, or 'viewer,' to describe or give details about a target that is hidden from the normal senses due to distance, time, or shielding."[1]

As examples he cites a location otherwise unknown to the viewer, who is nonetheless able to describe it with accuracy. He or she may also succeed in observing a forgotten event, finding an object in a concealed place, or supplying information not available through any other means about persons and activities, near or far. These observations are all made without the viewer being supplied any details whatsoever about the subject. Even names and general locations are withheld. According to Star Gate veteran Joseph McMoneagle, "remote viewing is the ability to produce information that is correct about a place, event, person, object, or concept which is located somewhere else in time/space, and which is completely blind to the remote viewer and others taking part in the process of collecting the information."[2]

With mixed results the Army officially dissolved Star Gate in November 1995. McMoneagle claims that "literally dozens of targets worked by viewers within the Star Gate Program made successful predictions relating to events involving people, places, or things."[3] Despite these successes, the project was hampered by occasional mismanagement and too many skeptics unable to accept the validity of psychic phenomena under any circumstances.

Out of the Star Gate experience emerged several remote-viewing organizations, some of them composed of former army participants but primarily with a following among professionals from various scientific backgrounds. The active participation of academically qualified and experienced individuals helps to defuse attempts by skeptics to debunk remote viewing and dismiss the phenomenon as delusional. Some of the IRVA's executive board members include:

- John B. Alexander, Ph.D., Colonel, U.S. Army (ret.)
- F. Holmes (Skip) Atwater, former Operations and Training Officer of the U.S. Army Remote Viewing Training Unit
- Angela Thompson Smith, Ph.D., research psychologist
- Marcello Truzzi, Professor of Sociology at Eastern Michigan University
- Russell Targ, retired senior staff scientist at Lockheed-Martin

Among IRVA's founding members is Stephan A. Schwartz, Research Director of the Mobius Group. Over the past forty years his organization of psychic volunteers scored perhaps the best-known remote viewing successes. In the late 1970s they claimed to have found the lost harbor of Alexandria on the Mediterranean Sea. The site included a palatial residence built for Cleopatra VII (the Great), dating back to the first century B.C.E. All was lost during a massive earthquake some nine hundred years later, when part of the Alexandrian shore suddenly collapsed into the sea.

Since then archaeologists scoured the murky waters of its suspected location, always in vain. Schwartz's Mobius Group not only identified the location of the subsurface ruins, but accurately described some of its artifacts—carved columns, sphinx statues, and a long causeway hitherto unsuspected by Egyptologists—eventually found by a French research diving team in the late 1990s. Remote viewing really does work. But how? Is it a rare gift limited to only a few naturally sensitive individuals? Or is its potential innate to every human being? If so, is special training required?

Researchers have been able to answer most of these fundamental questions about remote viewing, although explanations for precisely why it occurs are still limited to philosophical speculations. One theoretical interpretation goes back to the views of Pierre Teilhard de Chardin.

Ordained a Catholic priest in 1911, he won the Legion of Honor during World War One for his courage on the front lines as a stretcher bearer, was a highly respected teacher at the Catholic Institute of Paris, and later traveled to China, where he played a major role in the discovery of the skull of Peking Man, a find that pushed back evolution by 250,000 years. His subsequent research of Asian fossil deposits altered the development of twentieth-century paleontology.

Despite these influential achievements, Teilhard de Chardin's ideas about human evolution and its spiritual implications were suppressed during his lifetime by his religious superiors. They likewise prevented him from teaching his unconventional views at the Collège de France. All of his metaphysical work had to be published posthumously. Teilhard de Chardin's deepening understanding of evolution combined with his undiminished spiritual feelings convinced him that the invisible underside of the Earth's biosphere was an ordering intelligence—a *noosphere,* or "mental sphere," into which every human mind was subconsciously tuned.

Influences, he said, were reciprocal, with the combined mental activity of humankind morphing the whole world, just as the noosphere organized the rest of nature. Individuals experience this planetary interconnectedness when they feel their moods influenced by the emotional state of another human being or even their pets. Teilhard de Chardin went further to coin the term *cosmogenesis,* according to which the purpose of the noosphere was to make mankind the goal of all its strivings, because human beings alone of all creatures on Earth are able to recognize the Universal Mind, consciously interact with it, and thereby transcend it.

Remote viewers successfully tap into the noosphere, that global information resource connecting all things and ordering the world, using specific methodologies to accurately envision people, places, or things separated by time and space. While some methods may involve especially receptive individuals using complex procedures that require months or even years of training by experienced facilitators, remote viewing is not limited to naturally gifted adepts. It would appear instead that the capacity was developed as part of human evolution and may have atrophied only with the advent of civilization five thousand years ago.

During the previous millennia man lived on more intimate terms with Nature, and the struggle to survive energized every one of his senses to the utmost. Life itself depended on his sensitivity to each nuance in the environment. City walls and armies to protect him muted this sensitivity but did not destroy it. A close variation of remote viewing is remote sensing. The difference is small but significant. Swann describes remote viewing as "the ability to access information from a remote geographic location using something other than the known five senses."[4]

One of the original members of the 1980s military remote-viewing team says that remote viewing initially referred only to a set of protocols used to test, quantify, evaluate, and, if possible, conclusively prove innate psychic powers under scientifically controlled circumstances. Researcher Angela Thompson Smith adds that once remote viewing "gained scientific respect, almost anyone who had done anything 'psychic' jumped on the bandwagon and started calling what they did 'remote viewing.'"[5] Lyn Buchanan believes a distinction needs to be made between indefinite New Age versions of remote viewing and "Controlled Remote Viewing, as a definite protocol, with certain rules and regulations."[6]

In an effort to make that distinction, remote sensing might be described as distant viewing. This means that human consciousness is expanded to obtain the accurate image of a specific place or thing. Thompson Smith tells us, "According to Swann, the RV [remote-viewing] model consists of five definite components: a subject, active ESP abilities, a distant target, the subject's recorded responses, and confirmatory positive feedback. When one of these component parts is missing, remote viewing has not taken place."[7]

Remote sensing or distant viewing is thus defined by the removal of the final component, because "confirmatory positive feedback" is not required and does not necessarily occur. Recent finds being made in remote sensing are nothing new but rather represent the rediscovery of a lost talent latent in everyone. Given the universal character of that ability, the editors at *FATE* magazine invited readers to personally participate in the first distant-viewing experiment of its kind. Never before had so many "perceivers" been asked to join in remote viewing a common target. *FATE* requested that every person who read the article follow a simplified procedure aimed at envisioning an unknown feature of the same location.

If you wish to attempt a remote viewing, complete the step-by-step process described on pages 82–84. Regardless of your level of success you should at least experience an enhanced psychic receptivity. At most, you may become part of a dramatic discovery, with powerful implications for the rest of the world—because our remote-viewing target is the Great Sphinx of ancient Egypt. Perhaps the most famous man-made object on Earth, the Sphinx stands among the pyramid complex of Giza, near the Lower Nile.

The 240-foot-long structure was sculpted from a single ridge out of the living rock and stands 66 feet high. Although largely intact it suffers from both man-made and natural damage. Islamic Mamelukes in the eighteenth century peppered its face with rifle bullets and shot off the nose. Severe erosion at the base was caused by rainwater, a fairly recent discovery that in a single stroke dismantled archaeological dogma that insisted throughout the twentieth century that the Sphinx dated back no earlier than 2550 B.C.E.

But Egypt only experienced the kind of wet conditions that eroded the monument at least two thousand years earlier, after the last Ice Age. Obviously the Sphinx must have been created before the rains came. Its face has been officially ascribed to Khafre, the fourth king of the Fourth Dynasty, who was also supposed to have built Giza's second-largest pyramid, but both claims, however official, are bogus and easily dismissed. The so-called Inventory Stele found by Auguste Mariette, the nineteenth-century French Egyptologist, records that Khufu, Khafre's predecessor, built a temple beside the Sphinx, which was

Figure 14.1. The Great Sphinx.
Brooklyn Museum Archives
(S10|08 Giza, image 9627).

already standing when Khafre became pharaoh. Forensic comparison of Khafre's facial features as preserved in several portrait statues reveal that his is not the face of the Sphinx.

It is no wonder that Edgar Cayce, the so-called Sleeping Prophet, referred to the Sphinx as "that enigma that is still the mystery of mysteries."[8] He said that it was built as a cooperative effort between native Egyptians and newcomers arriving at the Nile Delta as refugees from the destruction of Atlantis. Deep under the left paw of the Great Sphinx, Cayce stated, the Ancients excavated a subterranean chamber, a Hall of Records. In it they placed written records describing the Atlantean catastrophe and the subsequent rebirth of civilization in the Nile Valley, where the surviving culture bearers settled to intermarry with the indigenous inhabitants.

The dynastic Egyptians were a happy hybrid of the two different but fundamentally complementary peoples. All this and much more is supposedly described in detail at the underground Hall of Records. During the mid-1990s subsurface soundings at the front of the Great Sphinx did indeed indicate that a subterranean corridor, at least, runs under the monument. Unfortunately, the Egyptian authorities forbade further work at the site for fear of damaging the fragile structure. It is at this yet undiscovered feature that we shall direct our collective consciousness.

HOW TO REMOTE VIEW

The target of *your* remote-viewing experiment will be the Atlantean Hall of Records that Edgar Cayce reported lay underground at the Sphinx. To successfully complete the exercise, you must follow a simple procedure known as controlled remote viewing (CRV). As experimenter Paul H. Smith describes it, "Information obtained through CRV is carried to the viewer on a theorized 'signal line' which the viewer's subconscious detects. The goal of CRV is to facilitate the transfer of information from the viewer's subconscious, across the threshold of

still fresh in the memory they were described in specific reports and/ or illustrations, some of which are reproduced here. As the first undertaking of its kind, the results were insightful, to say the least.

We are very grateful to the many readers who sincerely devoted their time and energies to this experiment. While each of their reactions was individually unique, the number of common elements they shared is remarkable. For example, all but two persons participating in the remote-sensing project identified the location of the subterranean chamber beneath the left paw of the Sphinx. One reader placed it between both paws; another, at the rear of the monument. Their observations were not necessarily incorrect, because many investigators believe that an entire complex of corridors and chambers, with numerous entrances at various locations, lies under the Sphinx. The left paw seems, however, to rest over access to the feature Cayce identified as the Hall of Records.

Frances Colvin remembers entering on the inner side of the left paw, although she "is not sure how to get in." Descending down a gradual incline, the subterranean corridor goes north. Finally arriving at the chamber, she found it faintly but clearly lit, a discovery Frances shared with virtually every remote sensor. Eva Martin wrote how the interior filled with "a shimmering light." A reader who preferred to contact us under a name appropriate to the occasion, Isis of the Lotus, described the room as illuminated by "an internal light of its own."

Mildred Bolton, Jeannette Buck, Patricia A. Davey, and Betty Wood all mentioned that the chamber glowed with "an inner light." To Sherri Gould, it seemed like "indirect lighting." According to Connie Roberts, the chamber was alive with "a golden light as though from a lantern made of material much thicker than glass, more like quartz." Evelyn Bell similarly described "a crystal light source."

To Phyllis Nash and Ruth Smith, the room was "dimly lit." The mysterious light perceived by our readers has its parallels on the Giza Plateau, which the Sphinx shares with the Great Pyramid. There, from ancient times to the present day, an irregularly occurring phenomenon has been seen by a few fortunate eyewitnesses and documented by trained observers. Visitors at the Giza Plateau sometimes see the summit of the Great Pyramid lit by a bluish haze, cloud, mist, or halo of varying luminosity.

Whatever we may think of the notorious cabalist, Aleister Crowley did spend a night inside the pyramid's so-called King's Chamber in 1903. He was surprised to see that the entire compartment was suffused in a blue glow, the source of which he could not determine. Crowley reported that he could read by the light, although it was very dim. The Great Pyramid's blue light continues to be observed by modern observers, who usually doubt the testimony of their own senses.

Another American visitor, William Groff, was equally astounded to witness a blue light illuminating the summit of the Great Pyramid. As a prominent physicist he was influential in bringing fellow scientists from the Institut Egyptien to the structure. Despite an exhaustive investigation of its internal passages, however, they were unable to find a cause for the phenomenon. While early reports of the event were filled with superstitious dread, investigators today believe the pyramid's inner light is generated by increasing stress within the Earth directly beneath the structure.

As tectonic forces building up to release their energies in an earthquake exert increasing pressures on granite and/or other crystalline rock in the planet's crust, a piezoelectric charge is emitted. The Giza Plateau with its Sphinx and pyramids sits within a seismically active zone, so the light sometimes seen flashing at its apex probably results from the same energies responsible for *earthquake lights* witnessed elsewhere, particularly in Japan, southern California, and Peru, where they are known as the *Andes glow*.

FATE readers who remote sensed the room under the Sphinx appear to have seen this seismically induced phenomenon, just as Crowley and others experienced a similar illumination inside the King's Chamber of the Great Pyramid. The similar reports of Connie Roberts and Evelyn Bell are particularly interesting in this regard, because they associated the subterranean light with crystal, which is an important component in harnessing, magnifying, and directing electrical power. In the case of the Sphinx, that power source is nothing less than seismic forces in the Earth itself. Perhaps the ancient Egyptians knew about the relationship between crystals and electrical energy and endeavored to put that knowledge to work for them.

When Ted Venske remote sensed the interior of the underground chamber he saw "some kind of an electrical device, like a battery or capacitor." Theresa Behnken also saw "machines that may have used some kind of magnetic energies." Frances Colvin visited several underground rooms interconnected by a series of corridors beneath the Giza Plateau. In one chamber she perceived a large collection of flying craft tracing the progress of aviation, not only as we know it from the early twentieth century but as it developed in previous civilizations unfamiliar to us. The same room was filled with large display tables featuring numerous, utterly strange mechanical devices, some of them apparently robotic.

Shirley Ann McDaniel reported seeing five crystals, each from seven to ten inches tall and five inches across, mounted on the wall of one room beneath the Sphinx. These oversized crystals "generated energy which they (the Egyptians) used for a variety of things, such as healing or rejuvenating the human body." Phyllis Nash felt the chamber had been made earthquake-proof, perhaps as part of the ancient technology aimed at harnessing seismic energies for electromagnetic conversion. Possibly as an example of that lost technology, some kind of mechanical "orb" was also seen at the center of the room.

This detail in her report is one of the most remarkable parallels of our study, because another reader, Mildred Bolton, wrote, "in the center of the room will be a silver-colored ball that rotates continuously. There will be evidence to show how different forms of energy can be used in the universe, and how thought is one of these energies." A more common parallel shared by our participants was their observation that the Sphinx is connected by underground passageways to the pyramids standing behind it.

J. Doss stated "at least one tunnel connects to the pyramids," while

Patricia Davey and "Isis of the Lotus" wrote that a passageway directly connected the Sphinx with the Great Pyramid. These interconnecting corridors underscore the supposition of many unconventional investigators who believe the three pyramids and Sphinx were conceived and built together as one sacred site. All but one of the participants in our remote-sensing experiment described the underground chamber with similar dimensions.

Mildred Bolton reported that it is about thirty feet across, while Shirley Ann McDaniel found it twenty-four by thirty feet. Everyone remembered its low ceiling, "only tall enough to stand in," according to Ted Venske, an observation seconded by Ruth Smith, who estimated its height at about five feet, eight inches. Heather Sickels and "Isis of the Lotus" likewise characterized the chamber as "low ceilinged." There was also a general consensus about the documents found inside.

Even hieroglyphs decorating the walls were, as Douglas White Jr. described them, "non-Egyptian." He was unable to read them, but somehow knew they were important. To J. Doss, all the preserved texts were "unexplainable." Their "unknown language," as Jeannette Buck characterized it, is probably Atlantean, because the records written in "an indecipherable language" on gold, silver, platinum, and copper tablets spelled out the history and achievements of Atlantis, according to Theresa Behnken.

Ted Venske likewise saw copper plates inscribed with histories, geographies, medical, and scientific texts. They were one-quarter inch thick and slightly smaller than their 3.5-inch-by-4-inch containers. So too, "Isis of the Lotus" reported that the chamber preserves records dealing with astronomy, mathematics, literature, history, prophecy, and acoustics. Sherri Gould also wrote that the records contain information about past and future events. But mention of acoustics seems especially pertinent in view of recent discoveries by mechanical engineer Christopher Dunn, implying that the ancient Egyptians applied high frequency sounds for construction purposes.

An email from a participant who identified himself only as "Moon Guy" stated that scrolls in the subterranean room tell of "mankind's origins." Other clues supplied by our readers suggest Atlantis. Theresa Behnken writes that the walls of the chamber's interior are composed of black, white, and red stone decorated with sheets of precious metals—precisely the same arrangement described by Plato, the fourth century B.C.E. Greek philosopher, in his dialogue the *Kritias,* for the building materials characteristic of Atlantean monumental construction. She also mentions the presence of *orichalcum* in the chamber. It, too, was cited by Plato as a high-grade copper alloy invented by Atlantean metalsmiths. Phyllis Nash likewise saw hieroglyphs in red and white with golden borders. She believes the original face of the Sphinx belonged to an important personage from Atlantis "with some Native North American DNA."

Mildred Bolton stated that the ceiling of the underground chamber is emblazoned with a zodiac, reminiscent of the Dendera Zodiac still visited by tourists to Egypt. Frances Colvin similarly noticed an astrological design on the ceiling. It was executed in blue and resembled the glyph for Cancer. In Greek mythology, Atlas, the first king of Atlantis, is portrayed as a man supporting on his shoulders the sphere of the zodiac, not the Earth, a common misunderstanding of his function as the inventor of astrology. Hence the origin of his name from *atla,* "to uphold," in the Sanskrit language, the parent tongue of classical Greek. It seems fitting, then, that our readers found a representation of the zodiac on the ceiling of a room dedicated to preserving information about Atlantis, the birthplace of astrology.

Frances also perceived a kind of underground museum displaying engineering tools and mundane items such as dishes, fabrics, eating utensils, and toys from "pre-Atlantean times." A majority of the participants describe the underground room as "gritty and wet," "damp," or "cool." Shirley Ann McDaniel explains that a subterranean river runs through the complex beneath the Sphinx, yet another parallel with the ancient Egyptians, who told the Greek travel-writer

Figure 14.2. Escape from Atlantis.
Original painting by Kenneth Caroli.

Herodotus in the sixth century B.C.E. that the Great Pyramid was built over an underground water source.

His report complements Theresa Behnken's observation that the subterranean complex at the Sphinx is a labyrinth or maze formed out of a natural cave, and Sherri Gould's contention that the monument and the chambers presently beneath it were originally constructed over an astrobleme, or meteor crater. Her statement takes on special significance for some researchers who conclude that the monuments at the Giza Plateau were intended to memorialize Atlantis and its destruction by some celestial catastrophe. Remarkably she and Mildred Bolton, respectively, characterize at least one of the chambers underneath the Sphinx as "a large oval room" and "rounded."

Many remote-sensing participants perceived a stone "table" or "altar" (often identified as granite) positioned at the center of the chamber. Strangely, at least one volunteer saw it collapsed and folded away, leaning against a wall, as though waiting to be set up. He and his fellow experimenters share other observations in common, such as the presence of metallic cylinders somehow preserving cosmic and even musical knowledge; jars of grain; numerous scrolls wound around ornate, wooden handles and well-preserved in animal hides, all neatly stored in pigeonholed ledges, as though in wine-bottle racks. Many participants noticed urns filled with jewels.

Frances Colvin entered a chamber filled entirely with precious gems. Other psychic observers, like Heather Sickels and Shirley Ann McDaniel, tell of collapsed sections of the underground complex with piles of sand and other debris somewhat filling the various rooms and corridors. Nancy Van Scriver found "sand traps" filling the corridor that led into the chamber. The damage perceived by Donald A. Buchanan was more serious. Water, not sand, had seeped into the repository over the centuries, rotting part of its timber construction and spoiling or destroying many documents. Most, however, are still in relatively good condition.

Both S. Gardner and J. Doss perceived images of young children associated with the Sphinx. The number and close resemblance of so many details perceived almost identically by dozens of men and women scattered across the country and unknown to one another go far to establish the veracity of their observations. Just as fascinating are those details of the Sphinx and its underground chamber uniquely reported by just one volunteer. For example, Eva Martin alone saw the sarcophagus of a woman in the chamber. Mildred Bolton said that the Sphinx—half-beast, half-human—was built as a monument to mankind, itself an experiment for the fusion of matter and spirit.

Connie Roberts was startled to find another composite image inside the chamber, this one something of an "ant-spider" carved into a sandstone rock. Shirley Ann McDaniel writes that the present face of the Sphinx is the third of its kind. It memorializes a blond, leonine people who created dynastic Egypt. A statue of this lost race is preserved in the nearly life-size statue of a man that can be found in the underground room. According to Theresa Behnken, translation problems posed by the various written languages found inside will be assisted by the discovery of a "Rosetta Stone" equivalent.

Phyllis Nash learned through her psychic journey to the Sphinx that its secrets were still known as late as the first century B.C.E., when another "Great," this one Cleopatra VII, shared them in confidence with first Julius Caesar, then Marc Antony. She was, after all, the chief priestess in the cult of Isis. An emblem resembling an S outlined in green and banded in red was seen by Jeannette Buck over the entrance to the chamber, although she could not determine its significance. Perhaps the S represents the serpentine (i.e., seismic) power that courses through the Giza Plateau, activating its monuments.

Betty Wood perceived a huge boulder at the rear of the Sphinx that must be moved aside before the entrance to the chamber is accessible. That done, a huge flight of stairs, almost as wide as the Sphinx itself and comprising ten steps, will be seen to lead down toward the subterranean room. Once there, visitors will discover another sphinx, this one just five inches high, writes Paul Cartwright. It will open to reveal a golden ring mounting a precious green jewel. Nearby, "a collective letter in homage to a god" will be found inscribed on a golden tablet. S. Gardner convincingly reports that the Sphinx was originally known to its Atlanto-Egyptian builders as the Great Face.

Dynastic Egyptians simply referred to the monument as Hu, or guardian. *Sphinx* is a much later Greek word signifying the combination or "binding up" of several diverse elements, as seen in the human- or god-headed lion. According to Gardner it once had "a female nose, and a neckpiece that went to the ground, with fancy shoulder details. I had a feeling of a long time past; this is as close as I can get to the feeling in words." The Sphinx has been repaired and reconfigured many times, not only in our modern era but during the Roman occupation and in Pharaonic times.

For Gardner the experience became progressively weird: "The face was waking, and its lips moved. I nearly lost it here. It was, to say the least, a most nerve-rattling event!"

After completing this report, inspired by the remote-sensing adventure undertaken by our readers, I decided to try the experiment myself. Following the six-step procedure, I found myself descending a narrow, somewhat steep flight of stairs into the ground somewhere in the immediate vicinity of the Sphinx. The entrance and exact location were never clear.

The stairway, dimly lighted from no discernible source, was clammy, almost cold. It ended about twenty feet beneath the surface in a very small, plain chamber of massive stone blocks. I had to walk around a square depression, whose function I could not guess, in the center of the floor to reach the other side of the cubicle.

There I passed into another, larger room, more brightly lit but still faintly and indirectly illuminated. The dimensions of this second chamber were about twenty-two by thirty feet, as similarly described by many of our participants, although the ceiling seemed a bit higher, perhaps seven feet. A large painted zodiac decorated the ceiling. In the middle of the floor was a round, black, stone table supported by a single center stand. Other than the zodiac, the interior was undecorated by hieroglyphs or illustrations. No chairs were in the room. The left wall supported three or four full-length shelves piled with oversized books and scrolls. The latter were at the far end.

The books were all very heavy and entirely unlike modern perfect-bound volumes. Instead, their pages were compressed between two cloth-covered boards bolted at the spine by great metal clamps. Seven of these enormous tomes comprised the history of Atlantis. The cover of volume 1 was a beautiful azure with gold trimming and a single large V or A (minus the middle cross stroke). I grabbed this book first. It was in new condition, with uncommonly thick pages, dull milky white, not papyrus, but something selected for durability.

The text was handwritten with heavy black ink in a cursive script that seemed hieratic or demotic. Both were much later developments from hieroglyphs, and consequently, they could not have been contemporary with Atlantis. Perhaps the book was a dynastic copy from earlier documents. In any case, the book was profusely illustrated with large, original color paintings of forests, fields, mountains, buildings, gardens, animals, even elephants. (Plato wrote that elephants were common in Atlantis.) While unable to read a single word, I somehow knew generally what all the dozens or hundreds of books described. Their subjects ranged from astronomy, biology, and civil engineering to navigation, geography, and incantations.

There were a great many medical texts. A bright red volume was *The History of Lemuria*. It, too, featured wonderful color illustrations. The wall at the far end was blank. In front of it, to the left, was a nearly life-size statue of a man standing with a staff in his right hand. It was typically Egyptian, although the bare head had been individualized to portray a specific person. This somewhat fleshy, middle-aged head contrasted with his stylized muscular torso. The gray eyes were made of glass. The statue was set up to honor the man who had been entrusted by his superiors to collect and preserve the rare documents contained in this chamber. His name was Thoaught-tor-et, Thaut-or-es, Tha-thor-tet, or something like that. I tried repeatedly to see the right wall, but could not.

FATE reader Myron Webb was similarly obstructed when he tried to remote sense the Sphinx and its underground mystery. "I find myself encountering some kind of shield," he reported, "that won't let me see what is inside the Hall [of Records]. I sense that it is trying to tell me that the time is not right for man to know these things yet. I do sense, however, that when the time is right and the portal to the Hall is opened, mankind will receive an enlightenment of all the knowledge therein. I was, however, able to partially make out one shelf supporting a line of model ships, all skillfully made of wood and cloth. They were mostly tubby affairs, apparently commercial vessels, but of an unfamiliar type."

I returned to pore over the attractive books, and gradually understood that this place was not the Hall of Records but only one room of it dedicated to Atlantis. I somehow "knew" that it was connected by a network of underground passageways to other chambers throughout the Giza Plateau. This was an enlightening realization, because it became clear that the *FATE* readers who participated in our remote-sensing exercise were seeing not the same subterranean space but various chambers, which accounted for the similarities as well as the dissimilarities of their reports. I was also aware that this secret network had been in use by privileged persons for thousands of years, long after the decline of Egypt itself.

As Phyllis Nash observed, Cleopatra was a visitor here. So, perhaps, was Jesus. Only with the collapse of Roman civilization in the fifth century were the entrances sealed to protect the Hall of Records from destruction at the hands of the same religious zealots who burned the Library of Alexandria and tortured to death its last librarian. The work of the guardians of the subsurface library was completed and perfected by centuries of neglect, as the sands covered all signs of the precious treasures that lay beneath. With the gift of this lost piece of the past, my stay in the chamber was abruptly terminated.

15
The Book of Living and Dying

Though a well-worn subject, stunning representations of the Pyramid of Khafre, Giza's penultimate monument, against the backdrop of a starry night sky never fail to amaze me, and it always gives me a sense of wonderment to discover a new fact about Egypt.

Joann Fletcher's *The Egyptian Book of Living and Dying* shows a delicate, perfectly preserved papyrus illustration from the reign of Thutmoses III (circa 1430 B.C.E.).[1] It is a symbolic rendition of the Primal Mound in Egyptian myth, which told that it rose from the bottom of the sea and was the first home of humans and gods. Two female figures pour jars of water, which encircles the island on which men are shown tilling the soil as the sun rises from behind a twin mountain peak. Just two pages later we encounter a golden statuette of the artificer-god, Ptah, resplendent in lapis lazuli cap. Fletcher points out that the name "Egypt" may have derived from the god's enormous temple, the *Huwt-ka-Ptah,* or Mansion of Ptah's Soul.

Another masterpiece is the perfectly preserved wooden statuette of a priestess dressed in a clinging gown. Her name was Tuya, the mother-in-law of Amenhotep III. But her career was apparently other than religious, because she was also known as "chief of the entertainers" and sang in the great temples of Amun and Hathor.

*Figure 15.1. Maat, the divine personification
of balance in all things*

The religion of ancient Egypt was a gentle, life-affirming spirituality. Missing is a wrathful Jehovah intent on punishment or the heart-ripping monsters of the Aztec pantheon. Instead, the central principle of Egyptian spirituality was the notion of *Maat,* personified in a goddess of that name (see figure 15.1 on page 97). All the other deities were obliged to follow her concept of universal balance and harmony. The only alternative was chaos. Maat represents perfect equipoise, the embodiment of truth, signified by a single feather standing upright. In the Hall of Judgment, it was weighed against the soul of a deceased person. If they balanced each other out, the soul was allowed to proceed to paradise.

If the scale tilted against the soul too heavy with sin, it was devoured by a crocodile-headed beast. But there was an alternative to this grisly fate. The mystery rites of the Benu bird, better known as the Phoenix, promised escape from the jaws of eternal death, not to paradise, perhaps, but in another go at earthly existence. The title of Fletcher's book directly refers to Maat, which regarded life and death as part of the pairs of opposites that comprise the universe and enable it to function.

The dynastic Egyptians believed human beings did not stand outside this process and could begin to lead successful lives once they grasped the significance of their place in the eternal struggle.

Although I have been a student of Egyptology since a child and traveled to Egypt several times, there is always something new to uncover.

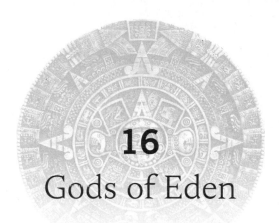

16
Gods of Eden

Andrew Collins is among the best-known investigators of unconventional archaeology, and deservedly so. In *Gods of Eden* he demonstrates that, as great as the dynastic Egyptians were, they nonetheless inherited an even earlier civilized greatness belonging to the Elder Gods.[1]

It was this class of culture creators who excelled in forms of technology only today being rediscovered. Surviving examples are granite cores produced by tubular drilling, the results of some kind of sonic tool comparable to space-age devices, but dated, incredibly, to the beginning of the Old Kingdom, just when the Nile Valley achieved political unification for the first time. Photographs of a part from just such a machine show a flywheel-like object beautifully carved from a solid block of schist and likewise dated to the start of Pharaonic civilization. Completely unlike any known cult item, it best resembles what it appears to be: a machine part.

But even these intriguing pieces of evidence from a lost, sophisticated technology were part of a cultural legacy. Collins describes a period defining the materially advanced Elder Gods, who memorialized their predynastic civilization in the Great Sphinx. The monument has already been credibly backdated by geologist Robert Schoch, through rain erosion he identified on its flanks, to seven thousand or ten thousand years ago. Collins supports these millennial parameters by pointing out that the Sphinx directly faced the helical rising of the

Figure 16.1. Pyramid of Khephren.
Photograph by Frank Joseph.

constellation Leo, which it appears to signify, in the predawn hours on the spring equinox of 9220 B.C.E.

He also points out that the nearby Great Pyramid was originally surrounded by a moat made possible by diverting the Nile River. But here too, conventional Egyptology is at odds with geology, because the structure is supposed to have been raised around 2550 B.C.E. The Nile, however, was then too far removed from the Giza Plateau on which the pyramid stands to have surrounded its base. Again, that would have been possible only about seven thousand years earlier, thousands of years before the official beginnings of Egyptian civilization. Hence both the Sphinx and the pyramid must have been built by a different, much earlier people.

How then can we explain the association of the names of dynastic kings with these monuments? Collins points out that at the commencement of Pharaonic times the Giza structures were already in advanced stages of decay. They were merely repaired by much later rulers who claimed the impressive features for their own glory. Khufu, Khephren, and Menkaure were the restorers of the pyramids and Sphinx, not their original builders. Indeed, the geological and astronomical evidence tends to support their predynastic provenance.

The use of ancient sonic technology is seen in other parts of the world, where traditions of building, particularly the levitation of massive stone, associate cyclopean construction with the deployment of organized sound. A Swedish visitor to Tibet in the early twentieth century, Dr. Hans Jarl witnessed great stone blocks being lifted invisibly into the air through the power of chanting monks arranged in a semicircle to direct and concentrate the vibration frequencies. The fate of Jericho was a reverse of this creative process, when the Ark of the Covenant was used as a weapon—a sonic disintegrator—in conjunction with a massed chorus of trumpets to destroy the city's outer fortifications. From the Ark's origins in Egypt, it was part of the acoustic technology devised by the Elder Gods, through the Hebrew Exodus and into biblical history.

When the veil is lifted the deep past is revealed as a technological world more advanced and older than ever suspected.

Places of Power
in America

17

The Valley of the UFOs

For most of my life I never saw a so-called Unidentified Flying Object—didn't know if such a thing actually existed, nor did I much care. My father was an amateur astronomer whose homemade telescopes afforded our family summertime observations of the night sky during my boyhood, but no unworldly craft ever hovered into view. Throughout my life I knew men and women who claimed to have seen strange phenomena in the heavens suggesting visitations from another planet, although I was not personally privy to extraterrestrial encounters of any kind until my early fifties when I rented an old log house in a remote area of northwestern Wisconsin.

The thickly forested area was sparsely populated, mostly spread over disconnected farmland, much of it destitute, in a valley running east to west for about thirty miles. The small village of Ridgeland was some five miles to the north, although Menomonie was the nearest city, a forty-minute drive away. Neighbors were few and far between, but I preferred nature to society, and felt relieved to have at last found refuge beyond the noisy distractions of modern life. I lived alone at the Wisconsin house, serenely content in its unspoiled isolation, for more than a year before anything unusual happened.

During all those months of seasonal change and unchanging solitude nothing in the wooded environment suggested anything paranormal or threatening, so I was unprepared for an event that took place shortly after 3:00, on the morning of April 18, 1999. The videotaped film I had been watching clicked off at its conclusion, leaving me in the dark living room to ponder my schedule of duties and events for the coming day. Thus self-absorbed, I hardly noticed a not very brilliant yellowish-green light that flashed briefly through the front window.

"Must be the police, checking on things," I assumed half-consciously, until realizing with a start that during my fifteen months residency near Ridgeland I never saw a single patrol car. I walked outside to the deck to investigate. The spring night was absolutely quiet, cool, and clear. There was not a cloud in the sky filled with stars, one of which caught my attention in the west. It seemed larger, brighter, and less familiar than the rest. And, it was moving slowly over a line of treetops about a quarter of a mile away. The yellowish-green light bobbed gently, as though suspended from a balloon, occasionally shining a faint ray, perhaps probing into the hilly forest not far across the gravel road.

I could not guess the object's size, although I felt somehow it was not very large. The perfect stillness of the night was not dispelled by a single sound as I watched the strange radiance drift above the trees for about ten seconds. It came to a sudden halt in midair, then vanished by degrees, as though a cover rotated over the light, concealing it. Irrational as it seemed in retrospect, I could not help feeling at the time that whoever controlled the object was somehow aware I observed it, and deliberately hid itself from view. Soon after its disappearance, the baying of farm dogs could be heard in the distance.

The next afternoon I asked a friend who ran the Ridgeland post office if anything unusual happened after 3:00 a.m. "Our dog started barking about then," she said. "He's never done that before."

Had I seen a UFO in the extraterrestrial sense? I wasn't sure. It made an unlikely plane, because there are no airports in the vicinity of Ridgeland. Moreover, the bouncing ball of light did not behave like an aircraft, nor did it produce any engine noise; sound travels far over the nighttime hills of northwestern Wisconsin.

Inconclusive as the sighting may have been, I gave it little thought until the following June 25. As before I stood on the deck admiring the night sky, this time hung with cosmic curtains of northern lights shimmering in ghostly folds of red, green, blue, and silver. While observing them I became gradually aware of two nutlike shadows growing larger against the backdrop of the celestial spectacle. In seconds the pair took on more defined shapes, and I could see quite plainly that they were solid forms resembling gigantic almonds, but their shared exteriors were matte black. They streaked over my barn faster than any jet plane I had ever seen, at perhaps just a thousand feet, the one in the lead differing from its companion only with the addition of a spar or antenna protruding horizontally from the forward section of its upper half.

Although their swift passage lasted but a few seconds I had a clear view of the objects, which appeared enormous. Both were at least two hundred feet long. Not a sound accompanied their high-speed flight, an impossibility because wind noise is generated even by motorless gliders during their descent through the air. In a moment the two objects vanished over the southern horizon, inexplicably leaving me more shaken than thrilled. They could have represented some human classified military technology, but my instincts felt otherwise.

At last I saw what appeared to have been authentic UFOs, and I more seriously reconsidered my previous sighting in April. The chances of seeing another one, I imagined, were more than unlikely. Before that summer was over, however, I was casually driving home and about to turn onto the road less traveled to my home, when what I took for the moon began to appear more angular than I ever noticed it being before. I stopped the car to watch it turn red, then slowly revolve and begin to disappear—not behind any clouds, because there were none. I then realized with a shock that this evening's untypical "moon" was vanishing into the south. Again a sensation of "knowing" overcame me—a feeling that whoever or whatever was in charge of the moonlike object tonight was aware of my observation and concealed itself from me.

In October, I married, and my wife, Laura, joined me as a fellow witness to additional encounters. Once, while we were driving back to

Ridgeland late one clear fall evening on Highway 25, a most unusual "shooting star" flew over the car. We glimpsed what appeared to be a large pitted boulder spinning wildly before it burst into a long, blue flame only a few hundred feet above us, or so it seemed. We wondered how many other observers had seen such a "meteor," certainly the most unusual we ever saw.

On the same road, driving across especially desolate areas, enigmatic searchlights occasionally rose from the ground into the clouded night sky. They did not belong to farm machinery, because we saw them during the dead of winter when the few impoverished fields in the vicinity were abandoned for hundreds of square miles in every direction.

More unusual and frightening were noises we sometimes heard long after sundown. Beginning in January 2000, the sound of large-scale drilling seemed to come floating on a southwest breeze late at night from an unimaginable location not too far away. On at least half a dozen separate occasions that winter we could hear serious grinding going deep into the earth. The sound was as eerie as it was inexplicable, and we prayed whatever caused it would stay away from us until the dawn gave us renewed courage.

In the morning we jumped into our car to find the source of the nighttime racket, even though I was already familiar with the economically depressed area for many miles around and knew that no one in that part of the state operated large drill rigs of any kind, certainly not at 2:00 a.m. in the middle of winter. Riding over the desolate acreages of often deserted farmland, we never saw anything remotely capable of producing the terrible grinding sound we heard after dark. Laura theorized "they" were drilling into the limestone aquifers that ran throughout the Wisconsin valley to remove some of its exceptionally good water.

We shared none of our experiences with others, however, until March, when the twenty-eight-year-old son of our landlord paid us a visit, ostensibly to inquire about the possibility of remodeling the place. Before leaving he looked at me with an uncertain expression and wondered aloud if we ever saw "anything strange around here."

"Such as?" I asked disingenuously. Before he could think of a proper response, Laura announced to my annoyance, "Frank's seen flying saucers!"

"That's it," he agreed with a smile. "You're not the only one. That's why I asked. Many people have been seeing UFOs in these parts for many years. You can ask just about any family around Ridgeland or in between the other towns. Most have had their own encounters."

"What about you?" I asked. "You grew up in this house."

"Well, to give you an example, when I was fifteen, back during the late '80s, on a summer evening I was standing with my dad and brothers in the driveway after hanging up our gardening tools in the barn. Mom was looking at us through this window, trying to tell us to come in for dinner, when she pointed excitedly at the barn. We turned around and saw a cigar-shaped . . . thing—hovering about fifteen feet over the roof. It didn't move or make a sound, like it was nailed in place but airborne. It was very dark brown, maybe only ten feet long, and looked something like a helicopter fuselage without propellers or the plastic bubble for a pilot.

"All four of us stared at it for a good half minute, then it just shot away up into the sky and disappeared in a second or two. We all had other sightings, individually, mostly late at night, but that was the only time the whole family saw the same thing, and during daylight."

Fascinated and relieved to learn that Laura and I were not the only ear- and eyewitnesses to extraterrestrial-like activities in Wisconsin's Great Northwest, I followed the young man's tip and began looking into other reports in the area. My research turned up something more than the usual sightings made around the world. It seems that Belleville and Elmwood recently vied with one another for the title of UFO Capital of the World. The thirty or so miles between these two small towns at opposite extremes of the valley including Ridgeland may indeed feature the highest number of such sightings on Earth.

A surge of similar reports began quite suddenly in 1975 when police officer Glen Kazmar reported a cluster of blue, red, and white lights hovering over Belleville. They were witnessed by fellow officers as well as a number of townspeople for the next several nights. Leading Elmwood citizens, including a schoolteacher, local police, and a deputy sheriff claimed to have seen bizarre craft flying in the vicinity of their town as well. Before the end of the decade, thirty-five such accounts had been filed with the city law enforcement authorities.[1]

A typical report was made in early October 1977 by Paul Fredrickson, a nursing home administrator, who, like myself, mistook something else for the moon. "I took one look at the speed it was approaching," he recalled, "and knew it could not be the moon. It was round and a bright orange, but as it came close, it turned out to be crescent shaped. The light was coming from the front end. As it hovered near us, we could see the underside very clearly. It was round, nearly saucer shaped, dark grey, and about fifty feet in diameter. Before it came over us it made no sound, but when it passed at about a thousand feet up from us, it made a *whoosh* as it passed over. It disappeared so fast, it was gone with a snap of your fingers. I felt elated and frustrated. I wish I had a piece of the ship so I could have concrete evidence of what I saw."[2]

Nearby Chippewa Falls is the home of the UFO Site Center Corporation, whose members announced the proposed construction of an extraterrestrial landing pad at Elmwood, where the alien craft seemed to be constellating. Although the venture was backed by Elmwood's mayor, it fell through for lack of funds in 1999, but over the past nineteen years this town of one thousand residents has staged an annual UFO Days festival, with floats and celebrations welcoming the space brothers.

More serious was an encounter of the worst kind experienced on the night of April 22, 1976, when police officer George Wheeler investigated a flaming-red object hovering a hundred feet or so over central Elmwood. As he drove up beneath the craft, his radio abruptly ceased to function. Sometime later David Moots, a local resident, saw the patrol car sitting silently and unlit in the middle of a downtown street. Inside, Officer Wheeler was barely conscious.

In response to ambulance technicians trying to save his life on their ride to the emergency ward, Wheeler claimed he had been hit in the chest with a painful red ray that shot from the UFO through his windshield. As his health rapidly deteriorated for causes his doctors could not determine, he repeatedly told them, to their consistent disbelief, that he was dying from the mysterious effects of internal injuries caused by alien beings. Within six months after his April encounter, Officer George Wheeler died "of unknown causes."[3]

What is it about the Belleville-Ridgeland-Elmwood area that attracts visitors from another world? Whatever the reason or reasons, the relationship between extraterrestrials and the territories where they are sighted cannot be discounted. Investigators hoping to learn some answers may wish to camp out in Wisconsin's Valley of the UFOs—if they dare.

18

The Disturbing Imagery of Pre-Columbian America

Since 1983 I have been investigating the remains of a lost North American civilization known as Aztalan. Actually, that is just the name of its capital, once a 175-acre ceremonial city about halfway between Madison and Milwaukee in southern Wisconsin. Three mighty walls with watchtowers regularly spaced every twenty feet encircled a trio of earth pyramids oriented to the movements of the sun, moon, and the planet Venus. An extended irrigation system connected the city with Rock Lake, three miles away, where the enigmatic leaders of Aztalan society interred their honored dead in stone sepulchers on small islets.

Behind their forbidding walls the ancient aristocrats lived in fine houses, traded great quantities of raw copper mined from the Upper Great Lakes region, and farmed gourmet crops. There they also conducted rituals of human sacrifice and cannibalism. Then, in the early years of the fourteenth century C.E., they suddenly and inexplicably abandoned Aztalan, burning its walls to the ground and vanishing forever into the American wilderness. Why they abruptly relinquished their empire, which spread throughout Wisconsin and into neighboring

Figure 18.1. Aztalan's Pyramid of Venus behind re-created stockade.
Aerial photograph by Frank Joseph.

Iowa, Illinois, and Indiana—with commercial links as far as the Gulf of Mexico and the Virgin Islands—continues to baffle researchers.

Since their unaccountable disappearance seven centuries ago, the Rock Lake necropolis has gradually sunk beneath the waves and into legend. All that remains of Aztalan itself are two reconstructed mounds and a modern version of part of the wall, together with several hundred broken artifacts in several Wisconsin museums. In conducting my own investigation of this little-known chapter in ancient American history, I have called upon many old and original sources, but none more startling than the work of Theodore Hayes Lewis, a surveyor who, alone and with little money, personally explored and documented the prehistoric ceremonial centers and effigies of the Middle West.

Beginning in 1881 he eventually covered some 54,000 miles, more than 10,000 of them on foot, often foraging through the most hostile terrain, to find, measure, and document hitherto little-known or newly discovered ancient earthworks before they were obliterated—sometimes before his very eyes, as he was in the process of sketching them—by the inexorable advance of agricultural development. Twentieth-century analysis of his line drawings showed that all the sites he documented before most of them vanished depicted authentically prehistoric, indigenous creations, not the work of white settlers or earlier explorers.

Because the fragile remains of pre-Columbian America were being destroyed by advancing civilization, Lewis knew he was working against time to at least preserve their memory. He was particularly interested in ancient rock art and the often-enormous effigy mounds—mostly animal representations, but some abstract designs skillfully sculpted from the earth itself. Lewis meticulously surveyed thousands of these premodern structures for fourteen years, dying in obscurity around 1930. Fortunately, his original artwork is preserved in dozens of large folders and microfilm copies at St. Paul's Minnesota Historical Center.

There I read his unpublished field notes written in his own hand, and paged through the vast collection of his illustrations. They range over the first to fifth centuries C.E., when North America's enigmatic civilizers raised an incredible ten thousand sculptures, a majority of them in Wisconsin, and Lewis succeeded in surveying most before they were forever lost. His accuracy in reproducing each one shows not only his dedication but also his professional expertise. He drew what he saw, bequeathing to new generations an exact likeness of a vanished world of gargantuan earth sculpture, commonly of giant creatures beautifully and precisely molded according to some forgotten standardized system of lengths and measures. Many are so realistically configured that the species of the animal portrayed can be readily identified. Others are bizarre, unfathomable abstracts.

As I paged through Lewis's illustrations I felt I was literally turning the pages of time to the late nineteenth century, seeing these wondrous images through his eyes and far beyond into the distant past. Clearly, most of the effigy mounds were accurate re-creations of what the ancient Americans saw on a daily basis. There were obvious figures of buffalo and deer, birds and fish, cats and dogs. Every so often, however, I came upon an image that riveted my attention in disbelief. Between the numerous representations of eagles or spiders appeared . . . elephants.

At first I doubted my own interpretation of the renderings. But there were others even more unmistakably elephantine. Nor were they images of mastodons, which did indeed inhabit our continent until about eleven thousand years ago. No, the ancient earth mounds represented modern elephants. Altogether, I counted six distinctly elephant effigies formerly located in Wisconsin's Rock and Vernon Counties, and Allamakee and Lansing Counties in Iowa. But the Lewis drawings held more surprises.

At Dodge County, Wisconsin, he surveyed the 176-foot-long image of an oceangoing Arctic seal. On the north shore of Lake Wingra, he found the effigy of a Peruvian llama, 127 feet long and 3 feet high. How a people living at least a thousand years ago and inhabiting the Upper Middle West could have been familiar enough with creatures from India, the Arctic, and South America to so accurately portray them in colossal earthworks is no small mystery. At Pipestone Mountain, Wisconsin, Lewis reproduced a cave drawing of a nude male figure with a knotted club raised in its right hand—a typical representation of Hercules throughout Classical Europe, but found most often along the Atlantic shores of North Africa.

Near the American Hercules appears an unusual design, a triangle within a circle, a symbol occurring among the Guanche, the original, pre-Spanish inhabitants of the Canary Islands off the Moroccan coast. Is the Wisconsin figure an example of cultural coincidence, or was it left behind by visitors from far over the sea centuries ago? A clue may have formerly existed in certain earth effigies Lewis surveyed around Aztalan itself. They were gigantic mounds shaped into the configuration of oars, often in excess of 160 feet long; their very size suggests sea power. Perhaps they were the emblems of a proficient maritime people, who navigated farther than present-day mainstream scholars give them credit for, and who perhaps saw many animals not indigenous to the Midwest.

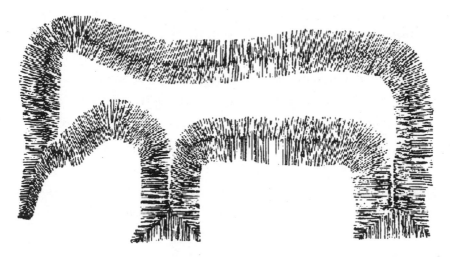

Figure 18.2. One of numerous elephant mounds in western Wisconsin illustrated by T. H. Lewis

This interpretation of the oar mounds as symbols of seamanship is underscored by the numerous examples of prehistoric American petroglyphs and cave art dealing with turtles and tridents, both indicative of travel by water. An even more perplexing image appeared in Rock County, near one of the elephant mounds, where Lewis discovered the 98.5-foot-long effigy of an animal with wheels instead of hooves. Historians are unanimously agreed that Native Americans had no knowledge of the wheel before the sixteenth-century arrival of Europeans. The singular earthwork self-evidently portrays a horse, a no less anomalous identity, because the animal was first introduced by the same modern Europeans.

The most famous wheeled horse in history, the Trojan horse, was invented by Bronze Age Greeks as a siege weapon in their war against Ilios, capital of Troy. Were the ancient creators of the Rock County effigy somehow familiar with Homer's epic? The mound is absolutely unique, lacking any other parallel among the many thousands of earthworks in North America or anyplace else. Together with the elephant and Hercules images, it at least suggests contact with Old World themes going back more than three thousand years. The atypical effigies surveyed by Lewis are not the only disquieting images in the North American landscape we documented.

The illustrations in question may portray a shaman's drug-induced hallucinations, or perhaps represent something else. Deep inside a large cave in Allamakee County, just west of the Mississippi River among yet more elephant mounds appeared an otherwise unseen figure. It seemed to Lewis related to a generally similar specimen of rock art he copied from inside a cave in La Crosse County on the east bank of the Mississippi. The subterranean walls of both the Iowa and Wisconsin sites were decorated with the profuse imagery of stars, suns, and crescent moons, implying a celestial setting.

Portrayed amid Allamakee County's heavenly depiction floated a kind of zoomorphic vehicle with two orderly rows of fourteen rectangular windows and something resembling a burst of radiant energy streaming from or behind its dorsal position. La Crosse County's cave contained the even more bizarre image of a vaguely humanoid creature descending from the night sky. Was this rock art the result of altered states of consciousness, or was it intended to illustrate mythic tales that were forgotten with their prehistoric creators?

Or were these extraterrestrial-like images, like the recognizable effigy mounds of Middle Western fauna, the re-creation of things the ancient artists actually witnessed? However one may attempt to answer such questions, they never would have been considered without the life's work of Theodore Lewis.

19
Illinois Sacred Sites

While the Land of Lincoln is best known around the world today for its Windy City, Chicago's mundane powers of money and politics are complemented by older influences of a subtler kind. A southward drive of about five hours brings visitors to the Shawnee National Forest, the largest natural preserve in the United States. And some say the most mysterious. Spirit apparitions and fantastic creatures furtively prowl its leafy shadows today just as they have for generations. The modern camper has his or her own accounts of spectral encounters similar to early settlers' tales of the *Whangdoodle,* a phantom tiger.

The resident Mohawk Indians still recall the ghostly giants who fashioned the weirdly formed canyons. The dark, extensive character of the Shawnee National Forest naturally lends itself to such accounts. It was here, for example, that the last-known wild mountain lion in the state was killed more than 170 years ago, but longtime natives of the area continue to catch fleeting glimpses of the allegedly extinct big cats, or hear their blood-chilling cries in the night. Old-timers wink knowingly and say, "That's the Whangdoodle!"[1]

While phantom felines and Indian ghosts certainly impart a strong sense of the unusual to Shawnee, they are less easily observed than the forest's foremost archaeological site. By no means confined to the exclusive interests of dispassionate academics, the so-called Lewis Wall is part of the mystical atmosphere pervading the park. Even cynical professionals are baffled by the gaunt rampart and confess their astonishment at its construction.

Beyond the Lewis Wall's marvelous engineering achievement, however, is the palpable magic of the place, a living sacred center. Spreading for several hundred acres in all directions are the natural stone columns and twisting canyons that gave this part of the Shawnee National Forest its name: Giant City. The fabulous sheer cliffs and colossal embankments do indeed seem to have been crafted by the ogres of Mohawk legend. No less impressive, the Lewis Wall is unquestionably man-made. But by whom?

Native American oral traditions assign its construction to the same alien giants who fashioned the rest of the park. They were said to have arrived at the southern shores (the Gulf of Mexico?) of Turtle Island (North America) as refugees sailing across the sea from some military disaster that rendered them immigrants in a new world. Sailing up the Mississippi River, they eventually reached the Shawnee Forest, which the gods had already sanctified—particularly a spot of ground atop a cliff.

Here the giants erected a stone wall to mark off the area as a sacred precinct. Over time they intermarried with the natives and died off. But their sturdy rampart, revered by subsequent generations of Plains Indians, defied the centuries. The old wall perfectly bisects the top of a steep cliff, running along a linear east-west axis for 285 feet. Six feet at its highest point, with an average thickness of four feet, the structure is a dry-stone battlement comprising an estimated forty thousand stones, weighing altogether about 200,000 tons.

All these stones were handed up the sheer incline from the dry riverbed more than fifty feet below. The labor necessary to build such an edifice was certainly gigantic, at least on a scale of social organization, and this style of building is not observed among the Plains Indians. The wall was raised ingeniously by fitting together mostly flat stones selected for size and a rough, uniform fit. Its age attests to the untypical skill of its ancient engineers. When Emperor Claudius ruled in Rome two thousand years ago, southern Illinois's wall was new.

The stone partition's construction has been radiocarbon dated to the mid-first century C.E. It is the work of an unknown people who occupied the area for only the next hundred or so years, then vanished for unknown reasons. That it has stood fundamentally intact for twenty centuries in this major earthquake zone is proof of its high-level construction. But the Giant City wall is not unique. It was once part of a network of stone ramparts spanning hundreds of miles. At least eight similar examples, likewise situated atop forested cliffs, were arranged in a line across southern Illinois.

Strangely, all were built, occupied, and abandoned within the same time period. Some of the old walls were demolished by European settlers during the early and mid-nineteenth century as building materials for cattle fences or wells, but a few are still hidden under thick woodland growth on private property. The Giant City wall is the only such ancient edifice in Illinois still accessible to visitors. The structure appears to define a sacred space on the south end of the cliff on which it was raised. It was here that the ancient officiants engaged in their ritual activities. Their altered states of consciousness supercharged the holy ground, interacted with the natural plenum of the site, and set up emotive human vibrations in the environment still very much in evidence to modern visitors.

To Native Americans, south is the Direction of Becoming, an ancient conception that may be a clue to the esoteric significance of the site, oriented as it is toward the south. The precinct may have been a shaman's arena for initiation into his mystery cult, a staging area for coming-of-age ceremonies, or a place for even more arcane acts of transformation, such as *the flight of the bird-man* (astral projection) and control of the weather. Supporting a mystery-cult interpretation of the site is its opening to a large cave below the overhanging cliff.

Caves are commonly associated with Earth Mother energies, and practitioners often sought out the privacy of such a place to better confront the interior spirituality of our planet. Also, the space at the bottom of the cliff suggests an assembly area, accommodating at least several hundred persons, who might have been addressed by the shaman standing dramatically at the edge of the drop-off. Interestingly, the natural acoustics here are extraordinary in that the human voice reverberates as though through loudspeakers.

But even these speculations cannot answer all the questions about Giant City. Nor should they, if this sacred site is to preserve its living aura of mystery. Visitors conveniently park their cars in the small lot directly across the access road from the cliff. They walk around to the west end following a cleared path to the top of the formation, the dry streamed at the left. It was from here that the unknown wall builders collected the heavy stones for their enduring structure some two thousand years ago. It is easy to appreciate the enormity of their effort while ascending the steep incline to the summit.

The Lewis Wall, named after the mid-nineteenth-century farmer on whose land it was found, is located in a quiet place under a shadowy canopy of oak trees. Approaching the stone partition, ruinous yet magnificent, a definite shift in atmosphere is apparent. Walking through a wide gap in the structure to the precinct at the edge of the cliff, the mood shifts to a sense of resident power. It is a physical link between the corporeal dimension and the ethereal. Fortunately, the site is not overrun with noisy tourists. It is well maintained and affords space and quiet for meaningful, uninterrupted meditation.

A better-known Illinois sacred site is also among the region's most spiritually powerful centers. Starved Rock State Park is an 1,850-acre forested paradise of sometimes hidden, always dramatic waterfalls spilling through bizarre canyons and titanic rock formations crafted into weirdly splendid towers by eons of erosional forces. Starved Rock's God-given beauty is the outward manifestation of an area supercharged with Earth power. Its name derives from an incident in September 1680, when the last of the Illini Indians were driven to the top of a high bluff overlooking the Illinois River.

Figure 19.1. Starved Rock.
Photograph by Frank Joseph.

The Illini had been for generations the foremost native people of the state, noted for their superb craftsmanship. But by the late seventeenth century, a coalition of enemies drastically reduced their influence through several vicious wars. A long, unbroken series of defeats substantially reduced Illini numbers, until hardly more than a remnant was left to make its last stand atop a high bluff. Around its base gathered large numbers of Potawatomi, Miami, and Kickapoo warriors, all bent on genocide. While protected from direct assault by their impregnable position, the trapped Illini's predicament was exacerbated by the onset of a smallpox epidemic.

Schick Shack, who later became a famous chief respected by the white man, was a nine-year-old witness to the standoff. He recalled that the disease suffered by the Illini "caused them to dig pits around the outside of the rock in the soft dirt, in which they could roll to ease their agony."[2] Their situation became more desperate still when food and water began to give out. Some Illini tried to make a break for freedom through the surrounding woods, but were caught, bound, and brought to a high precipice just east of the bluff.

Here, at what was subsequently known as Camp Rock, the Potawatomi tortured their captives to death in full view of the beleaguered Illini. A young man and his new bride, however, escaped execution when, hand in hand, they broke from their fiendish captors and leaped to their deaths into the canyon four hundred feet below.

Taking courage from their example other Illini similarly killed themselves by stepping from the ridge of the bluff. Interpreted as an omen for attack, the Potawatomi and their allies stormed the top, only to find the corpses of old men, enfeebled women, and children who had already died of disease and starvation. But Starved Rock's human history predates that bloody event by many centuries. Sometime after 900 C.E. a large and prosperous town operated near the base of the Rock, along the banks of the Illinois River.

It was an important way station or clearinghouse for many kinds of trade goods, including shells for mother-of-pearl decoration, nuts, raw copper, furs, brightly painted pottery, stone effigy pipes, arrowheads, and most of the religious-ceremonial items precious to the enigmatic Mound Builders. About midpoint between the great, prehistoric capital cities of Cahokia in southwestern Illinois and Aztalan in southern Wisconsin, the nameless Illinois village witnessed vessels traversing water routes from south to north and back again for two centuries. Then, around 1100 C.E., the site was suddenly, inexplicably abandoned in the midst of its prosperity, and the Illini's ancestors occupied Starved Rock for the next five hundred years.

But archaeological digs have recovered an even older human imprint in the vicinity. Graves of Woodland Indians interred just above the remains of the Mound Builders' river town prove that societies of hunter-gatherers lived throughout the area as early as three thousand years ago. Today Starved Rock draws seekers on a spiritual quest along its meandering trails and up the infamous bluff. Whenever great, natural Earth power and dramatic human actions interact, they produce a sacred center of extraordinary numinosity. Such is certainly the result at Starved Rock, where human beings have been drawn to its spiritual radiance for at least thirty centuries.

The prehistoric response to its environment, despite a relatively primitive level of society prevailing at the time, was essentially no different from our own. Those ancient Illinoisans felt the magic of the place, probably more effectively than most modern visitors, if only because their community absolutely supported all its members in their vision quests to glimpse the Divine. Human beings are instinctively drawn to places like Starved Rock because of their inherent need for personal empowerment and spiritual replenishment.

When the natural spirituality of a place has been irrevocably stamped by traumatic social interaction, the local energies become still more powerful. Despite the tragedy at Starved Rock, its enduring energies are almost entirely positive. The terrible things men did to each other have left only a faint impression in the landscape. What remains is a location in which human and natural spiritual forces have melded over time to generate a potent sacred center. From the information booth at the east end of the parking lot, visitors follow the clearly marked trail to Starved Rock itself. Alert pilgrims will pick up on the resident energies rippling beneath their feet and all about them soon after entering the wooded area.

As the path ascends to the fateful bluff, some persons experience a sense of nameless anticipation. The top of the rock affords thrilling vistas of the serpentine Illinois River and adjacent cliffs. It was at this tranquil spot that a race died. But there is less sadness here than a sense of liberation. Generally regarded as the high point of one's visit, Starved Rock is really only the beginning. More persistent explorers descend and follow the trail marked "To Lovers' Leap." Their hike through the ravine and up the other bluff is perhaps even more weirdly beautiful, with Hobbit-like architecture of natural pinnacles and rocky towers molded into fairy villages of sandstone and glittering mica.

Native Americans believe the surrealistic structures are the ancient abodes of protective, helpful spirits. In truth, the nature-made monuments are points of living Earth power, telluric capacitors concentrating the planet's inner energies. Such energies were not only intuited by prehistoric Americans but concentrated and focused in the Middle West centuries before Columbus sailed from Spain.

An outstanding example of their spiritual engineering is a structure known today as Rockwell Mound. It is the largest and most visually impressive ancient structure in the Illinois River Valley, erected at the same time Emperor Hadrian ruled the Roman Empire, more than eighteen hundred years ago. Although only fourteen feet high, approximately 1.7 million baskets of soil went into the two-acre, circular earthwork. Standing near the east bank of the Spoon River (made famous in the last century through *The Spoon River Anthology* by local dramatist, Edgar Lee Masters), it belongs to the so-called Hopewell Culture (named after a Mr. Hopewell, on whose farm the first artifacts of their kind were found) that flourished here beginning in 200 B.C.E.

The Hopewell were mound builders, miners, metallurgists, and townsmen who inexplicably disappeared around 400 C.E. Their Rockwell Mound was the main feature of a populous settlement and ceremonial center stretching three miles across the river. Most of the village's features have been obliterated over time, but the modern Dickson Mounds Museum displays large dioramas re-creating prehistoric living conditions, together with superb examples of ancient copper workmanship. Appropriately, the local Indian name for the earthwork before it was renamed by archaeologists was the Great Speaker's Hill, from which, according to native legend, a powerful chief had once admonished his people during a time of desperate war.

Test diggings at the site revealed no trace of burials, results that in addition to the structure's flattened top suggest it was built for large-scale ritual activity, ceremonies, and public pronouncements by leaders of society. If this interpretation is correct, an interesting synchronicity appears in the subsequent history of Rockwell Mound. Havana, the pioneer town surrounding the earthwork, conducted its first community meetings atop Rockwell Mound, from which Illinois politicians orated in the spellbinding histrionics of nineteenth-century rhetoric. The most famous of those statesmen was Abraham Lincoln, who felt drawn to speak from its summit.

One of his famous debates with Stephen A. Douglas took place there in October 1858. Since then the mound has witnessed numerous public gatherings, including open-air concerts under an old-fashioned gazebo. It would appear ancient energies of a ceremonial nature in Rockwell Mound continue to elicit specific human behavior. The structure is most dramatically approached from the south, up a short flight of stone steps. At the summit lies a brilliant flower garden in front of the gazebo. To the right is what appears to be a large grave. It is instead a former lily pond filled in with dirt, although how or why an early nineteenth-century headstone got there, no one knows.

Springtime views to the west, across the gentle Spoon River, represent rural Illinois charm at its most ideal. Although a public park, Rockwell Mound is often deserted, despite occasional high school band concerts at its gazebo. The place generates a nonspectacular but somehow compelling effect when visitors ascend the south stairway. Even though the mound is not very high, traffic noises seem to diminish with each step until, at the top, they are so muted, they almost vanish into thin air, perhaps absorbed by the great heap of soil itself.

Here, it is easy to feel the presence of the *axis mundi,* the World Center piercing the structure, the enormous bulk of which is a telluric battery charged with spirit power. This is the mound's spiritual focal point, its esoteric wellspring. Undoubtedly it was this very planetary quality that led the original mound builders, more than eighteen centuries ago, to choose the Havana site as the location for their massive earthwork. It was for them chiefly a gathering place where the inner and outer worlds of human experience met. Something of that function still survives at Rockwell Mound, if only modern visitors are open to its surviving energies.

Illinois is host to many more spiritual centers than the Lewis Wall, Starved Rock, and Rockwell Mound. But no others can match them for the atmosphere of mystery and ghostly presence that lingers at these premiere sacred sites.

20

The Forgotten Enigmas
of Kansas

The world was unrecognizable 520 million years ago. In that inconceivable past the entire 82,276 square miles of present-day Kansas lay beneath the waves of a vast sea. Over the millennia it drained away into the south, only to be succeeded by one inland ocean after another. Curiously, this process of recurrent inundation and evacuation came to an abrupt halt at the same moment the age of the dinosaurs ended with great suddenness. Something of planet-wide proportions must have shaken the Earth 65 million years before present.

But during the succession of North American seas, chemical and organic deposits built up rising layers of sedimentary rock: limestone, sandstone, gypsum, salt, clay, shale, and chalk—immense quantities of chalk. So much so, chalk was designated the state rock of Kansas, just as the sunflower and cottonwood tree are the state's official plant life. But it was the last great flood that gave the state its singular formation. Known to geologists as the Cretaceous Sea, it was alive with numerous varieties of shell-enclosed microscopic animals. As they died, billions of their shells piled up on the bottom.

Then the Cretaceous Sea, like all those that preceded it, retreated, leaving the accumulated shells. They were subsequently buried by enormous quantities of sand and gravel washed over them by the weathering of the Rocky Mountains. The gargantuan fossil-chalk sculptures were hidden underground for the next 64 million years until they were released by the combined energies of wind and water at a time parallel with the appearance of the first human beings. Composed of soft rock, the formations known as the Chalk Pyramids are ever changing as erosional forces constantly remold them into new shapes.

Within and against the gray shale are bands of yellow, white, and orange chalk, which are effused with an uncanny glow in the direct rays of the sun at twilight. The roughly pyramidal structures stand about four hundred feet above the Kansas plain and suggested the monumental architecture of ancient Egypt to early visitors. A feature at the far end of the group is still known as the *Sphinx* for a faint similarity to its man-made counterpart at the Giza Plateau in the lower Nile Delta. Much of the Nibrara Formation, as it is referred to by geologists, comprises natural chalk pyramids, some resembling ruinous examples of Pharaoh Khufu's famous structure.

Others rise like great pyramidal towers. One of these, a 100-foot-tall, 200-ton specimen, toppled over in earthshaking self-destruction during the late 1980s. The weird formation, in some places no more than a single foot thick, has been exposed to wind forces for the last million years, so dramatic occurrences of this kind are not entirely rare events. The Chalk Pyramids in western Kansas are as old as humankind. Both they and *Homo erectus,* our earliest direct ancestor, were born from the Earth at the same time. But the bond between humans and western Kansas's stark environment is more than coincidental.

Resemblance of the site's milieu to the ruined precinct of dynastic Egypt was and is evocative enough to justify its sobriquets, the Chalk Pyramid and the Sphinx. Strangely, this parallel to the mute memorials of the Nile Valley stirs similar human responses of awe and wonder. The Kansas pyramids emerged simultaneously with humankind from the womb of the same Earth Mother. They were fashioned by powers far greater than our own to resemble humanity's early civilization.

Figure 20.1. Chalk Pyramids of Kansas.
Photograph by Wistar92.

The human evolutionary and archaeological connection between humankind and nature in Kansas is part of our mysterious relationship with our common planetary destiny. The Chalk Pyramids occupy a solitary sacred site. They receive few visitors, but their loneliness is part of their enchantment. They stand with quiet significance on the otherwise vacant Kansas plain, surrounded by deep silences vaster than themselves, but sometimes their voices may be heard in the occasional high winds that whistle through their sandstone ledges.

Another bizarre sacred site worth seeking out lies in the north-central part of the state. Dominating the Kansas plains is a mystery that has generated controversy for more than a century. Visitors to the site one hundred miles north of Wichita soon find themselves caught up in its controversy, because the human mind cannot resist the compelling enigma of Rock City. It is named after two hundred immense, spherical rocks occupying an area the size of two football fields and dotting the flat landscape like gigantic bowling balls weighing several tons apiece. The largest specimen is twenty-seven feet in diameter, but there are many others of comparable size. All share a weird uniformity and there is an oddly disconcerting order in their placement, as though they were deliberately set up by some thoughtful ogre.

But geologists are almost universally agreed that these marbles of the gods are entirely the result of natural forces. According to the state authority, the spheres are caused by differential erosion of the Dakota sandstone. Both of these areas were once covered by a considerable thickness of sandstone. Ground water circulating through the sandy rock deposited a limy cement that grew outward in all directions from calcite crystals or limy fossil fragments scattered throughout the sandstone. As the softer uncemented portions of the sandy rock were weathered away by erosion, these spherical zones of cemented sandstone remained. There are some difficulties with this pat, wholly geological interpretation, however.

While spheroid formations similar to the Kansas example occur

Figure 20.2. Spheres of Dakota Sandstone.
Photograph Nationalparks.

elsewhere (although very rarely), Rock City's samples are unique because they do not appear in such size and number anywhere else in the world. If the geologic causes cited above were entirely responsible for the oversized spheres, they would not be the unique phenomenon they are in Kansas. Even the official researcher for the National Monument Project of the Kansas Academy of Science had to admit, "Analyses show that the cementing material is calcium carbonate, which was precipitated in the pores between the sand grains by circulating underground water. Why the cementation process was localized and why the material was deposited in more or less spherical fashion is not known."[1]

Jim Brandon in *Weird America,* his late twentieth-century classic of the abnormal, stressed the unlikelihood of a "concretion" interpretation.[2] More recently world explorer and popular archaeological writer David Hatcher Childress reaffirmed Brandon's lack of faith in an entirely geologic explanation of the rocks: "Although all are severely weathered, it is quite clear that the rocks are much more uniformly spheroidal than could be expected in a natural random formation. They may be ancient, man-made balls, and are highly similar, though more eroded, to the strange stone balls found in Costa Rica. These stone spheres are admitted by scientists to have been man-made, though what their purpose was has never been figured out. Was Rock City in Kansas made for the same, enigmatic purpose many thousands of years ago?"[3]

The Costa Rican balls Childress mentions represent one of American archaeology's most baffling mysteries. In 1940, while land was being cleared for a banana plantation, an artificial, almost perfect sphere carved from solid granite was found half buried. It was seven feet in diameter. Since that first discovery, several dozen similar balls have been found across Costa Rica, from mountaintops to the seashore. Some had been arranged into linear and triangular formations, but their significance, singly or in groups, has never been determined, nor has the culture responsible for their creation been identified.

A few have been broken open only to reveal that they are solid stone. There are no local traditions associated with them, and relative dating through a few pottery shards, which may or may not have been related to the objects, places their creation over a vague 500-year period from the sixth to eleventh centuries C.E. The Kansas balls are laid out in three distinct sets along an east-west strip 125 feet across and 1,700 feet long, the same horizon-to-horizon arrangement found at some of the Costa Rican sites. Rock City's immediate surroundings likewise suggest that something other than geologic forces alone were responsible for the colossal globes.

They are located near the confluence of the Salt and Solomon Rivers, a strategic spot for any civilization, and north of the state's other ancient sites—the stone council circles and solstice-oriented serpent intaglio of Rice and MacPherson Counties, both of which are directly connected to Rock City by tributaries of the Solomon River.

One can still ride a boat from one site to the next. If the stone spheres are indeed man-made, then they belonged to some long-forgotten civilizers who once set up their mysterious monoliths on the lonely, windswept plains of central Kansas. Archaeologists theorize that at least some of the great stone balls of Costa Rica (and possibly those in Kansas) are oriented to various celestial phenomena.

A few of the formations lie on an east-west axis following the general traversal of the sun across the sky, but such alignments appear to be only simulated parallels, not actual orientations. Childress speculates that the spheres were like magnetic crystal balls used by the ancients to scry the future. The Kansas balls are perplexing because they at once appear both natural and man-made. Their uniformity of configuration, linear layouts, groupings, and nearly perfect circular proportions seem convincingly artificial. But their severe external weathering implies great age and the millennia-long work of busy erosional forces. The extraordinary results of a vanished sea or of a vanished race, the great stone spheres of Rock City constitute a genuine sacred site.

Another sacred center in the state worth seeking out is Castle Rock, a natural formation similar to the Chalk Pyramids. Like its companion pieces, it is an Earth-energy terminal radiating deep telluric power. Castle Rock is one of the most solitary places on the face of the planet. An unquestionably man-made location is the Madonna of the Trail. The spot on which the outdoor shrine was erected in the 1970s may have been a sacred site from ancient times, as suggested by local pre-Columbian artifacts displayed in the nearby Kaw Mission. The Kaw Mission Museum at Council Grove is near the southeastern shores of Council Grove Lake. Rather than having usurped the prehistoric power focus, the Madonna of the Trail preserves the site's holy nature.

On the otherworldly side of the rich fields and plains most Americans associate with our country's Sunflower State, lesser known sacred sites pulsate with mysterious Earth energies. Visitors who experience their transcending power are sure to exclaim, as that famous Judy Garland character once did, "I don't think we're in Kansas anymore, Toto!"

21

The Sacred and Profane in Southern Wisconsin

For more years than anyone can guess, a broad, indefinite expanse of southern Wisconsin has been regarded by successive generations of diverse residents as a sacred region unique for its compelling, sometimes dark qualities. The famous writer of fantastic tales, August Derleth, often spoke of the area's "*Cthulhu* power-zones," concentrations of supernal energies so focused they could transform mere mortals into either angels or demons.[1] The denizens of Aztalan, a walled pyramid city that flourished forty-five miles west of Milwaukee eight hundred years ago, appear to have succumbed to the dark side of Cthulhu, as their civilization dissolved into human sacrifice and cannibalism, culminating in the fiery destruction of their great ceremonial center around 1325 C.E.

At the polar opposite of Aztalan is the modern Buddhist monastery of Deer Park, just south of Madison, the state capitol. The center is home and school to monks from Tibet who were forced to leave their homeland during the Communist Chinese invasion of 1959. His Holiness, the fourteenth Dalai Lama, left with 100,000 followers, most of whom resettled in India. The Wisconsin retreat is the Midwest outpost of that twentieth-century Diaspora. But the Buddhists do not

Figure 21.1. The Deer Park Temple.
Photograph by Frank Joseph.

proselytize, even though their teachings are open to interested persons. And while they long to return to their despoiled country, our own is made richer for their serene, unobtrusive contribution to America's spiritual life.

Their teachers offer classes throughout the year on theological topics and ritual practices, as well as the Tibetan language. The monks, who dedicate their lives to following the traditional moral discipline set out in Buddhist scripture, perform ancient ceremonies. The abbot, Geshe Lhundup Sopa, is among the most outstanding Buddhist scholars in the world. He established Deer Park in 1976. Its name derives from the grove in ancient India where deer were allowed to wander freely, the same grove where Buddha first enunciated the Four Noble Truths. In the past 42 years, the monastery has built an authentic Tibetan temple furnished with numerous *tankas,* or illuminated scrolls, and graceful statuary. The library contains extensive collections of Buddhist literature in Khangyur (the Tibetan language), Chinese, Japanese, Hindi, and Sanskrit. A large house provides living quarters, offices, and a conference hall. The outstanding physical feature of Deer Park is its *stupa,* a sacred monument of glistening white marble and gilt decoration, roughly pyramidal in shape, about eighteen feet tall. From its base, the state capitol dome, itself a white monument of another kind, appears floating on the distant horizon, separated from this Little Tibet by a gently sloping valley.

Deer Park's newly built stupa was personally dedicated by the Dalai Lama himself, when he visited the monument in 1989. He turned on the power, as it were, but admonished those attending the dedication ceremony that it was more important to build a stupa in their hearts. Even so, the impressive monument, incongruous as it may seem in the pastoral Wisconsin countryside, is a focal point of local telluric energy and part of Buddhist thought. Buddhism's chief aim is the personal attainment of a state of mind transcending mundane existence to achieve inner peace and self-mastery.

To attain that goal, the Four Noble Truths must be recognized. These are: (1) suffering is endemic to the human condition; (2) suffering is most often caused by ignorance, hatred, and attachment to those material things that keep us from our higher destiny; (3) freedom from suffering is possible; and (4) the means are available to win that freedom. These methods include the Hinayana and the Mahayana, or the Lesser and Greater Vehicles. The Hinayana establishes a strong sense of morality, improved concentration, and insight into the underlying nature of reality. The Mahayana graduates from the Lesser Vehicle toward genuine enlightenment, omniscience, and heartfelt compassion. Thus attained, the Mahayana divides into the Perfect Vehicle, with its emphasis on generosity, perseverance, and wisdom, plus the Tantra Vehicle, largely concerned with advanced levels of meditation.

The stupa represents all these realizations of the Buddha, the Enlightened One. But as a sacred form it predates his era, going back to far earlier, distantly related concepts of the oldest Hindu beliefs, as shown in the Adytas. These are gilded human figures along the base of the monument, supporting the level signifying the sky, or floor of heaven. The Adytas are themselves even more venerable than the Hindu style in which they are executed, because they were originally representative of Atlas, the mythic character preserved in the religion of the classical Greeks (themselves a people with roots in the East) as a Titan supporting the sky.

Atlas was the eponymous figure of Plato's Atlantis, inflected throughout many esoteric traditions as the cradle of the world's mystery religions. An Atlantean parallel with Buddhism does not end with the Adytas' Atlas-like appearance on Wisconsin's stupa. The monument features a representation of the Cosmic Egg from which all things came and to which they will eventually return in a self-renewing cycle. The same concept traces back to the Greek memory of their Pelasgian ancestors, an Atlantean Sea People, whose emblem was the Cosmic Egg emerging from the jaws of a serpent, itself symbolic of the vital power of the universe.

It is wonderful to see in Deer Park's modern stupa the collected spiritual ideas of perhaps five thousand years. In fact, the dome of the stupa is referred to as the *anda,* or egg, and sometimes as the *garbha,* or womb. *Garbha* is a particularly appropriate term in view of the name of the chief religion allegedly practiced in Atlantis, the Navel of the World. The stupa's four gateways, signifying the four cardinal directions, repeat this world-center symbolism. Interestingly, even the term *Dalai Lama* derives from *ta-le,* or ocean.

Modern Tibetan Buddhism appears to preserve esoteric concepts and symbols from its Atlantean origins still in evidence at Deer Park. The deer is an appropriate emblem of the monastery not only for its early association with the Buddha's basic teaching. The animal personifies rebirth through the process whereby its antlers regenerate themselves. Its symbolic origins are no less old than Atlantis itself, and perhaps even more so, because the Neolithic sites of Çatal Hüyük, which flourished eight thousand years ago in what is now central

Turkey, connected the deer with the sun's capacity to rejuvenate life.

Deer Park is certainly a hallowed site on a high level of mysticism over an equally deep level of living esoterica. The monks' choice for this location for their retreat tends to reaffirm the numinous character of southern Wisconsin as an extended sacred region. While the stupa is Wisconsin's most recent sacred site, the state features another monument of spiritual power about forty-five miles north and many centuries older. This is the so-called Man Mound, one of the more than ten thousand prehistoric earth sculptures known to have adorned the Upper Midwest before the arrival of modern Europeans.

Fashioned into the images of bears, panthers, turtles, birds, and beasts from the subconscious, these effigy mounds were usually crafted on a colossal scale. None were more mysterious than the Sauk County geoglyph near Baraboo. Originally about eighty feet long from crown to toe, three feet high, and twelve feet broad at the shoulder, it is the representation of a faceless man wearing a horned helmet and artistically molded into the northern slope of a hill overlooking a declining prairie. This mutilated survivor is one of a handful that still remain scattered throughout Wisconsin.

The majority were obliterated during the nineteenth century, mostly by way of the farmer's plow. The effigies were the earthen artworks of an unknown people who occupied territories from the Mississippi River to Lake Michigan from the third century B.C.E. to the fifth century C.E. However, this time frame is almost entirely speculative, and fresh evidence implies a greater antiquity for their creators. After the turn of the last century, engineers laying Sauk County's first paved road eradicated the Man Mound below the knees. Local citizens were outraged by such callous destruction and formed a foundation for the preservation of what remained of the desecrated terraglyph.

The similar (although not identical) effigy of a human giant could still be seen in neighboring La Valle until the 1930s, when an irrigation project buried it under thirty feet of water. Today, the Sauk County effigy mound is maintained as a wayside park, lonely and seldom visited.

Figure 21.2. This early twentieth century photograph of Wisconsin's Man Mound (showing it upside down) has been chalked-in to highlight the effigy's anthropomorphic configuration.

A wooden observation tower affords an improved view. But who or what was the Man Mound supposed to represent? When French immigrants were settling in the town of Baraboo during the early 1830s, the resident Sauk Indians still revered the geoglyph as the sacred image of Wakt'cexi.

This was the anthropomorphic water spirit who saved their ancestors by leading them to safety on the eastern shores of Turtle Island (the North American continent) after a Great Flood drowned their original lodge place, or homeland, in the Sunrise Sea (the Atlantic Ocean). The Sauk legend is more than a little reminiscent of Plato's story of Atlantis. In the fourth century B.C.E., the Athenian philosopher told of a splendid island-city in the Atlantic Ocean swallowed by a natural catastrophe. Its survivors scattered throughout the world.

Comparisons between the Native American and ancient Greek accounts do not end here. Incised in the well-preserved stone walls of a Twentieth Dynasty temple in Egypt's Valley of the Kings are the individualized portraits of invaders wearing horned helmets. Referred to as the *Meshwesh,* or Sea Peoples, they were soundly defeated in a series of large-scale military campaigns ranging from the Lower Nile Valley into Palestine. The Egyptian defenders were led by a vigorous pharaoh, Ramses III, who built a Victory Temple to his triumph over the marauders. Their testimony was recorded on the limestone walls.

It tells how the Meshwesh invaded Egypt because their oceanic capital sank, flaming, beneath the sea. These historical events took place around 1200 B.C.E., and although that date cannot be positively identified with the Wisconsin effigy, it can be connected to the Man Mound's British counterpart. This similar figure is found in the south of England, not far from Bristol. Known as the Long Man of Wilmington, it is the chalk outline of another faceless man cut into the slope of a hill and reliably dated to the late Bronze Age.

It too originally wore a horned helmet, all traces of which were erased in the early nineteenth century. About three times as large as the Sauk County effigy, it nonetheless has the same orientation—on the north side of a hill overlooking a low-lying area. Both the Baraboo and British earth giants were intended by their creators to be seen from a distance and appear proportionate at ground level. Viewed from the air the two hill figures are elongated distortedly, proving that the makers of both effigies understood the principles of applied proportion through foreshortening, suggesting the geoglyphs were produced by a common culture. An explanation for the Man Mound's location in southern Wisconsin might be found in its relation to the ancient copper mining that took place in the Upper Great Lakes region.

Ore was extracted in tens of thousands of tons from 3000 B.C.E. to 1200 B.C.E. by a people unknown to archaeologists. Here again occurs

Figure 21.3. England's Long Man of Wilmington.
Photograph by Frank Joseph.

the date for the final destruction of Atlantis (circa 1200 B.C.E.), that same time period in which the Sea Peoples invaded Egypt and left their testimony of a sunken city on the walls of Ramses III's Victory Temple. At the same historical moment, England's Long Man of Wilmington was created, and ancient North America's copper mining enterprise was abruptly halted. Combined with the Sauk tradition of the Man Mound as a water spirit from an ancestral deluge, the evidence points persuasively to an Atlantean identity for the Wisconsin terraglyph.

Significantly, when the Long Man of Wilmington was cut into its hillside, Britain was known as the Cassiterides, or Tin Isles, for its abundant deposits of the metal. Copper combined with tin (and lesser amounts of zinc) produces bronze, and both the English and Wisconsin hill figures probably date back to the late European Bronze Age, 3,200 years ago. The Sauk themselves were also known by their

Algonquian tribal name as the *Osakiwug,* or People of the Outlet, a reference to the landing of their ancestors on the eastern shores of North America after the Great Flood.

It seems more than ironic that the Man Mound's companion earthwork at La Valle—likewise a memorial to the Deluge—should itself suffer a modern flood when the modern irrigation project covered it under five fathoms of water. Emphasis has been placed on the historical features of Wisconsin's Man Mound because the hill figure derives much of its mystical milieu from its Atlantean origins. By tapping into its resident energies we may also reestablish that very ancient bond with mankind's lost homeland.

For unknown centuries, the anthropomorphic earthwork was the site of neo-Atlantean ceremonial activity, which supercharged the very soil with reverberating forces still sensed by visitors. Its faceless features are in some measure a part of its mysterious, powerful appearance. Although Deer Park's stupa and Baraboo's Man Mound are vastly separated in time, their shared location in southern Wisconsin is a survival from the high spirituality of Atlantis, which left evidence of its impact around the world.

22

Prehistoric Landscape Sculpture of the Middle West

Our schools are very deficient in educating their students about the human prehistory of North America. For example, most Americans are unaware that their predecessors here created an art form on a colossal scale unmatched anywhere else in the world. More than ten thousand earth sculptures once spread from eastern Minnesota, throughout Wisconsin, down to northern Illinois, across Indiana, and into Ohio.

The majority of these effigy mounds were concentrated in Wisconsin; many of these were documented by T. H. Lewis as discussed in chapter 18. Sometimes over a thousand feet long, they were superbly molded images of birds, dogs, snakes, bears, panthers, buffalo, men, fish, and turtles, referred to by archaeologists as *biomorphs*. Others, known as geoglyphs, were abstract shapes, linear embankments, ridge-topped mounds, and conical pyramids. Still others were crafted into designs clearly representing beasts that the pre-Columbian inhabitants of our continent were supposed to know nothing about—namely, elephants and horses.

To these early artists the rolling plains of the Upper Midwest comprised a vast canvas for a regional menagerie of oversized animal figures. But they signified far more than artistic achievement, however monumental. Each effigy mound marked a particular sacred site, a concentration of Earth energies used by tribal shamans and their initiated followers. The effigy mounds were places of spiritual power epitomized in the shapes of animals. Birds were synonymous with the soul, bears signified rebirth, as did snakes, but what the other creatures symbolized to the prehistoric mound builders is less certain.

Comparably ancient hill figures such as the White Horse of Uffington or the Cerne-Abbas Giant can still be seen in Britain, while Peru's Nazca desert is famous for its prehistoric and gigantic illustrations of animals such as spiders and condors. But North America once boasted by far the largest collection of zoomorphic landscape art on Earth. Tragically, most of it was destroyed by the farmer's plow as settlers moved across the Upper Middle Western states in the early decades of the nineteenth century. Archaeologists hurried from one effigy mound to another, preserving them at least in pencil sketches and surveyed measurements prior to the earth sculptures' obliteration, sometimes before the very eyes of scholars.

Only a few examples survive as testimony to the creative skill and nature-oriented spirituality of a vanished people. The most impressive specimen lies atop a steep hill in the Ohio Valley. Visitors enter the site off the main road via an ascending driveway that ends in a parking lot before a small museum. An aerial view of the quarter-mile-long geoglyph is afforded by climbing to the top of a twenty-foot observation tower nearby. From this overlook the snake appears to writhe across the ridge in seven humps, its huge jaws agape before an egg-shaped mound, its tail ending in a spiral.

With an average width of twenty feet and a height of five feet, the serpent's overall length is 1,254 feet, following its coils and humps. Although the Great Serpent Mound is clearly discernible at ground level and more so from the observation tower, it can be fully appreciated from the vantage point of an airplane at three hundred to five hundred feet above the structure. From any point of view, however, its

Figure 22.1. Ohio's Great Serpent Mound

fine proportions testify to the technical and artistic sophistication of its creators. Who they may have been and when they built the mound are questions still debated by investigators more than 170 years after its discovery.

Answers range from the dogma of conservative scholars certain the image was built by ancestors of local Indians only a few centuries ago, to the controversial conclusions of archaeo-astronomers who argue that the structure, which appears to represent the constellation Draco, was oriented to that area of the night sky around 2000 B.C.E. Whoever its builders may have been, they thoroughly cleaned up after themselves. Not a trace of tools, implements, or weapons of any kind have ever been excavated from the site. Its construction involved careful planning. Flat stones were selected for size and uniformity, and lumps of clay were laid along the ground to form a serpentine pattern.

Then, basketfuls of soil were piled over the pattern and finally molded into shape. This process formed an interlinking reinforcement of various materials that have preserved the Great Serpent Mound's configuration over centuries or millennia. The effigy lies in proximity to other significant archaeological sites. Among these are Fort Hill in neighboring Highland County, an enormous stone enclosure above the Ohio Bush River; Mound City, near Chillicothe; and Fort Ancient, another walled enclosure.

Farther still from the Ohio Valley, at the shores of Lake Nell near the port town of Oban, Scotland, winds a serpent mound less than half the size of its American counterpart but closely resembling it in other respects. The intriguing correspondences linking the Ohio earthwork with ancient Old World myth convince some observers that it is the handiwork of overseas visitors in prehistoric times. Others reject such parallels as just so much coincidence. The Serpent Mound was never a habitation site, and served instead as a ceremonial center attracting worshipers from great distances.

In Old Europe the serpent-and-egg theme was associated with the deified physician of ancient Greece, Asclepius. He was regularly portrayed in surviving classical art beside a snake with an egg in its mouth. The same image was known much earlier to the Egyptians as *Kneph,* the sky serpent, from whose jaws the Cosmic Egg, the source of all life, emerged. As it happens, the Great Serpent Mound's location is unique, situated as it is near the western edge of a crater formed by a meteor that struck the Earth about three thousand years ago. Did the effigy's creators witness a meteor strike and raise the biomorph as a visual explanation of the event?

In any case, its position at the edge of an astrobleme, or impact crater, implies that archaeoastronomers may be correct in suggesting that the mound was made in reference to some celestial happening. In October 1983, a dispassionate researcher with no interest in the paranormal was visiting the Great Serpent Mound for the first time. He was alone after closing time at the archaeological park near sunset, when an uneasy feeling gradually crept over him. He could not shake the sensation of being watched. The nameless anxiety grew by degrees until it seemed the woods entirely surrounding the site were filled with the presence of unseen people silently and intensely staring at him. He noticed, too, that not a breath of wind stirred. No birds sang in the trees. The whole area was absolutely calm and still as though under a glass dome.

"It suddenly seemed like the inside of a cathedral," he later remembered. He felt strangely welcome and at peace. The feeling of being watched was so strong he almost expected to see native faces peering out at him from behind the leaves. Years later he was surprised to read in *Mystic Places,* from the famous Time Life Mysteries of the Unknown series, that another visitor to the Great Serpent Mound described a similar encounter, although of a decidedly less amiable character.[1] This person, too, experienced the abrupt calm and feelings of being watched. But as he walked around the jaws of the effigy, hundreds of dried leaves suddenly swirled together, rising in the form of a large man. The visitor fled in horror, never to return.

While the world's largest surviving zoomorph is found in Ohio, another effigy mound in Wisconsin is no less impressive a sacred site. At Lizard Mounds, in the eastern part of the state, the visitor approaches the site by car, driving through open sparsely populated farm country. But the moment he turns onto the road leading into the public park, the site stands out boldly—a small but dense forest of tall pine trees alone among an ocean of fields. From the parking lot a marked trail winds through the woods to each of the thirty-one large effigy mounds masterfully sculpted from the earth itself into the vibrant images of birds, reptiles, panthers, buffalos, and unidentifiable creatures. They seem to move among powerfully centered linear structures, including embankments and conical pyramids.

Altogether, these earthworks comprise the largest surviving collection of geoglyphs in North America. No other group is so numerous, well preserved, or diversified in form; no other group exhibits such outstanding examples of prehistoric art on so colossal a scale. The figures are expressionistic, though stylized. Nothing about them bespeaks the crude, the savage, or the primitive. They are all proportional, refined,

Figure 22.2. A sign from Lizard Mounds, Wisconsin.
Photograph by Frank Joseph.

and graceful, reflecting the ordered minds that conceived, molded, and appreciated them, to say nothing of the skillfully organized system of labor and surveying technology responsible for their creation.

Who their builders and worshipers were, not even the resident Menomonee Indians can tell. The place is, therefore, a prehistoric enigma. All that seems certain is that it was finally abandoned around 1319 C.E. for reasons unknown. Even the dates of its construction and occupation are doubtful. It would appear, however, to have been laid out by the same people who built Aztalan, a city flourishing about seventy-five miles to the southwest, because identically styled earthworks once surrounded that remarkable ceremonial center. Aztalan's final phase, when the population within and outside its stockaded walls may have reached ten thousand or more inhabitants, began around 1100 C.E. and ended suddenly at the same time

Lizard Mounds was deserted. In any case, a few of the Lizard Mounds effigies served as tombs.

The deceased were placed in pits beneath the geoglyphs with decorated clay pots, bone harpoons, pipes, copper arrowheads, and ritual crystals. The precinct was used exclusively for spiritual purposes. No one ever resided within the sacred arena; settlement was in surrounding villages. The largest effigy of the group is three hundred feet in length, but the site derives its modern name from a 238-foot-long figure thought to represent a lizard. Even so, the figures are not so large that they cannot be made out at ground level.

Seen at altitude, however, they assume a startling perspective to appear in their proper proportions, implying that they may be appreciated only from the sky. In this feature, at least, they can be compared with Ohio's Great Serpent Mound. The modern park trail appears to follow closely the original ritual path used by the ancient worshipers as their processions wound from one effigy to the next. Today's pilgrim walks for about 250 feet through the woods before coming to the first structure, the longest of the slender linear mounds, some two hundred feet in length.

It marks the real beginning of the sacred precinct. Beyond it stands a small, conical pyramid, followed by a teardrop figure pointing at another cone of the same size. All the mounds are only three or four feet high. Despite having endured unknown centuries of erosional forces, the earthworks were probably not much larger at the time of their creation than they now appear. The first animal effigy encountered is the so-called Panther Mound. Visitors come upon it gradually, imperceptibly, from the point of its tail. The tail thickens by degrees as the bioglyph takes form. As it does so its power seems to gather momentum, increasing along the arched back to the massive head. It is flanked by a pair of large conical mounds.

The trail forces each visitor to walk between the two cone pyramids. These are followed by a smaller linear structure. A few paces more brings the forepart of the most massive of the panthers into view. There are three more such earthworks before visitors reach the focal point of the site—a pair of elongated figures facing each other in a combined spread of 425 feet. The trail leads directly between their heads, narrowing the site's inherent energy into a narrow gap. It is important to know that the sole surviving Indian tradition of Lizard Mounds involves this very spot.

The Menomonee remember that each winter solstice their ancestors gathered behind these twin zoomorphs to observe sunset before the longest night of the year, marking the world's transition from darkness back into the light, and the human soul's reemergence from death to light. Tribal leaders stood at the twin-headed focal point. At that critical moment, as the sun shed its last ray precisely between the two animal heads, the great shift between darkness and light—death and life—took place. Curious if this Menomonee tradition had any basis in fact, James Scherz arrived at Lizard Mounds on the late afternoon of 1989's winter solstice. A professor of Civil Engineering and Environmental Studies at the University of Wisconsin in Madison, and pioneer of archaeoastronomy in his state, he was highly qualified to test any scientific basis for Native American myth.

As he observed dusk on the longest night of the year, Professor Scherz saw the sun go down precisely between the two earth-sculpted birds' heads, just as described by the Menomonee Indians. Just beyond the zoomorphs lies the effigy mound after which the set has been named. The lizard represents the underlying motive force of all living creatures, the vital spirit of action. In native South American symbolism the lizard is associated with precipitation, from dew to deluge, although that meaning does not seem to apply at the Wisconsin location. The trail leads away from the eponymous earthwork to smaller effigies, including a pair of linear embankments pointing to the only oval mound at the site.

While not so spectacular as the others, it is the key to this sacred center, representing as it does the Cosmic Egg, the Womb of Life, earlier encountered at Ohio's Great Serpent Mound. More than any other figure, the oval earthwork identifies the site as a sacred center. The trail passes between the heads and along the outstretched wings of two enormous bird effigies. Perhaps they were meant to signify the uplifting experience of walking among the colossal figures of Lizard Mounds.

Although America's surviving effigy mounds are few in number, they still resonate with at least some telluric power of the Earth from which they were so beautifully fashioned long ago.

23

Illinois's Gold Pyramid, Iowa's Grotto of Gems, and Tennessee's Greek Temple

Drivers speeding along Highway 94 forty miles north of Chicago occasionally catch a glimpse of a glittering anomaly in the otherwise ordinary suburb of Wadsworth, Illinois. Built in 1974, America's own pyramid is the private home of the James Onan family, who, until the mid-1990s, opened their untypical domicile to the public each summer. Visitors were confronted by the forty-foot-tall colossus of a pharaonic figure, the largest freestanding statue of its kind outside Egypt. It continues to guard the eighteen-acre estate in which the gleaming pyramid stands surrounded by an eight-foot wall decorated with hieroglyphic motifs.

South of the 200-ton statue is a gift shop where jewelry, clothing, statuettes, plates, prints, and numerous other items reflecting Egyptian themes can still be purchased via the internet. Leaving through the east exit of the gift shop, visitors used to skirt a large gravel mound to the left until they arrived at a flight of stone steps leading to a darkened doorway at the top of the mound. The structure is a re-creation of the tomb of Tutankhamun, who ruled Egypt 3,350 years ago. A ramp descends gently through a corridor painted with scenes from the

Figure 23.1. The Gold Pyramid House.
Photograph by Frank Joseph.

Book of the Dead (an ancient Egyptian guide for the soul's progress to the Otherworld) and opens into an exact copy of the boy-king's burial chamber.

The tomb contains an abundance of real gold crafted into furniture, a dagger, a large death mask, and statues. This brilliant collection is surrounded by far greater treasures in the next chamber, where a full-sized, accurate version of the pharaoh's enormous sarcophagus is reproduced in 14-karat gold. The walls surrounding it are decorated with scenes from his funeral and soul's ascension to godhood, identical to the Egyptian original. In the adjacent room gold statues of protective goddesses stand at the four corners of a canopied shrine seven feet high and ten feet long, wrought entirely in real gold.

Visitors emerged from these dazzling sights through a south exit and followed the sidewalk to the Pyramid House, about 150 yards to the east. The house is surrounded by a moat, and its twelve thousand square feet of walls are covered with 24-karat gold plate gleaming amid the spring-fed waters. Access is across a bridge and walkway flanked on either side by rows of sphinx statues. At fifty-five feet in height, the Gold Pyramid is a 1:100-scale replica of Egypt's Great Pyramid on the Giza Plateau. Like the original, the six-story structure is oriented to true north. Its interior contains seventeen thousand feet of living space, featuring a full-sized re-creation of Tutankhamun's ceremonial chariot covered entirely in gold.

The Chariot Room also displays some authentic Egyptian artifacts, many statues of gods and goddesses, another solid-gold coffin lid, and hundreds of marvelous objects to catch the eye and delight the senses. The Pyramid House is unquestionably an evolving sacred site, one of the latest in North America, although that is not the original intention of its builder and owner. Yet from its very inception it has evidenced many qualities typically identified with sacred centers.

As an experienced and successful contractor, James Onan knew not to build over an underground water source. Even so, weeks after the foundations of the Pyramid House were laid, a freshwater spring inexplicably bubbled forth at the very center of the construction. It grew so large that it completely surrounded the structure, making the pyramid an island. Remarkably, archaeologists know that during its civilized heyday the Giza Plateau was likewise completely surrounded by water from the river Nile. Access to the Great Pyramid then was via a bridge, just as the Illinois Gold Pyramid is reached today.

What mysterious forces required that North America's twentieth-century version of the Great Pyramid be encircled by a moat like its ancient Egyptian counterpart? Tests of the spring surrounding the Gold Pyramid House reveal its excellent purity and high mineral content. Onan bottled the water, and people from around the world have come to swear by its remarkable curative properties. Just before the unexpected arrival of the freshwater spring, a bulldozer broke its steel teeth against a large, immovable outcropping of black rock. Chunks of it were sent to the Colorado Assay Office in Denver for analysis.

Meanwhile, the spring continued to rise ever higher, eventually drowning the black rock lying just outside the perimeter of the foundation under twenty feet of water. It was then that the Colorado report arrived, informing the astounded Onan that the sample pieces were gold ore! He is the only person to have found gold in Illinois, and at the very spot of his Gold Pyramid. So far he has been unsuccessful in retrieving the submerged mass of gold at the bottom of the moat. Clearly, he had been directed to build the Gold Pyramid at this appropriate place.

Claims that pyramid structures exert some kind of preservative influences are borne out at Onan's unusual home. He experimented with different kinds of food placed at various locations inside and in its immediate vicinity. They naturally spoiled over time, save one banana that he left at the midpoint between the very center of the Gold Pyramid and its south wall, halfway up the structure, on its second floor. Incredibly, the fruit desiccated but refused to rot. To this day, more than forty years later, Onan still shows visitors the dried banana, preserved through the unseen energy coursing through the Gold Pyramid House.

Soon after its completion he installed a lightning rod at its apex. He was surprised and annoyed the next day to observe that the rod was completely bent over. Cursing its poor quality, he immediately replaced it with another rod made by a different manufacturer. Within twenty-four hours it too was bent over.

All subsequent attempts to top his pyramid with lightning rods, no matter how well made or professionally installed, met with the same result. Onan eventually gave up his attempts to thus equip his home, which has since stood at the center of numerous electrical storms, some of them very ferocious. Not once has the Gold Pyramid been struck by lightning in the forty-four years of its existence. During the late 1970s one of Onan's sons, a normal lad in all respects, lived on the ground floor directly over the spring of freshwater beneath the house. Shortly after setting up his room there, the boy was overcome with an inexplicable urge to perform bodybuilding exercises. Claiming that the barbells with which he worked daily were substantially lighter inside the

Gold Pyramid than anywhere else, he went on to win several national weightlifting championships.

Indeed, the place does seem to exert unusual influences on human behavior. Some years ago I was fortunate enough to be an overnight guest at the Gold Pyramid House. In its living room I experienced a deep sense of inner calm, as did many other visitors, but nothing more. I did, however, have a precognitive dream about the Gold Pyramid House. The vivid psychodrama featured a small aircraft that narrowly missed colliding with the structure to crash on the street just outside the main gate. Later that same month a private pilot, while sightseeing over the Gold Pyramid, lost control of his single-engine plane and crashed on the street out front, just as foreshadowed in the dream.

But humans are not the only creatures apparently affected by the Gold Pyramid House. Strange animal events are also known to have occurred there. For two summers running, beginning in 1986, hundreds of jellyfish suddenly appeared in the moat, *an impossible event in the Midwest,* according to experts at Chicago's renowned Shedd Aquarium. As suddenly as they arrived, the creatures vanished and never returned. No similar occurrence has ever been reported in Illinois, or anywhere else. The Pyramid House has been home to other bizarre animal phenomena.

Families of vicious birds roost above its eaves outside the north exit of the Chariot Room, which is no longer usable because the birds boldly swoop to attack anyone approaching its glass doors. Coincidentally, the Chariot Room contains the faithful replica of Pharaoh Tutankhamun's coffin lid, its golden side panels illustrating his judgment and spiritual apotheosis. In ancient Egyptian religion the king's resting place was guarded at its northern end, the Pathway of the Soul, by Sokar, a bird that attacked anyone seeking entry to the royal burial chamber.

An ancient arcane principle states that the faithful re-creation of a sacred object or place infuses some energy of the original into the duplicate. This explanation accounts for the sacred power, say, of even a cheap, plastic crucifix, which nonetheless resonates with at least something of the power of the Cross it is meant to simulate. The same principle appears to be at work at Illinois's Gold Pyramid House, whose faithful if downsized reproduction of the Great Pyramid has attracted to itself a portion of the mysterious power still in evidence at Egypt's Giza Plateau.

The singular creation of another man arose some two hundred miles west from the Gold Pyramid House, in northwestern Iowa. Sprawling more than a city block is a series of nine handmade alcoves. With an estimated value in excess of $3 million, the complex comprises the largest grotto and most extensive mosaic ever created. Hundreds of thousands of precious and semiprecious stones have all been bonded by a specially cured, erosion-proof cement to form colossal columns, archways, niches, and shrines. One grotto, the Bethlehem Cave, is made of sixty-five tons of petrified wood. The combined weight of the entire complex is so prodigious that solid iron foundations needed to be sunk twenty feet into the ground to support it.

The Grotto of the Redemption was constructed with stones from every state in the union and from every region of the globe. There is alexandrite from the emerald mines of Russia's Takiwaya River, and purple amethyst from the Andes Mountains of South America; green jade from China and dark blue lapis lazuli from Egypt. There is even a specimen brought back from Admiral Byrd's expedition to the South Pole. Agates were cut and polished in Brussels, but the vast collections of quartz crystals came from all over the Earth. Everywhere there is a glittering profusion of orange coral, yellow jasper, pitch-black onyx, golden zircon, sea-green turquoise, deep purple sapphires, fiery rubies and bloodstones, pale moonstones, green malachite, rich amber—more than the eye and mind can take in during the course of a single visit.

Although the grotto is a monument portraying the biblical Fall of Man and his redemption through Christ, the brilliant variety of its costly materials and the peculiar shapes determined by their mineralogical character give the whole complex an almost Asian appearance.

*Figure 23.2. View of Lower Arcade: Small Stations of
the Cross at the Grotto of the Redemption.
Photograph by MissouriRichardson.*

It changes mood during daylight hours, sparkling after dawn, ablaze
with rainbow colors at noon, and dimly glowing at dusk. Artificially lit
after sundown by a dozen large spotlights atop sixty-five-foot poles, the
grotto resembles some impossibly gigantic jewel set against the black
velvet of the night sky.

Throughout the site are many superbly sculpted statues, all
of white Carrara marble from the Apennine Mountains in Italy,
imported at a cost more than $100,000. The most outstanding piece
is a faithful re-creation of Michelangelo's *Pietà* set atop a forty-foot-
high hill of minerals. Close by is an artificial lake where white swans
glide through the grotto's reflected image. Walking distance away is
St. Peter and Paul's Church. The Christmas chapel inside contains
a single Brazilian amethyst weighing over three hundred pounds.
The twenty-two-foot-high maplewood altar was hand carved for the

Chicago World's Fair in 1893, when it won first prize in an international carpentry competition.

As though the Grotto of the Redemption was not impressive enough in itself, the story of its creation is even more amazing. It is the conception and work of one man, Paul Dobberstein, a physically slight man from Germany who arrived in the United States to study for the Catholic priesthood. Father Louis Greving, who much later became Dobberstein's helper and took over construction of the grotto, relates how the young seminarian became critically ill with pneumonia.

"As he fought for his life," Greving stated, "he prayed to the Blessed Virgin to intercede for him. He promised to build a shrine in her honor if he lived. The illness passed, the student completed his studies, and, after his ordination, he came to West Bend [Iowa] as a pastor, in 1898. For over a decade, he was stockpiling rocks and precious stones. The actual work of building the grottoes began in 1912. Before 1947, all the work of the grottoes was by hand labor; that is, the cement, mortar, rocks, steel, and precious stones were moved to the building site and placed on the building platform or scaffolds by bucket and wheelbarrow.

"Only in 1947, when perhaps eighty percent of the gigantic project was completed was an electric hoist installed to make the work lighter for the ailing artist. Most architects and contractors would hesitate a long time before undertaking a project such as the Grotto of the Redemption. It is doubtful whether it can or ever will be duplicated. The sheer bulk of the achievement is startling when we consider that most of the manual labor was done by two men, and practically all the artistic endeavor was done by Father Dobberstein single-handed."[1]

No less remarkable, Dobberstein resorted to no architect's plans, no blueprints or sketches, no paperwork of any kind to construct the grottoes. The vast project, from its conception after the turn of the twentieth century until the man's death in 1954, was carried entirely in his imagination. Nor was his work completed. For the next forty years Father Greving continued to expand it, adding more precious stones.

All the materials—minerals, labor, and equipment—were donated over the decades by numerous persons inspired by Dobberstein's vision and achievement.

He suffered many personal hardships in its construction, including several serious accidents, once when scaffolding on which he was standing collapsed. His hands were often bloody with the work he felt compelled to complete before he died. The priest's final resting place is in the parish cemetery overlooking the monument he engineered.

The grotto is a powerful sacred site because of the sacred will and high spiritual intention that went into its creation. For those who appreciate the esoteric qualities of the stone Dobberstein chose, the location's capacity for physical or emotional appeal is great. Each year about 100,000 visitors pass through the Grotto of the Redemption.

Another modern American re-creation likewise demonstrates the ancient principle of sympathetic magic: Tennessee's Parthenon. The architects, Ictinus and Callicrates, who built the Greek original in 439 B.C.E., never dreamed it would come to be regarded as the most beautiful structure ever raised by man. The white marble temple is an epitome of the so-called Doric order, the simplest and most refined of the Hellenistic systems of proportion and decoration. Its twenty-five fluted columns support a low triangular pediment of relief sculpture at the east and west ends depicting the Olympian gods and goddesses.

The interior comprised a walled rectangular chamber, the *cella,* which contained one of Western civilization's greatest treasures, the Athena Parthenos, a thirty-eight-foot tall statue of Athena the Virgin, after whom the building was named; literally, Hall of the Virgin. Made of gold and ivory, the colossus portrayed her standing erect in battle gear holding a diminutive goddess, Nike (Victory), in her hand. Light admitted through an eastern doorway and reflected off the gold ceiling was the single source of interior illumination for the 101-foot-wide by 228-foot-long structure.

The Parthenon remained intact for eight hundred years until Christians transformed the pagan temple into a fifth-century church.

The new owners tore down the huge chryselephantine statue of Athena and sold off its pieces of ivory and gold. Later, Islamic Turks trashed its installed Christian paraphernalia, replacing them with their own, including a minaret in the southwest corner.

In their battles for Greece with the Venetians, the besieged Moslems used the cella as a powder magazine. During the course of one bombardment it received a direct hit, destroying the center of the building. Further degradations occurred when an English noble-man bought most of the surviving sculpture from the obliging Turks. Other sales went to French and Danish connoisseurs. Today, the bat-tered, raped Parthenon still stands essentially intact—at any rate, its basic structure exists.

Its Nashville counterpart is a re-creation of the Parthenon in its original condition, complete with restored and duplicated statuary. One of the few concessions to modernity is the use of concrete. The employ-ment of marble on so grand a scale would have been impossibly expen-sive. The Tennessee replica was completed for the 1897 Centennial Exhibition, celebrating Nashville's reputation as the Athens of the South. The brick, wooden lathe-and-plaster temple survived the exhibi-tion because of popular demand.

By the 1920s, however, the structure was crumbling badly. So a ten-year restoration project was proposed by the city park board. Reopened to the public in 1931, it attracted more than ten thousand visitors from forty-six states and a dozen foreign countries during the first month of its new lease on life. More than fifty years later, a twenty-month reno-vation upgraded the site to its present level. But the restorers' crowning achievement was unveiled in May 1990 with sculptor Alan LeQuire's plaster statue of Athena (see page 165).

Portals at either end of the temple frame the largest set of matching bronze doors on Earth. The Greek originals were so heavy, mule teams were needed to open and close them. The Nashville Parthenon's doors weigh 721 tons each and are decorated identically to those found in the Athenian original. Visitors enter at the east end and should not miss the

Figure 23.3. Nashville's Parthenon.
Photograph by Jud McCranie.

gift shop, or the three galleries of original American art on the lower level. Outstanding is the Parthenon's permanent Cowan Collection, featuring the works of Albert Bierstadt, William Merritt Chase, and Winslow Homer.

The Tennessee Parthenon is not a substitute for the original. It is instead the other missing half of the Parthenon experience. Those fortunate enough to visit the Greek Acropolis will feel their perception of this renowned sacred site completed after having seen the temple in its pristine condition. Although the Nashville Parthenon is a modern replica consciously unconsecrated to any supernal concept, it is nonetheless a rapidly developing sacred center through the influences of sympathetic magic. This term refers to the transference of spirit power from its first source to another location resonating with the same or closely similar theurgic vibrations of the original.

Perhaps the most apparent instance of sympathetic magic generally encountered in the Parthenon is a kindred presence experienced here, as at the Greek source. Some ascribe this uncanny, respectful feeling to our human responses to the gods, and cite as an example the hushed tones into which most visitors naturally seem to fall when confronted by the Athena colossus. Others believe our genetic memory is at least partially reactivated in the presence of the Nashville simulacrum, as the image of the great temple that epitomized our spiritual instincts for centuries.

Whatever the cause, America's Parthenon is certainly pervaded with the milieu and feel of a genuinely magical place. Interestingly, the hill in Nashville's Centennial Park on which the modern Parthenon stands was already a sacred center long before construction began in the late nineteenth century. The Tennessee replica occupies a unique position on the 475-mile-long series of interconnected trails and waterways linking the Cumberland and Mississippi Rivers. Known as the Natchez Trace, it was traveled by Spanish explorers, tribal Indians, earlier Mound Builders, and even more enigmatic culture bearers over three thousand years ago, more than two millennia before the original Parthenon was raised in classical Greece.

Numerous ancient structures—mounds and earthworks—line the trace, at the northern terminus of which is located the Nashville Parthenon. Coeval with Athena's warlike protection of civilization, it was at the hill that later became the site of her re-created temple that General Andrew Jackson rallied his army for one of the most politically significant (if militarily untimely) victories in American history, the 1812 Battle of New Orleans, which frustrated British ambitions to reconquer America—although it was fought after the peace treaty was signed. Forty years later the same hill was a focal point of the Northern armies during the American Civil War.

In 1897 it was named part of Centennial Park, commemorating the one hundredth anniversary of Tennessee's constitution. So it would appear that the Parthenon and its colossus of Athena are but the latest additions in a developing sacred center consecrated to the humanizing forces of civilization. Before actually going inside the temple, tourists can climb the broad staircase to the upper level and stand in front of the towering bronze portals decorated with mythic themes. Some claim to have experienced feelings of expectation, as though the fifteen tons of doors were about to slowly swing open at the touch of an Olympian hand.

For these perceptive visitors, a walk down the peristyle face across the west entrance and back up the south side completes a ritual circuit of the sacred center and sublimely prepares them for the greater inner experience of the Parthenon. They enter at the east end, ascending a short flight of stairs to the cella. There stands the impressive representation of Athena Parthenos poised magnificently under soft natural light streaming into her holy precinct from the 150-foot-high ceiling. At nearly forty-two feet tall, it is the largest piece of indoor sculpture in the Western world. The spear Athena supports with her left arm is thirty-six feet long. She stands on a five-foot-high marble pedestal decorated with golden panels depicting the immortal Olympians present at Athena's birth. Surrounding her, beyond the cella columns, are casts made of the original Parthenon sculptures of gods and goddesses. Even persons not spiritually inclined feel compelled to speak softly, as though out of reverence for the great living power that resides here. Behind her shield at her left side coils a huge serpent, a multisymbolic device signifying the Pelasgian, or Sea People, origins of the Greeks, together with the spirit of regeneration as implied in the snake's ability to slough off its old, dead skin for a new one.

In her right hand is Nike, the little goddess of winged victory. The white marble base is surrounded by gilt panels depicting Greeks and Amazons in combat. Other relief sculpture reproduced and surrounding the cella represent battles between men and centaurs, and the *Titanomachy,* a primeval war in which the Olympian gods overthrew the Old World order of the giants. All these portrayed conflicts demonstrate the victory of order and creative intelligence over chaos and ignorance.

The Amazons characterized unbalanced female energy, just as the centaurs stood for baser masculine passions, while the giants were identified with the forces of brutality. Athena personified the civilized triumph of harmony, self-mastery, and reason. Standing before her much larger-than-life image we realize that she is the potential for triumph

Figure 23.4. The largest indoor sculpture in the Western world is Alan LeQuire's re-creation of the lost original Athena Parthenos statue. Photograph by Dean Dixon.

within ourselves. With her own hand she literally offers us victory over all our imperfections that undermine happiness.

Walking around the Athena Parthenos to the western section

behind the cella, visitors will find casts of original sculpted reliefs from the Greek Parthenon representing the birth of Athena in the company of all the Olympians and her contest with Poseidon, the sea god, for possession of Athens. This contest signifies the triumph of the conscious mind over subconscious chaos. Authentic Hellenic vases, executed in all the colorful grace, adroit liveliness, and skill for which they are prized, are also on display.

Illinois's Gold Pyramid House, Iowa's Grotto of the Redemption, and Tennessee's Parthenon exemplify the sympathetic magic that connects our time with the past through the numinous power of a shared spiritual relationship. And when we visit these modern sacred sites, we partake, at least partially, of the mysterious energies that went into their creation.

24
The Inscrutable Mysteries
of Coral Castle

In 1993 I went searching for Florida's—and perhaps the world's—most bizarre place. I had seen the strange complex known as Coral Castle on a television documentary, and my curiosity was aroused. Because I was already in Florida for a book convention, I decided to combine business with investigation. I drove south on Highway 1 toward Homestead, where Coral Castle is located. The town is better known as the focal point for Hurricane Andrew, one of the worst tropical storms in U.S. history. Even though this natural catastrophe had occurred a full two years before, dramatic evidence of its impact was still visible from the highway.

On the way, through Princeton, Naranja, and Leisure City, there were lingering reminders of the disaster. The shell of what used to be a bank stood beside a roped-off supermarket, its roof buckling under the impossible burden of an upside-down semitrailer truck. Block after block, private homes, mostly little brick bungalows, were individually smashed almost beyond recognition as though by some giant's hammer. No structure stood undamaged. Numerous heaps of unidentifiable rubble shoveled together by relief workers were all that remained of many buildings.

Mile after mile, south Florida resembled an atomic bomb testing site. The devastation increased the closer to Homestead I got. I assumed Coral Castle had been badly damaged by the storm, if not obliterated. Homestead had taken the brunt of Hurricane Andrew's fury. Although violent desolation lay at the castle's very gates, the peculiar site stood intact, the only structure untouched by the swirling carnage. But what is Coral Castle, and how could it have defied a cataclysm that devastated everything around it for hundreds of square miles? The fortress-like complex is constructed of massive coral blocks, many of which exceed five tons. These are imaginatively arranged and fit together to form a central courtyard surrounded entirely by dominating walls.

Entrance is made through a gate fashioned from a single coral block weighing nine tons. This miraculous monolith is approximately eighty inches wide, ninety-two inches tall, and twenty-one inches thick. It fits within a quarter of an inch of the walls on either side and pivots through an iron rod resting on an automobile gear. The enormous block balances so perfectly on its center of gravity that a visitor can easily push it open with one finger. Modern construction engineers are at a loss to explain how such a ponderous object could have been set with such a high level of precision.

Another gate, this one a great triangle, at the opposite wall, weighs three tons. Inside the courtyard, to the visitor's immediate right rears a broad, square tower with a flight of stone steps ascending to a single doorway near the top. They lead to the highest point in the area and a small room. This chamber is occupied only by a leather hammock and a crude wooden table piled with primitive tools—chains, saws, many kinds of drills, wedges, hammers, chisels, and crowbars. Tools also festoon the walls. This imposing tower was raised with approximately 240 tons of coral cut into cyclopean blocks weighing from four to nine tons each.

The roof alone is comprised of thirty one-ton blocks neatly fitted together. Although modern electricity and plumbing are absent, oil lamps and a well of fresh water serve the living quarters—a sleeping chamber with twin beds, an outdoor cookery, and a bathroom. Usually overlooked by visitors is a low but massive altar comprising two coral blocks set against the south wall. To what god or gods it was dedicated, no one knows. Through a single window looking out over the courtyard below, the extent of this peculiar place can be perceived in a glance. Among its oddities is a scattering of oversize chairs made of coral, each one weighing a half ton. Although they look extremely uncomfortable, the chairs are, in fact, exceptionally restful and balanced into perfect rockers.

Remarkably, not a single tool mark has been found on any of them. Many chairs resemble contour lounges oriented to the sun after dawn and at noon. But they are not the only Coral Castle features with celestial orientations. Strolling through the castle I noticed numerous stone representations of planets, moons, and suns, many—perhaps all—deliberately aligned with various sky phenomena, as were the twenty-five huge chairs carefully positioned throughout the precinct. The site appears to be some kind of celestial observatory dating back to a time before the invention of the telescope.

Figure 24.1. Coral Castle overflows with celestial imagery.
Photograph by Christina Rutz.

Twenty feet outside the wall stands the Great Pelorus—a lensless, telescopic structure, twenty-five feet tall and weighing twenty tons. Crosshairs inside its aperture resemble those in a bombsight, and they are aligned with Polaris, the North Star.

Figure 24.2. Coral Castle's Great Pelorus.
Photograph by Frank Joseph.

Nearby is a massive sundial calibrated to noon of the winter solstice, December 21, and the summer solstice, June 21. The sundial is adjacent to a fountain adorned with representations of the moon in its first and last quarters and when full. On the north wall are sculpted images of Saturn and Mars. The latter is shown next to a palmetto plant, signifying the artist's belief that life exists on the Red Planet. Other astronomical depictions and alignments abound throughout Coral Castle.

The castle's astronomical identity is subtly reinforced throughout the site. For example, a feature referred to by guides as the bird bath comprises three concentric circles 124 inches, 62 inches, and 18 inches in diameter, respectively. These measurements represent the solar system. The concentric rings correspond to the three major divisions of planets. The innermost group includes Mercury, Venus, Earth, and Mars. Jupiter, Saturn, and Uranus make up the middle group, and Neptune and Pluto are represented by the outermost circle. An appreciation of the extraordinary labor that went into building it may be gained by inspecting this same north wall.

The center section, surmounted by the representation of a crown, is the site's heaviest single block at thirty tons. Almost as massive is a forty-foot obelisk set in a hole six feet deep. In addition, Coral Castle has a two-and-one-half-ton banquet table surrounded by half-ton rocking chairs. The stone chairs are so perfectly balanced that they continue rocking long after a light touch has set them in motion. But Coral Castle was not built by stone-dragging slaves of an ancient civilization.

No less incredible than its own stupendous construction is the fact that the entire complex was built between 1920 and 1940 by and for one man working alone and in secret. His name was Edward Leedskalnin. He was born in 1887 into a farming family at Stramereens Pogosta, a small village near Riga, Latvia, but emigrated to North America before the outbreak of World War One.

While working in a Canadian lumber camp Leedskalnin contracted tuberculosis and fled to the warmer climate of Florida. With his puny savings, he purchased an acre of land near then-obscure Florida City for twelve dollars. Here he began building the first structures of the castle. At five feet tall, weighing one hundred pounds, and in uncertain health, Leedskalnin would be an unlikely candidate to quarry and move the tons of coral that even a robust man would have found impossible to budge. And his fourth-grade education hardly qualified him as a construction engineer. His tools were handmade saws, chisels, chains, hoists, and hammers of the most primitive kind, and his only mode of transportation was an ancient, dilapidated bicycle without tires.

Leedskalnin was a fanatic for secrecy and worked only after sundown, when he was certain no one was watching him. If anyone did stop by to inquire how he was getting along, he would immediately stop working and chat pleasantly with visitors until they left, when he would resume construction. When we consider that he cut, moved, and positioned all of the structure's megalithic blocks in the dead of night, the man's achievement assumes a truly incredible scale. Some teenagers spying on him one evening claimed they saw him "float coral blocks through the air like hydrogen balloons," but no one took them seriously.[1] If their testimony can be believed, they were the only witnesses to the construction of Coral Castle.

In 1936, when developers threatened to set up a subdivision near Florida City, Leedskalnin bought ten acres in nearby Homestead with money saved through years of performing odd jobs for neighboring farmers. He dismantled the largely finished castle and transferred it block by block to the new location. Each piece was placed on a pair of iron girders mounted on a makeshift truck chassis and transported over ten miles to Homestead. For this major operation he relied on outside help for the first and last time. He hired a tractor but insisted that its driver not be present whenever the blocks were placed on his truck. The driver showed up at 9:00 every morning, and returned in late afternoon to find the chassis loaded with coral monoliths.

Once, the driver absentmindedly returned after less than half an hour for a lunch pail he had forgotten on the seat of the tractor. He was

astounded to see several multiton stones already laid neatly on the girders. "It was impossible to have stacked those gigantic blocks in under
thirty minutes," he recalled, "even with a steam-powered derrick. And
Ed had no equipment, just a simple tackle and chain hoist. Yet, there
they were, piled like cord wood."[2] Their mysterious mover was nowhere
in sight, and the driver, somewhat apprehensive, left before Leedskalnin
returned.

Relocating Coral Castle progressed with an easy haste. Leedskalnin
accomplished this amazing engineering feat in less than a month and re-
erected his stone complex, working under cover of darkness all through
the night until dawn. It took him four years of unrelieved labor, during
which time he added walls eight feet high and four feet wide at the
base, with an average thickness of three feet. These forbidding ramparts
weigh at least six and one-half tons. After Coral Castle was completed,
Leedskalnin opened it to restricted tours, charging twenty-five cents per
visitor, but he preferred to live behind the great walls in seclusion.

He never shared the secret of its construction with anyone, saying
only that he had rediscovered the laws of weight, measurement, and
leverage used by the Ancient Egyptians, and that these lost principles
somehow involved the relationship of the Earth to certain positions of
the heavenly bodies. Leedskalnin is quoted as saying, "I have discovered
the secrets of the pyramids. I have found out how the Egyptians and the
ancient builders in Peru, Yucatán, and Asia, with only primitive tools,
raised and set in place blocks of stone weighing many tons."[3]

The very stones of Coral Castle support his story—at an average of six tons, they are twice the weight of the blocks in Egypt's
Great Pyramid at Giza. Carrol A. Lake, a colonel in the U.S. Army
Corps of Engineers, stated that "Leedskalnin proved for all the world
to see today that he knew the construction secrets of the ancients."[4]
He was seconded by one of America's leading investigators, Vincent
H. Gaddis, who said of the mysterious Latvian immigrant, "There is
no doubt that he applied some principle in weight lifting that remains
a secret today."[5]

Even the purpose of Coral Castle was deliberately obscured. When asked why he assumed such an enormous undertaking, Leedskalnin smilingly explained that it was built entirely for his Sweet Sixteen, Agnes Scuffs, a woman he once asked to wed but who never left Latvia, where she married even before he arrived in Florida. Revealingly, he never contacted Agnes after coming to America. He seems to have used this tale to politely put off unwanted curiosity.

Little is actually known about Leedskalnin, a friendly though private person. His dedicated isolation once got him into trouble, however, when he was beaten by a gang of local yahoos who threatened to kill him if he did not divulge the location of what they believed was a treasure hidden inside Coral Castle. He suffered their savagery and told them nothing.

After his death, $3,500 was found in the tower—his life savings, mostly from land sales—but that was all. Leedskalnin's work was his life. Material pleasures meant nothing to him, and he merrily subsisted on a diet of sardines, crackers, eggs, and milk. His meager garden produced green vegetables and some fruits, and he trapped the occasional rabbit. He worked tirelessly from sunset to sunrise and spent much of his day reading from his library about magnetic current and cosmic forces, resting only a few hours in the late afternoon.

Edward Leedskalnin passed away in his sleep during 1953 of malnutrition and kidney failure. His only living relative, Harry, inherited what was then known as Rock Gate Park. Shortly before he died, Harry sold the property to a Chicago family, who gave it its present name. Thirty years later Coral Castle was placed on the National Register of Historic Places. Nearly seven decades later, Leedskalnin's marvelous home is still explored each year by thousands of visitors from across the country and around the world.

Coral Castle has attracted the international attention of professional construction engineers, astounded and mystified by the apparently impossible achievement of this diminutive wonder worker. In the mid-1970s, for example, a large bulldozer was hired to manipulate a coral block equivalent to the Castle's thirty-ton monolith; the bulldozer could not even lift it. Alternative science investigators suggest that Leedskalnin somehow learned the secret of the World Grid, an invisible pattern of energy lines surrounding the Earth that concentrates points of telluric power where they intersect. It was here, at one of these intersections of Earth energy, that he was supposedly able to move his prodigious stone blocks using the unseen power of our planet.

Researcher Ray Stoner suggests that Leedskalnin moved the Castle not because it was threatened by an encroaching subdivision but because a surveying error misplaced the site ten miles from an Earth-energy vortex or focal point. In order for the structures to maximize this energy the entire complex needed to be relocated in Homestead, where the telluric forces were focused.[6]

Investigator Bruce Cathe writes, "the site of Coral Castle is mathematically related to the world energy grid, as are the other remarkable structures which, however, date from ancient times. Ed Leedskalnin had not moved on to the Florida site by chance. This geometric position was extremely close to one that would be ideal for setting up harmonics related to gravity and light harmonics. The fact that [he] had access to secret knowledge is much more evident in the relationship of Coral Castle to the world energy grid system."[7]

Stoner argues that "some fundamental conditions must be met before a structure like Coral Castle can be made to function as intended. It must be exactly situated over an energy vortex, aligned with a celestial event or events sufficiently precise to predict their recurrence, constructed in a specific shape, and built with certain materials. Finally, activities at the site may be successfully undertaken only at the moment the celestial events to which it is oriented take place."[8]

Stoner's prerequisites for particular shapes and building materials are reminiscent of experiments in pyramid power in the mid-1970s, when the precise angles (variants of 15.2 degrees) of the pyramid and its special construction elements (crystalline granite and nonconducting limestone) determined their success. Author James Wyckoff writes, "The ancient Egyptians knew that the shape and angle of pyramids contained a mystical energy force."⁹

Traditions from various parts of the ancient world describe levitation as the construction means used by the unknown builders of miraculous structures. In Britain, Merlin was said to have originally found Stonehenge in Ireland, where, like Leedskalnin, he single-handedly took apart its massive stones and transported them through the air to England's Salisbury Plain. A world away in distance and time, the South Pacific islanders of Ponape still tell how the twenty-ton basalt columns of Nan Madol, an enormous megalithic site, were floated across the sky by two Merlin-like magicians. Recalling the teenagers' report of multiton blocks floating through the air, it may be easier to believe that Leedskalnin was using Earth energies after all.

Cathe suggests that "at certain positions on the globe there are localities where the forces of gravity can be manipulated by the application of certain geometric harmonies. Where these geometric conditions exist, it is evidently possible for people who have the knowledge to use gravitational forces to construct great buildings of massive material. Stonehenge, the ancient pyramids, the temple at Baalbek, and perhaps the pyramids in Central and South America were the results of a combination of knowledge and gravitational anomalies. Coral Castle, I believe, occupies one of these positions."¹⁰

But how Leedskalnin built Coral Castle is no more mystifying than why he did it. He had little interest in money, consistently resisting efforts by entrepreneurs to advertise his place and turn it into a tourist attraction. Indeed, outsiders could gain entrance only after pulling on a bell cord, to which he may or may not have been in the mood to respond. He rarely left the site, and what he did behind its sheltering walls no one ever knew.

Like the enigmas of its construction, its real function is unknown. Why did he make so many sculpted references and astronomical orientations to the heavens? For whom were twenty-five, half-ton rocking chairs designed? To what or whom was his barbaric altar dedicated? What need could have demanded so massive a complex as Coral Castle? And why did Edward Leedskalnin devote his whole life to it? Today, Coral Castle is open to the public as the self-made monument of a reclusive man's mysterious genius.

Extraordinary
Personalities

25

Four Thousand Years of Prophets

There are many colorful varieties of prophecy, from the altered states of consciousness deliberately induced by shamans to the spontaneous utterances of unconscious seers like Edgar Cayce and the visionary works of Jules Verne. Over the course of time many seers have revealed notable events to come.[1] Particularly credible is an interpretation of the much-debated Revelation, the last book in the bible, interpreted by Tony Allan.

It becomes clear, he states, when it is understood that John (perhaps the same John responsible for the fourth gospel) was writing about Rome near the end of the first century C.E. Thus perceived, the Revelation accurately foretold the barbaric invasions three hundred years later, the collapse of classical civilization, and the rise and millennial permanence of Christianity. But such an interpretation shows a dark side to the Revelation. According to John, after a thousand years Christianity will die out in a world war to be reborn a thousand years later, but in a drastically altered form. Troubles predicted for the Church were also spoken by the medieval abbess of the Rhineland, Hildegard von Bingen. Thanks to modern recordings of her compositions, her name has emerged from obscurity and is today well known among music lovers.

*Figure 25.1. German 10 DM commemorative coin (1998)
designed by Carl Vezerfi-Clemm on the 900th anniversary
of Hildegard of Bingen's birth. Photograph by Johel.*

But in her own time she was more famous as a prophetess who was sought out by popes and emperors. She told them that she foresaw a time when people and princes would forsake the Church and its fabulous wealth would shrink. Individual nations would switch their allegiance to national leaders rather than the papacy. Hildegard von Bingen's vision, expressed in the twelfth century, came to pass in the Reformation that swept over Christendom 350 years later.

Western readers will be less familiar with the story of Himiko, or Sun Child, the legendary first queen of Japan, who owned a sacred mirror that allowed her to see into the future. Remarkably, on the other side of the vast Pacific Ocean, the first Inca, Pachahutec, was said to have likewise possessed a magical mirror into which he accurately glimpsed coming events.

In our own time, the words "Remember Pearl Harbor!" were painted on a sidewalk in front of the entrance to a grammar school in Owensville, Indiana, on December 7, 1939—precisely two years before the day of the Japanese attack. The sinking of RMS *Titanic* on April 15, 1912, was accompanied by the largest known number of presailing cancellations on record. Although the ship was universally regarded as the greatest technological achievement of her time, hundreds of would-be passengers were beset with premonitions of the ocean liner's doom, which proved to be tragically correct.

Some predictions came in the form of nightmares. A mechanical engineer, John William Dunne, suffered from vivid dreams of a volcanic eruption on an island somewhere in the French Caribbean, where four thousand persons would be killed. A few days later, Mount Pele exploded, killing forty thousand victims on the island of Martinique. Dunne's vision had been correct in every detail, save the addition of one zero.

Similar anecdotal materials provoke us to wonder what seers in the modern world are prophesizing today.

26

Jules Verne,
the Clairvoyant Author

The name Jules Verne is synonymous with visionary science fiction. He described atomic-powered submarines, a trip to the moon, helicopters, television, and other twentieth-century technologies a hundred years before they came to pass. Verne's books were published to international popularity that continues today, and he still reigns supreme as France's most translated author. Surprisingly, however, Verne's most far-sighted novel was rejected by publishers in 1863—at the height of his career. Pierre Jules Hetzel, whose company published a sixty-four-volume series of Verne's work, returned the manuscript for *Paris in the Twentieth Century*, saying, "No one today will believe your prophecy."[1]

It portrayed life in the City of Light specifically during the 1960s, and differed radically from the author's imaginative fantasies in which he optimistically lauded technological evolution as the beneficent wave of the future. In his rejected novel Verne reversed himself by depicting the society to come as degraded by uncontrolled development and spiritual disorientation. In Verne's future Paris, popular culture has sunk to juvenile levels, with a general obsession for electromechanical gimmicks that are mere toys for transient self-gratification and triviality among the masses.

Figure 26.1. Jules Verne in 1878

After its rejection the manuscript disappeared. In 1989 Verne's great-grandson, while in the process of selling the family home, found a large safe. The safe's bronze door had to be cut open with a blow torch. The perfectly preserved, handwritten pages of *Paris in the Twentieth Century* lay inside under a pile of linen. Its publication 131 years after Hetzel's rejection caused a global stir when the novel was translated into dozens of languages. Readers were intrigued by the nineteenth-century writer's amazing descriptions of fax machines, automobiles, elevators, and so many other technological innovations that have become part of our daily lives.

But even Verne's knowledgeable fans were disturbed by his biting characterization of the vulgar materialism he saw as the end result of rampant technology. It seemed he had suddenly switched over from technophile to technophobe. Some reviewers compared the novel with the later classics *Brave New World* and *1984*. According to early twenty-first-century English editors of *Paris in the Twentieth Century,* "Its predictions are much closer to the truth. It is astounding how accurately Verne managed to predict our contemporary world."[2] Verne's future Paris is a megalopolis that teems with a confusion of self-propelled vehicles and includes twenty-four-hour convenience stores, an elaborate subway system, and car-shattering concerts of "electronic music."[3]

A typical condominium is "an enormous structure in wonderfully bad taste, sporting a multitude of plate glass windows, a veritable barracks transformed into a private residence, not so much imposing as ponderous."[4] The schools of the future—which Verne equates to academic credit unions—contain classrooms where information is dispensed through modern audiovisual equipment. Businesses use fax machines to communicate with far-flung branch stores. There is an electronic bank alarm, "an apparatus of virginal sensitivity," with which "electric lights are automatically turned on."[5]

There are even personal computers: "Operating by a sort of keyboard, sums are instantaneously produced, remainders, products, quotients, rules of proportion, calculations of amortization and of interest compounded for infinite periods and at all possible rates."[6] Verne also foreshadows two hotly contested aspects of today's legal system. Writing sixty-five years before the invention of the electric chair, he describes how in twentieth-century Paris, "criminals were now executed by an electric charge."[7]

He also predicts how he thought plea bargaining would come to dominate the system: "Lawyers no longer plead, they compromise; a good transaction is preferred to a good trial; it's faster and more profitable."[8] He deplored what he envisioned as a general decline in literacy: "Classical authors and the entire book trade in Sallust and Livy peacefully crumbled to dust on the shelves of the old publishing house; but introductions to mathematics, textbooks on civil engineering, mechanics, physics, chemistry, astronomy, courses in commerce, finance, industrial arts and whatever concerned the market tendencies of the day sold millions of copies."[9]

In Verne's futuristic Paris, not only literature but all the arts are dying through neglect. While Gioachino Rossini, of *Guillaume Tell* (William Tell) fame, still maintains a place in the repertoire, Giacomo Meyerbeer, composer of *Les Huguenots* (The Huguenots), has been, as Verne accurately portrayed him, almost totally "forgotten." So are Louis Herold and Daniel Françoise Auber, the founders of grand opera. Their kind of music is replaced by the hysterical ravings of sounds as discordant as they are stentorian: "Yes, an electric concert, and what instruments!"—all of them wired together to generate the loudest possible noise for the broadest commercial success.[10]

But there are sadder consequences than cultural sterility in Verne's twentieth-century Paris, including social disintegration and technology's calamitous impact on the natural environment. Verne argues that the transient material gains cannot compensate for the resulting social and personal losses. If a future dominated by relentless traffic, anonymous architecture, and supermachines must be purchased with cultureless wealth, broken families, and a polluted environment, he writes, then humanity has been catastrophically shortchanged.

Skeptics argue that Verne's prophetic novels about our century were possible only because he was a keen observer of scientific developments in his own time, trends he followed to their logical end in a hypothetical, though credible, future. While rooted in the technology of his day, the accuracy of Verne's predictions went far beyond anything his contemporaries could invent—so much so that paranormal abilities cannot be ruled out of his fiction. It seems clear that Verne did indeed peer into our time. Perhaps he saw more about ourselves than we are willing to recognize.

27

Amazing
Mother Shipton

England's Mother Shipton is not as generally well known outside her homeland as her better-remembered contemporary, Nostradamus. Still, she lacked none of the more famous Frenchman's powers to foresee the future. Her own mother was Agatha Sontheil, who lived near an unusual formation combining a cave and waterfall called Dropping Well at Knaresborough, an old market town in North Yorkshire, on the left bank of the river Nidd.

Orphaned at fifteen years old, Agatha was made pregnant by a handsome stranger who promised her the gift of prophecy in compensation for her sorrows. Thereafter she could foretell coming events. Local people liked her cheerful prognostications, until she came to the attention of the authorities. They charged her with witchcraft but acquitted her because of her advanced maternity.

In July 1488 Agatha bore a particularly ugly infant girl who she named Ursula. The baby was deformed; she was big-boned with bulging eyes and misshapen legs. Soon after, Agatha died in the care of a convent. Her daughter was thereafter reared by the parish nurse, who instilled a sense of compassion in the orphan. Despite her alarming physical appearance Ursula Sontheil grew up in possession of a brilliant mind, a supple wit, and a heart of gold. This inner beauty attracted a young man from York, Toby Ship, who married her when she was twenty-four years old. From then on, she was known as Mother Shipton, even though she never had any children of her own.

The name was given to her by the many people who experienced her kindness and generosity. Over the next forty-nine years her reputation for accurate prophecy drew visitors from many miles around, and she won the support of the Abbot of Beverley, who copied down a number of her pronouncements. Always good-natured, she offered her services in an informal setting in her small home, although she often returned to the Dropping Well cave. During her life and for centuries thereafter, many pubs throughout the south of England were named after her. Only two survive today: one, near her birthplace in Knaresborough, named after her preferred place of prophecy—the Dropping Well; another in Portsmouth, with a statue of her above the main entrance. A fundraising campaign in 2013 raised £35,000 (about U.S. $50,500) to erect another statue of Mother Shipton in Knaresborough.

While she appears to have been British, her name is German. *Sontheil* is Old Middle German for "sun health," "the healing sun," or "part of the sun." This is a particularly appropriate name for a woman who called upon the ancient Greek sun god of prophecy, Apollo—a singular practice for anyone in sixteenth-century Christian England. Apollo kept a cave at Delphi, atop a mountain in southern Greece, where his priestess, the Pythia, foretold the future through his auspices—all of which recall Mother Shipton's Dropping Well cave. In German, *Ursula* means "primeval knower," likewise appropriate for her calling as a seer.

The name of her birthplace, Knaresborough, was an Anglicization of the German Narresburg, or "Fool's Place." In esoteric tradition, as exemplified in the Major Arcana of the tarot card deck, the Fool is not a laughable clown but represents the pure innocence of a pure-hearted person open to the revelation of knowledge higher than that available to mundane, merely rational humans. It is this concept of the Fool that is associated with prophecy.

Mother Shipton's birth near the Nidd River is remarkable because

Nidd (also known as Nudd or Ludd) was the Keltic god of light and prophecy, the British Apollo. And who was that handsome stranger, Ursula's father? Some of the myths belonging to Apollo recount his female conquests, to which he bestowed the gift of prophecy, such as the Trojan princess Cassandra. We cannot interpret the ultimate significance of these biographical details, but merely make them available as part of the mystery that was Mother Shipton.

Most of her predictions dealt with everyday concerns in the immediate future, because the local people who called on her were interested only in matters that directly concerned them, and she only prophesied when asked. A few learned visitors, primarily clergymen, questioned her about contemporaneous political events that went beyond her own century. And while the wonderful accuracy of her predictions firmly established her credibility as a seer, the rise and fall of kings she foretold belong to a period of English history obscure to most Americans. Fortunately for us a few of her guests were foresighted enough to ask her about things to come beyond her own time, and these prognostications form our chief interest in Mother Shipton. Some prophecies concerning the fate of her famous countrymen bear repeating:

> *When war shall begin in the spring,*
> *Much woe to England will bring.*
> *But tell what's next, oh, cruel fate!*
> *A king made martyr at his gate.*[1]

The English Civil War did indeed begin in spring 1642, and ushered in widespread suffering throughout England. It concluded with the execution of Charles I. In his last words he described himself as "a martyr for my people."[2] And the axman's blade with which the king was beheaded was referred to as "a swinging gate." Her detailed account of major events beginning in the year of her self-predicted death are remarkable:

Great London's triumphant spire
Shall be consumed with flames of fire.
A widowed queen
In England shall be headless seen.
The harp shall give a better sound.
An earl without a head be found.[3]

St. Paul's church steeple was destroyed by fire in 1561, while widowed Mary, Queen of Scots, was beheaded, as was the Earl of Essex. His position as Ireland's governor may account for Mother Shipton's reference to a harp, the Irish national emblem. Speaking more directly to the twentieth century, she foresaw a time when

Carriages without horses will go,
And accidents will fill the world with woe.
Around the world thoughts shall fly
In the twinkling of an eye.
Under water men shall walk, shall ride,
    shall sleep and talk.
In the air men shall be seen
In white, in black, and in green.
Iron in the water shall float,
As easy as a wooden boat.
Primrose Hill in London shall be
And in the centre a bishop's see.[4]

During Mother Shipton's day, Primrose Hill was a full two miles outside the London city limits. Today it lies in the heart of the city and contains the See of the Bishop of London. She was no less on target concerning an event that occurred three centuries beyond her life:

In eighteen hundred and thirty-five,
Which of us shall be alive?

Mother Shipton

Figure 27.1. A popular engraving of Mother Shipton
made during her lifetime

But when from the top of Bow
Shall the dragon stoop full low,
When all men shall see them meet
On the land, yet by the Fleet. [5]

The meaning of these verses was unfathomable until the year she cited—1835—when repairs on St. Paul's Cathedral required that the cross and ball adornments had to be taken down. At the same time, Bow Church was also being reconditioned, and the Dragon façade was removed. All three items—cross, ball, and dragon—attracted public attention ("when all men shall see them meet"), because they were carried through the streets together to the same repair shop located beside Fleet Prison ("by the Fleet").

Mother Shipton referred at least once to the United States, which only came into existence more than two hundred years after she died:

Figure 27.2. The Callistege mi, *or "Mother Shipton moth."*
Photograph by Chrkl.

When the North shall divide the South,
An eagle shall build in the lion's mouth.[6]

Here, she described the Union victory over the Confederacy in our Civil War. The eagle was the emblem of Northern forces, and the lion—Great Britain—lost the lucrative cotton market in the South because England had supported the defeated rebels.

Mother Shipton also spoke about the end of the world. But we must not take her too literally. A "world" does not necessarily mean the planet Earth, but may also stand for an epoch of global significance, such as the Ancient World, the Western World, the Scientific World, and so forth. Indeed, the Aztec astrologers of prehistoric Mexico referred to eons of time as "worlds." Thus understood, perhaps Mother Shipton accurately prophesied the collapse of international Communism and the dissolution of the Soviet world power when she said:

The end of the world will come
In nineteen hundred and ninety-one.[7]

Shortly after her death in 1560, local residents began noticing an unusual moth fluttering around the Dropping Well and the Knaresborough countryside. A pattern on the insect's forewings bore a striking resemblance to popular engravings of the prophetess made during her active years. Among various cultures around the world, moths are human archetypes for the human soul. Today the *Callistege mi* is more commonly known as the Mother Shipton moth.

28

The Man
with X-Ray Eyes

In 1975, on an otherwise uneventful summer's day, Rollie Hillesland was casually riding his motorcycle near Fargo, North Dakota, when he was broadsided by a car running a stoplight at 65 miles per hour. The woman driver suffered serious head injuries and both vehicles were utterly demolished. Hillesland lay lifeless on the pavement as emergency teams covered him with a sheet and awaited the ambulance that would take his dead body to the city morgue. They were astonished a few minutes later to see the shroud suddenly cast aside as the bearded, six-foot, six-inch biker rose angrily to his feet, swearing vengeance on the unknown wrecker of his Honda CBX.

Paramedics managed to calm Rollie sufficiently for an examination, but he was too heavy for them to lift into their ambulance, so he got inside himself. At the hospital, physicians checked him over thoroughly but found him in excellent health. He suffered not so much as a scratch. Less than an hour after being admitted he was discharged and walked twelve blocks to his home. There, friends gathered around the wreckage of his Honda were certain no one could have survived such a collision.

The information discussed in this chapter is based on an interview of Rollie Hillesland by Frank Joseph, July 1995.

Rollie's unexpected appearance came as something of a shock, but he was unable to recall much from his ten minutes of legal death save for a sudden flash of white light below his right elbow, followed by a series of visions he was reluctant to share with fellow members of the Outlaw Motorcycle Club.

Rollie had been a truck driver before the accident, and something of a wild man, not unlike his Viking ancestors on the Norwegian island of Hillesland, or "Hilly Land," from which his family derived its name. The atypical visions persisted over the next three years, as a new, unfamiliar sensitivity began to open up in Rollie's head. While listening to digitally recorded music—whether Beethoven or rock—Rollie was surprised to find that his mind's ear could distinguish and separate each one of the performing instruments, isolating them from all the others.

On one occasion, while Rollie was thus excluding one sound from the rest, Secret Service agents were in the process of clearing an alternative landing space for a presidential visit just four miles away when their ultrahigh frequency receivers began picking up an "intruder signal," or possible enemy code in music. Tracing the anomalous broadcast to its source brought them into contact with Rollie Hillesland, who had been unwittingly transmitting his music appreciation to the suspicious G-men. The agents unceremoniously "recruited" Rollie for study and training purposes, intent on making some military or counterespionage application of his mental ability. The classified experiments to which they subjected him went against the grain of his conscience, however, and he eventually walked away from the government program. "It was not for the good," he recalled, "but for the bad," refusing to elaborate.

Meanwhile Rollie had ascended to another stratum of inner awareness. He was now able to merely look at someone in order to meld with their mind and body on levels even deeper than they felt themselves. In so doing he could instantly envision everything that ailed them, and simultaneously cure whatever undermined their physical health. Beginning with a few close friends he initiated the first of his "body readings," during which he sat quietly but informally with someone, engaging in casual conversation while he felt his spirit move inside the other person's corporeal form. He so identified with others that he experienced their physical discomfort. If they suffered stomach problems, his stomach ached as well.

"I picked up their same sensations," he said. "Everything that was wrong inside them, I felt and knew about." But Rollie knew much more. He saw the root causes of their suffering, and in diagnosing them simultaneously effected a cure. These were mostly minor discomforts, but sufferers were impressed with the accuracy of his "hunches," as most of them characterized what he preferred to call "frequency transposing."

A woman he had known for twenty years but had not seen for some time learned of his uncanny ability and came to him one day for help. Her doctors had informed her that she was afflicted with an advanced case of pancreatic cancer. They declared her condition terminal and predicted she would be dead in three months. Rollie sat with the woman for twenty minutes, focusing his consciousness on the region of her pancreas. She experienced a sensation of internal heat, and with its passing, her pain vanished.

Two weeks later, to the utter bewilderment of the professionals who had confidently pronounced her death sentence, her pancreas had completely healed. She is still cancer-free and actively employed some fifteen years after her miraculous recovery. Rollie never advertised his success, but word of mouth soon spread news of his restorative ability to persons he did not know. Just one day following his "body healing" of another woman afflicted with breast cancer, she was totally cured. In answer to how he could have achieved so thorough a result in so short a time, he said only, "I actually become the person in trouble. I know where to go inside and what needs to be done. To read somebody is to heal them at the same time. I make our bodies resonate at a common frequency."

The stepfather of a young man suffering from advanced cancer contacted Rollie for assistance. The lad was slated to have an entire lung removed, plus half of the other. Instead, he met with Rollie for treatment. As in all such sessions there was no physical contact between the two, and the patient was required to do nothing but ask to be healed. Two days later, when the young man was scheduled for drastic surgery, he was sent home instead. All the tumors in both lungs had totally evaporated.

"Cancer," Rollie says, "is a state of mind that becomes physical. I know that what I have belongs to every human being in the world. Actually, I do not heal anyone. Rather, I assist them to heal themselves, activating the natural, though hidden, potential for self-regeneration in everyone. This power is our natural birthright. I believe our body is a life-support system for an unevolved brain. My mind activates some underdeveloped part of the mental facility in others. The only difference is I know how to use that power. I cannot explain it, but if you were to die, as I did, and come back, then we could talk." Rollie admits to only one historic counterpart, whose work sheds some light on his own.

In the first half of the last century, Dr. Royal Raymond Rife invented a variable frequency flashing light source that allegedly killed bacteria, rickettsias, protozoa, fungi, and viruses. He claimed to have identified the frequencies needed to eliminate such microbes, all of them associated with major diseases, including carcinoma and sarcoma cancers. Dr. Rife's 1939 invention was a precursor of today's ultrasound instruments, although, like Rollie's natural gift, it not only diagnosed cancerous tumors but obliterated them.

"Dr. Rife found that he could cure certain diseases by bombarding them with radio frequencies, causing the germs to die," Rollie says.

Rife and Hillesland have something else in common: both failed to receive recognition from the American medical establishment. Rollie believes that, since his 1984 motorcycle accident, he has been able to tap into 20 percent of his brain's capacity, about twice as much as the rest of us use. "If everyone could do that, most diseases would disappear, and people would live to their normal lifespan of 143 years."

Remarkably, Rollie has found that he could effect a "body healing" even if physically removed from the sufferer by great distances.

"All I need is a photograph of the person, their name, and location. Sometimes, one of their personal possessions I can hold in my hands helps." His remote healing appears to be a form of the better known remote viewing, a phenomenon that, according to Rollie, is entirely authentic: "Again, the ability is naturally born in every human being. Anyone can access it if they put their mind to it."

A man whose enzyme test for cancer came up positive went to Rollie as a last resort. Despite exhaustive, costly testing, including x-rays and MRIs, doctors were unable to locate the tumor they knew threatened his life. Within moments of establishing a frequency transposition with the man, Rollie pinpointed the precise position of the five-centimeter-long cancer, which had eluded examining physicians because of its small size. Rollie claims that his sessions, typically less than an hour long, are the equivalent of sixty or seventy hours of conventional medical testing. To date, these consultations have saved more than 140 men and women from terminal diseases.

For the sake of comparison, of the 4,324 miracles documented in the entire history of the Catholic Church, no more than four were allegedly performed by any single saint. That is 136 less than Rollie's miraculous cures. Occasionally an ailment may return, usually as a result of complications set in motion by the original complaint. But Rollie's follow-up treatments usually succeed in thoroughly eliminating the problem. During their thirty- to fifty-minute sessions, Rollie's clients commonly experience some internal movement at the precise location of their distress. But the feeling of warmth often accompanying these sensations seems more reassuring than distressing.

Rollie is particularly proud of his skill in locating internal issues standard medical practitioners may be slow in detecting or neglect altogether. The smallest tumor he has so far discovered in a sufferer was only one-seventh of a centimeter long. "It took me a little longer than usual to find it," he said. "About five minutes." The same tumor was located at Minnesota's renowned Mayo Clinic, where doctors found it after half a year of examinations.

Rollie's healing rate is exceptionally high, greater than any claimed by mainstream physicians. "When all this began, I made a deal with 'Someone' that He would get 20 percent of the persons I tried to cure." Rollie's 80 percent success rate occasionally takes strange twists of fate, however. He learned shortly after healing a twenty-five-year-old man of lethal cancer that his former client had been arrested on charges of fraud. Before meeting Rollie, and convinced he was about to die in a few weeks, the foolish spendthrift maxed out all his credit cards and bounced a large number of personal checks in living the high life—one last fling before escaping debt by dying. Although restored to robust health, he now faces a lifetime of legal and financial difficulties.

Rollie works not only with cancer patients but quadriplegics as well. "I feel certain I could have cured the *Superman* actor, Christopher Reeves, because the man had such a positive attitude." More recently, Rollie was asked to help another newsmaker, Terry Schiavo, but she passed away after her feeding tube was removed by a court order and before family permission could be obtained for his ministrations.

"The mind holds a complete record of everything that has ever happened to our bodies, no matter how small," he says. For example, he "saw" inside the subconscious of a Vietnam veteran who had both legs amputated, but was able to verify that the ex-infantryman had suffered foot and knee injuries as a boy.

Rollie does not limit his "body healings" to fellow human beings. "The first animal I healed was a purebred wolf in Sedona, Arizona," he says. Since then his most usual four-footed clients are horses. "Animals are better to work with because they're completely open to the kind of frequency transposition I do. They're more used to it, since they do it to each other all the time, anyway."

Ironically, for all his inner gifts, Rollie is unable to heal himself. He suffers from a serious knee injury conventional surgical operations have aggravated more than cured, while his own energies are powerless to effect positive change. "My knee can only be fixed by another frequency transposer more powerful than myself. So far, I haven't found anyone of superior healing strength."

While he recognizes the deficiencies of modern medical science, Rollie urges all his clients to return to their physician immediately after frequency transposition for verification. "What I do does not supplant the doctor's art, but should be used in cooperation with it."

With each individual session Rollie experiences real fatigue as his own body, following such close identification with another, begins to shut down. In an attempt to restore his energies and clear his thoughts, he has invented a personal form of meditation, during which he rests his chin against his chest.

"This position seems to open the mind, as though a natural break opens between the base of the skull and the top of the spine." While in this position, he slips into a brief meditative state lasting only a few moments, enough to reset his diagnostic faculties. Unaffiliated with any religious organizations or marketing schemes, Rollie puts his energies at the disposal of anyone asking for physical healing. A simple flyer briefly describing his curative technique is his only promotional material.

Interestingly, its frontispiece is emblazoned with the likeness of an *Uachtet*—the stylized, all-seeing Eye of Ra, the ancient Egyptian sun god, long ago believed by Pharaonic inhabitants of the Nile Valley to bestow healing on all his worshippers suffering from otherwise incurable physical ailments. Perhaps Rollie, the Man with the X-Ray Eyes, has something of the old Uachtet about him. The crash that sent him on a ten-minute, round-trip visit to the afterlife forty-three years ago certainly appears to have opened his inner vision to the physical troubles afflicting this highly complex biological mechanism we know as the human body.

Fees for his assistance vary, but in any case, they are substantially lower than the sometimes-crippling hospital bills incurred by patients seeking the same cures. For example, Rollie tells of a fellow North Dakotan cancer patient who virtually bankrupted himself before he was finally healed by the unorthodox but more effective method of frequency transposition.

"I know I can't save the world," Rollie admits, "but I hope to reveal to people the great, unused potential for healing as part of their human inheritance."

29

The World-Shattering Secret of Sir Francis Bacon

Although I thought I was familiar with the grounds of the Minnesota State Capitol in St. Paul, I was unaware of any Columbus statue alleged to be there. But then I approached a small group of people gathered in rapt attention around the pedestal of a generally overlooked monument on the east lawn. I guess those are the folks I'm supposed to interview, I thought, and interrupted their apparent reverie by announcing, "I'm looking for Fletcher Richman."

The three men and five women made way for a spritely fifty-two-year-old man sporting a Stars-and-Stripes tie and a winning smile. He was the historical consultant of the group styling itself "Sir Francis Bacon's Sages of the Seventh Seal," of which I knew nothing, save that he and his colleagues—some from as far away as England—had gathered at the state capitol for some arcane purpose. Richman attempted to enlighten me as we walked around the base of the bronze statue in the bright May sunshine.

The information discussed in this chapter is based on a May 1996 interview with Fletcher Richman.

"Throughout the ages, men and women have been anointed with the sacred task of preserving, protecting, and often 'hiding in plain sight' original documents of ancient wisdom, historical archives, and the treasures of the advanced civilizations of centuries long passed," he began.

"In order that future generations may benefit once more from these remarkable evidences of human achievement, they utilized intricate coding and ciphering systems. These brilliant messages of the past laid a pathway of discovery for those individuals and small groups who were sensitive and receptive to an inner prompting to begin this unique journey of discovery. Through diligent purification of the human being, extraordinary dedication of study and practice, and the willingness to persevere in spite of obstacles and challenges to the contrary, great strides have been made in the twentieth, and now twenty-first century, to once again reveal the locations and contents of many of these sacred vaults in America and throughout the world. Each capital city has at least one such treasure trove, and St. Paul, Minnesota, is no exception."

Richman called my attention to the left hand of the larger-than-life-size statue of Christopher Columbus. "Notice it is pointing to a specific spot about fifteen feet south of the monument. That is where one of the vaults has been buried about twenty feet beneath the capitol lawn. Soon, we hope to meet with [Minnesota] Governor Pawlenty for permission to rope off this area and go over it with ground-penetration radar, which should verify that one of the brick chambers is indeed where we claim it is. Once its existence has been thus confirmed, we will file an application with the Governor's Office to excavate it."

The vault's subterranean location was apparently known to the sculptor and Italian government authorities that donated the statue and erected it in 1931. A few feet farther south of the vault's suspected whereabouts is the likewise unmarked site of Saint Paul's first white settler. Like the statue's maker, she was Greek, a not inconsequential coincidence to Richman, who argues that Columbus himself, contrary to mainstream opinion, was actually born Prince Nikolaos Ypsilantis. As a late-fifteenth-century student he traveled from his home in Chiosas, Greece, to Genoa, where he received a classical education, went on to become an accomplished navigator, and was initiated into the rites of one of the numerous secret societies that flourished throughout Italy during the Renaissance.

Sixty-nine years after Columbus discovered America another initiate was born in York Place, England. Conceived by the inappropriately entitled Virgin Queen, Elizabeth I, and Robert Dudley, the infant was packed off to grow up under surrogate parents, Sir Nicholas and Lady Bacon. The lad's exceptional intellect soon manifested itself, as Francis Bacon was early recognized as something of a boy genius in school. Not until late adolescence, however, did he learn the shocking truth about his royal origins, a revelation that immediately preceded his exile to France by a suspicious queen.

According to Richman, "in the grandeur of the French court, young Francis, at the age of eighteen, gathered with other philosophers and metaphysicians, among them Rosicrucians, Knights Templar students, and Theosophists. Under his leadership, they formed a movement of Freemasons, who were dedicated to recording the true history of their age, the contents of their work secured in copper cylinders, then placed in brick vaults and buried carefully in the earth for future generations to locate, excavate, read, study, and apply such knowledge for the upliftment of the human spirit and condition worldwide."

But far more than history books was allegedly buried in the brick vaults. Bacon and his associates supposedly worked out an ideal form of world government diametrically opposed to the monarchy of Queen Elizabeth—hence the need for secrecy. The principles of this democratic doctrine were clearly spelled out for use in some future period when Bacon's radical ideas would find greater acceptance than during the sixteenth century. He concocted these subversive concepts with his friends after his return to England after a three-year absence.

"These brilliant men and women, known as his 'Good Pen,'" Richman explained, "included such luminaries as Christopher Marlowe,

Figure 29.1. Sir Francis Bacon

Ben Johnson, Edmund Spenser, Sir Tobie Matthew, Sir Walter Raleigh, Sir Francis Drake, Lancelot Andrews, and Sir Thomas Meautys. Keenly aware of the dangers of publishing under their own names, the Good Pens hid their true identities under the greatest nom de plume in history: William Shakespeare. The true meaning of this unique name is 'The Will of the I AM will shake the spear of wisdom.'" Bacon and his illustrious friends cloaked their politically incorrect intentions in the worship of the Greek goddess Pallas Athena, said to "shake the spear of wisdom of truth."

Richman went on to point out, "There was a pretender, poacher, horse handler, and minor actor during the time of England's 'Divine Awakening,' but the spelling of his name was 'William Shagspur.' He was known to be illiterate, with a serious drinking problem, and could have never been the true author of such beautiful, classic plays and sonnets during his lifetime."

These famous works were written by the Good Pens, most particularly Sir Francis Bacon. They "paid this man [Shagspur] to be their 'muse,' using him as a cover for their true identities." According to Richman and his colleagues, Sir Francis additionally edited the King James version of the Bible in 1611, although his original rendition was altered by ecclesiastical authorities alarmed at Bacon's egalitarian sentiments, which they expunged.

In the midst of growing political oppression Bacon faked his own death in 1626, thus enabling him to carry on his work of enlightenment under another form of concealment. About this time members of the Good Pens sailed for the New World with their manuscripts, biblical translations, and political treatises—together with hordes of jewels, gold, and silver. Bacon did not follow them, but a relative, Nathaniel Bacon Sr., the acting governor of the Jamestown colony, was said to have interred the priceless collections under its first brick church. Fifty years later all these items were relocated to the Bruton Parish Churchyard, in Williamsburg, Virginia, in thirty-three copper cylinders buried twenty feet deep in a ten-by-ten-foot brick cube.

"Included within the Bruton Vault," says Richman, "is physical evidence for the true lineage of the English monarchy, the original Declaration of Independence, the United States Constitution, the lost writings of Shakespeare (actually, Sir Francis Bacon), the original King James version of the Bible as edited by Bacon, the exact location of all other vaults belonging to the legacy of colonists, pioneers, explorers, conquistadors, and individuals who were anointed with the sacred vision of true Christianity. The wealth contained within these sacred vaults is to be used to prepare, educate, and relocate the masses of humanity before, during, and after massive changes of the Earth during these latter days, and to rebuild communities after the settling of the aftermath."

Richman and his fellow researchers believe the combined contents of the vaults have the potential to stop the current Iraqi conflict, which they say is a prelude to World War Three, the biblical Armageddon. In addition to these treasures the vaults are also said to contain either unpublished chapters from or a sequel to Bacon's most famous published book, *The New Atlantis,* a utopian vision of world peace and prosperity, together with a master plan for bringing mankind into global harmony and order. Writer Tedi Trindle concluded in the three-part *Return of the Vault People* that this story "is as mysterious and convoluted as the human brain."[1]

Indeed, the tale becomes more fantastic the further it unravels. Some enthusiasts are convinced CIA operatives are suppressing all public information about the vault in the name of national security. These true believers suspect the CIA is using a Nazi-built time machine enabling agents to travel back and forth into the past and future, gathering intelligence and predicting the reincarnation of Jesus Christ and Mary Magdalene, who threaten to disclose the secrets of the vault. Extremist opinion also places the lost secret of alchemy—the transmutation of base metals into gold—and the power of immortal life in the Bruton vault.

While skeptics may shake their heads at what must seem to them a self-deluding fantasy, Sir Francis Bacon himself contributed to the controversy in one of his last written statements, recorded, significantly enough, at the Bruton Parish vault site, in 1676: "I have held up the light in the obscurity of philosophy, which will be seen centuries after I am dead. It will be seen amidst the erection of tombs, theatres, foundations, temples, of orders and fraternities for nobility and obedience; the establishment of good laws as an example to the world.

"For I am not raising a capitol or a pyramid to the pride of men, but laying a foundation in the human understanding for a holy temple after the model of the world. I shall not then doubt the happy issue of my undertakings in this design, whereby concealed treasure, which now seems utterly lost to mankind, shall be confined to so universal a piety, and brought into use by the industry of converted scholars whose wretched, opinionated books have impartial laws, or shall have dedicated as an untimely feast to the worms of Earth in whose tomb these deserted riches must ever lie buried as lost abortments, unless those be made the active midwives to deliver them."[2]

Yet another famous name has been drawn into the Baconian enigma, the occult writer of the early twentieth century, Manly Palmer Hall. Born March 18, 1901, in Peterborough, Ontario, Hall grew up to establish the Philosophical Research Society, which still hosts a wide range of lectures, seminars, workshops, and performances on philosophical subjects. Located in Los Feliz, California, since it first opened its doors in 1934, it was designated a Cultural Site by the Los Angeles City Council eleven years ago. During his long life Hall rose to the highest rank possible in the Scottish Rite by becoming an honorary 33rd-degree Mason, a privilege bestowed on such renowned personalities as Norman Vincent Peale and Senator J. Strom Thurmond.

Hall, too, was sure that Sir Francis Bacon was the real author of the so-called Shakespeare plays, but had better cause than most other investigators for reaching such a conclusion. In *The Secret Teachings of All Ages,* he explained, "The philosophic ideals promulgated throughout the Shakespearean plays distinctly demonstrate their author to have been thoroughly familiar with certain doctrines and tenets peculiar to Rosicrucianism; in fact the profundity of the Shakespearean productions stamps their creator as one of the *Illuminati* of the ages. Most of those seeking a solution for the Bacon-Shakespeare controversy have been intellectuals. Notwithstanding their scholarly attainments, they have overlooked the important part played by transcendentalism in the philosophic achievements of the ages. The mysteries of super-physics are inexplicable to the materialist, whose training does not equip him to estimate the extent of their ramifications and complexities. Yet who but a Platonist, a cabbalist, or a Pythagorean could have written *The Tempest, Macbeth, Hamlet,* or *The Tragedy of Cymbeline*? Who but one deeply versed in Paracelsian lore could have conceived *A Midsummer Night's Dream*?"[3]

Thanks to Hall and his wife, Marie, "the challenging task of

Figure 29.2. Skull and bones at the Bruton vaults.
Photograph by Sarah Stierch.

deciphering intricate cipher codes upon the tombstones at Bruton Parish Church has been, for the most part, completed," Richman says. "Diligently, with exacting precision, patience, inspired deciphering techniques, and months of metaphysical research, Marie and her friends were able to locate, for the first time since 1676, the original foundations of the first brick church in the middle of the cemetery in the churchyard at Bruton Parish."

But that was about all she was able to find during the course of two digs beginning in 1938. In neither excavation was the alleged vault unearthed. As testimony to the enduring nature of the Bruton controversy, attempts were again made in 1988 and 1992, when a geologist took twenty core samples at a depth of as many feet. He found no evidence of any human presence in the churchyard. Since then local authorities have forbidden any further archaeological work, professional or otherwise, in their cemetery, and posted signs in clear language to that effect for would-be discoverers.

"It's a pity," said Richman, who believes the vault lies under a pyramid-shaped structure in Bruton graveyard known as the Bray monument: "Beneath it is a spiral staircase that goes down to a Freemasonry library." Undeterred by these reversals, the ten men and women who comprise today's Sir Francis Bacon's Sages of the Seventh Seal are not discouraged. They have pursued their goal for the past twenty-two years and studied directly under the Halls at their Los Angeles home.

Before Manly passed away in 1990 he and Marie presented Richman and his associates with maps, cipher code translations, and their personal library—materials that have proved invaluable for their ongoing search for the 144 brick vaults buried around North America. Excavating and opening these underground repositories of Baconian wealth and wisdom, they believe, will usher in a new age of enlightened civilization and sustain mankind through the catastrophic Earth changes just ahead.

The time for the rediscovery and disclosure of the brick vaults has come, Richman says, despite the low number of his following. "Through the centuries, individuals and small groups have been anointed with the consecrated task of holding these truths and locations in silence until Providence initiated the permission for their release." Thus motivated, the quest for the lost wisdom of Sir Francis Bacon goes on.

30

The Mad Count of Alternative Archaeology

If there was ever a real-life "Indiana Jones," his name was Count Byron de Prorok, an early-twentieth-century Hungarian and naturalized British citizen who repeatedly endangered his life and the lives of everyone around him in search of ancient mysteries. World famous for his exploits during the interwar years, he is today almost totally forgotten, save by a few unconventional investigators who treasure his rare, long out-of-print titles.

Unavailable for more than sixty-five years, De Prorok's *In Quest of Lost Worlds* is witty, fast-paced, luminously descriptive at times, and delightfully incorrect—politically, that is.

"Gsell's room was thick with tobacco smoke, mostly his. Through the flood of his volcanic exhaust I saw him move to an old book on his shelf. 'I am an explorer in slippers,' he said. 'No, I cannot make this expedition. I am not so sure that I approve of all this digging, all this discovery, this bringing to light of new material which alters much of what I have written and more of what I still have to write.'"[1]

De Prorok, a university-trained scholar working for the French government and a member of the archaeological establishment, was an outspoken believer in the sunken civilization of Atlantis, a viewpoint that would today have him unceremoniously tossed out headfirst

Figure 30.1. Count de Prorok

from the tallest ivory tower. Shows you how things have changed.

"Absolve me from any daydreams of Atlantis," he pleads insincerely, "although I have consciously and unconsciously searched for the lost continent for years. I am not alone in the search." His quest took him into the most forbidding Mexican jungles, where he found an extremely primitive tribe on the verge of extinction huddled in their last generations among the crumbling remains of a splendid stone temple he speculated might have been built millennia ago by Atlantean refugees from the catastrophe that obliterated their overseas kingdom.

De Prorok's Yucatán experience is one of the great adventure yarns, the highlight of which takes place when a native boatman throws him into an alligator-infested river. Similarly nail-biting incidents punctuate description of some fabulous discoveries, since shelved by official archaeology most likely because of the man's interest in Atlantis. He nonetheless found a huge, megalithic city in central Algeria, naturally shunned today by excavators for that land's political chaos, and the tomb of Tin Hinan, the "legendary" Queen of the Tuaregs, ancient rulers of North Africa, in the A'Haggar Range of the Sahara Desert.

His expeditions conclude with an unsuccessful search for King Solomon's mines in the mythical Land of Ophir that he thought might have been in Ethiopia. In the process he provides firsthand insights into an Ethiopia on the verge of being conquered by Mussolini's army but with tantalizing, unmistakable roots in the Old Testament.

De Prorok was the first archaeologist to use motor caravans, motion picture cameras, spotter aircraft, and aerial photography, yet he is never so credited in modern archaeology texts. De Prorok is maverick archaeologist, high adventurer, and great writer—all of them rarities these days.

31

The Visionary of Atlantis

Alone and surrounded only by the high shelves of his beloved books, the short, stocky man sat writing at a large walnut desk. A Franklin stove shed radiance and warmth throughout his quiet library, while the blunt-edged winds of a Minnesota autumn battered the windowpanes. He wrote by the steady, yellow beam of an oil lamp, but his thoughts were as bleak as the darkness outside, gathering against the midnight. Ending by the minute was his birthday, made all the more poignant, mournful, and ironic by the loving congratulations bestowed on him some hours earlier by his adoring family.

Undistracted now, he vented all his heartache into the pages of his diary: "November 3rd, 1880. Alas and alack! Today is my forty-ninth birthday, and a sad day it is. All my hopes are gone, and the future settles down upon me dark and gloomy indeed. My life has been a failure and a mistake. My hopes have so often come to naught that I cease to hope. Well, well. All I can do is to face the music, and take my damnable fortune as it comes. A gloomy view for a man entering on his fiftieth year."[1]

He closed the little notebook and stared into the lamplight. His mind raced over the years that had brought him to this point. The utopian dream of building an ideal community on the banks of the Mississippi River had gone bankrupt. Once lieutenant governor of the state, his political career lay in ruins. All his hard labor as publisher and editor had come to nothing. Even a farming enterprise in neighboring Steven County, hit by drought followed by swarms of locusts, was collapsing.

Bedeviled by mounting debt and mortified by his inability to better provide for his family, he pushed away from the desk and strode across the room in an effort to shake off his cares. He ran the strong fingers of his hands through his thick auburn hair, took a deep breath, then let it out in a sigh of resignation. Turning for consolation to his cherished volumes neatly stacked against all four walls, his eye fell on a lidless, half-forgotten box hiding in a dark corner of the library. He knew what it contained and carried it back to his desk into the light. He vaguely skimmed over the huge collection of written material, the result of many years personal research beginning in his hometown, Philadelphia, and later amid the stacks of the Library of Congress at Washington, D.C.

All his life he had been an avid history buff, and his voracious reading tended toward understanding the saga of human development from its ancient origins. But for all his study he could not discover what he suspected must have been a missing link between savage and civilized man, a lost piece of the historical puzzle. The lingering mystery had assumed an importance in his mind on a par with the political problems of his own day. All the while he played at being founding father, gentleman farmer, or heretical statesman, the question preoccupied him, simmering, always simmering on the back burners of his high-powered imagination: Where, when, and how had civilization first arisen? The answer, he felt, lay somewhere in all these thousands of notes.

In a lightning flash of recognition the night's despair vanished at once. A new plan, a fresh hope, sprang full-blown from his mind. He would organize the haphazard collection of disparate materials into a book as unprecedented as it must be controversial, yet buttressed by impressive documentary sources and logical argument; its publication must ensure success. With it he would win the glory and income denied him by all previous endeavors. Past failures and present disappointments melted away in a blaze of enthusiasm and creativity. The man's brain was afire with purpose, ideas, and expression. By mid-March the following year, the work was done, and he embarked for New York City with his loosely bound manuscript in search of a publishing contract.

The journey from St. Paul took four days and cost him thirty dollars first class. Once in the Big Apple, he started at the top with America's largest publisher at the time, Harper's, and immediately struck pay dirt. The editors were so taken with his easy, dramatic prose and original ideas, they not only agreed to release his work but planned to actively promote it. During his return to Minnesota, the new author stopped over at Chicago's famous Palmer House, on East Monroe Street, to treat himself to a steak dinner for thirty-five cents. On July 22, he received the first galley sheets from Harper's, exclaiming in his diary, "I feel like a mother listening to the first cry of her first born. It may grow up to be an imbecile, but the fibers of my heart will cling to it."[2]

Receiving extensive, almost universally favorable reviews in the country's leading newspapers, the book caught on like proverbial wildfire, outstripping his highest expectations. Seven years after its release it had gone through twenty-three American editions, with an additional twenty-six British editions, leaping almost overnight from a national to an international bestseller.

When a four-page, personally-written letter arrived from British Prime Minister William Gladstone, congratulating him on his effort, the Minnesota writer confided in his diary, "I looked down at myself and could not but smile at the appearance of the man who, in this little, snow-bound hamlet, was corresponding with the man whose word was fate anywhere in the British Empire. The leg of my pants was torn; my coat was nearly buttonless."[3] But in a short time, the success Ignatius Donnelly received from *Atlantis, the Antediluvian World* put buttons on his coat—gold ones.[4]

He had come a long way since that night of despair on his forty-ninth birthday. His was a strange, fateful book, written by a driven man. With its publication, he became the modern founder of Atlantology, the serious study of everything connected to Atlantis. Until his research, the lost civilization was little more than a collective-conscious dream in the imagination of poetry. Although alluded to in the traditions of many cultures almost around the world, the earliest known account of its kind was composed during the early fourth century B.C.E., in a pair of dialogues, the *Timaeus* and *Kritias,* by Plato.

According to him, the original story of Atlantis was brought to Greece two hundred years before by Solon, the Athenian legislator, who heard it recounted firsthand by the chief priest in the Temple of the Goddess Neith (the Egyptian version of Athena), at the Nile Delta city of Saïs. No literary invention, the tablets inscribed with the account were seen and examined for centuries after Plato's death. One of his followers, Krantor, an illustrious philosopher in his own right, personally traveled in 260 B.C.E. to Lower Egypt, where he found Plato's narrative enshrined detail for detail. Krantor was also a respected scholar at the Great Library of Alexandria, the ancient world's center of classical learning.

There, the story of Atlantis was regarded as a credible episode in early history by the leading minds of the age, including Strabo, chief chronicler of the Roman Empire. Referring to the research of a Spanish historian—Poseidonous of Rhodes—Strabo wrote, "He did well in citing the opinion of Plato that the tradition concerning the island of Atlantis might be received as something more than fiction."[5]

Briefly, Plato's account tells of a great city that flourished in preclassical times on an Atlantis island outside the Straits of Gibraltar. Atlantis was the capital of a materially prosperous and politically powerful empire with all the scientific technology and artistic splendor of an exceptionally high civilization. Although its residents were originally virtuous and spiritually enlightened, successive generations gradually yielded to avarice and aggression, finally engaging in an imperialist war against Greece and Egypt. During this period of far-flung hostilities, Atlantis was suddenly wracked by massive geologic violence that, "in a single day and night," carried the entire island and many of its inhabitants to the bottom of the sea.[6]

Alexandria's Great Library contained a wealth of material describing Atlantis. Virtually all of it was lost when the magnificent complex was torched by Christian fanatics at the close of the Roman Empire. Plato's report was subsequently condemned as heresy by churchmen on two counts: Atlantis did not appear in the bible, so accusing Jehovah, by inference, of such an insight was blasphemy. Nor did Atlantis fit into the curious chronology of theologians, who dated God's creation of the Earth to little more than seven thousand years ago. During the collapse of the Classical World in the mid-fifth century, Atlantis, along with most civilized life, was forgotten.

A thousand years later, as the European Renaissance began to shrug off the Dark Ages, Plato's story was resurrected by Spanish explorers struck by obvious comparisons between the New World they were conquering and the *Antipodes,* or Opposite Continent he mentioned. Francisco Lopez de Gomera, Madrid's royal cartographer; Athanasius Kircher, seventeenth-century Germany's Master of a Hundred Arts; and the English polymath Sir Francis Bacon were among the intellectual luminaries that revived serious interest in the sunken city. But they were mostly unable to add anything new to Plato.

Over the next several centuries Atlantis began slipping back into the realm of fable, and could more often be found as a recurring theme in Western literature, most famously in Jules Verne's *Twenty Thousand Leagues under the Sea*. Donnelly's singular achievement was to apply the scientific method to Plato's dialogues, thereby elevating them from questionable philosophic narrative into credible history. He bolstered his modern approach with the latest findings in geology, comparative mythology, archaeology, anthropology, botany, and linguistics, and presented his well-established argument in a clear, rational, persuasive, highly readable exposition.

His conclusions took him far beyond Plato to show that Atlantis had been the very fountainhead of modern-style civilization, the place where humanity first arose from barbarism to organized society, and the original source from which derived the earliest high cultures on both sides of the Atlantic Ocean. It was a startling, entirely novel deduction, but the logical marshaling of abundant, up-to-date source material seemed appealingly irrefutable. The immense popularity he experienced as the founder of Atlantology surpassed and long outlived his reputation as a populist crank, because even old political rivals, such as those at the *St. Paul Dispatch,* could not help but publicly admire his effort as the author of one of the notable books of the century.

His *Atlantis* was the theme of both the New Orleans Mardi Gras and the Baltimore Oriole Festival in 1883. Three years later, he was good-naturedly declared the Duke of Atlantis in St. Paul's Winter Carnival. As his late-twentieth-century biographer wrote, "Thousands of people who normally did not read or hear of current books were exposed to Donnelly's work, and many of them bought it."[7] But why did this volume, as interesting as it was, generate such widespread enthusiasm among ordinary persons, as well as the intelligentsia of America, Europe, and Asia?

An explanation may have arisen from the times themselves. Late-nineteenth-century Americans felt that with the recent conclusion of the disastrous Civil War and the rise of industrial high finance in its aftermath, the nation had entered into a serious departure from the idealistic, even innocent or naive path that began in the antebellum period, when most of their fellow countrymen were farmers. The United States, they knew, was born with the glorious expedition of Christopher Columbus, got a foothold through the selfless rigors of the Pilgrims, grew into history's greatest political achievement, and expanded across a vast continent of illimitable wealth and beauty.

This grand epic of liberty was accomplished through individual heroism, self-reliance, rugged idealism, and a feeling of community. This seemed a particularly American story that was being steadily debased into mere shoptalk for ambitious politicians interested in personal power and wealth, not in building a free republic. Atlantis too, had been a great, happy country—rich, powerful, expansive, a beacon of enlightenment for the rest of the world. But a war interrupted the

Figure 31.1. Ignatius Donnelly

peaceful course of her culture. Her people turned away from the ethi-cal standards and idealism of their forebears in the unending pursuit of self-indulgence. They carelessly threw off their noble legacy to become a debased rabble interested only in self-gratification.

For this betrayal of their former greatness the gods passed judgment on Atlantis, sending her to a catastrophe so horrific that memory of it was seared forever into the collective subconscious of humanity and dimly recollected in worldwide traditions of a Great Flood. Perhaps, many intuited, heaven was preparing a similar fate for an America that was learning how to compromise its old principles with new greed.

The ominous parallel between predeluge Atlantis and post-Civil War America did not go unnoticed, and that awareness—admittedly, at different levels—accounted for its underlying general fascination. The appearance of Donnelly's book could not have been more timely.

Atlantis was and is a history lesson successive generations need to appreciate; therein, as Plato inferred, lies its highest significance. It is not enough to know that Atlantis was the origin of modern civilization, and that its people were highly gifted in the arts and sciences, while Egypt and Greece were still cultural backwaters. "We cannot escape history."[8] The portentous words of Abraham Lincoln still ran in the thoughts of Americans who saw in Donnelly's lost island an unsettling reflection of their own time. He was, however, the perfect—indeed, the only—man who could have brought Atlantis back to life. The job was too big for any university-trained scientist, especially a Victorian-age scholar, really a specialist indoctrinated in the restrictive discipline of that epoch.

Donnelly possessed a pair of virtues that better qualified him for the task. He had by all accounts a truly encyclopedic mind that ranged with natural authority over an enormous variety of subjects. An insatiable, rapid reader since youth, his persistent curiosity and passionate interest in the past made him a renaissance man on a nineteenth-century scale. It was not for nothing that he was known as the Sage of Nininger, the town he helped found in the 1850s. Just as importantly, Donnelly had an uncompromising reverence for the truth.

Yet he often bewildered his political contemporaries because he changed his party affiliations with as much facility as other men changed their coats. His alliances, quickly assumed and just as abruptly cast off in turn—from Republican to Democrat to all sorts of independent affiliations—ranked him among hypocrites and crass opportunists in some eyes. To them, he seemed "a veritable conundrum with the key thrown away," "a cryptogram and its key lost." Even long after his death "his inconsistencies and consistencies baffle understanding."[9]

But his mercurial political allegiances were only expedients.

However inflexible he may have been in his ideals, he was entirely flexible in the means employed to effect their realization. As the modern historian of Nininger rightly puts it, "it was the political parties that were inconsistent, and Donnelly merely aligned himself with the party that most favorably promoted his point of view. He was a man concerned with the wisdom and the principles of government, rather than politics for the purpose of personal or party gains."[10]

It was, however, just this freedom of intellect that made it possible for him to collect the vast material evidence for Atlantis and present it in a fashion that could be clearly understood. And in this he revealed himself not as an intellectual snob seeking to impress learned colleagues with his powerful brain, but as a true scholar striving to communicate something worth knowing to as wide an audience as possible. As a recent commentator wrote insightfully of Donnelly, "unquestionably, there was something in his message and his personality, insofar as it shaped that message, which a significant body of his contemporaries found appealing."[11]

And Donnelly, more than anyone, recognized modern America's parallel with old Atlantis. He knew from personal experience what it was like to battle as a state senator and congressman against a soulless money power on behalf of farmers and miners. It was a fight he was to lose, but he learned a broader lesson from defeat and transformed personal failure into the disquieting, historical irony implicit in his antediluvian world. Even before its first edition had gone to press, Donnelly was already hot at work on a sequel. Recurring throughout his voluminous collection of mythic traditions from every continent was an explicit theme describing a cataclysmic celestial occurrence he interpreted as a comet collision with the Earth sometime in deep antiquity.

He felt the event tended to reveal something about the nature of the destruction of Atlantis, but in 1882 there was not sufficient supportive data available for him to establish a firm connection. Based on the geological findings of his day he concluded that the last ice age was caused by a comet strike. Although incorrect, he was less wrong than his scientific contemporaries, who believed glacial epochs resulted in shifts in the Earth's axis or reversals of its magnetic field. Only as recently as the 1950s have geophysicists generally concurred that ice ages are caused by Earth's periodically changing, angular relationship to our sun.

While the chief argument in Donnelly's *Ragnarok* (named after the Norse legend of a cosmic disaster, the Breaking of the Gods) has been faulted by scientific discoveries made nearly one hundred years later, the book's secondary theme is not only persistently valid, but visionary.[12] Donnelly was the first writer to assert that Earth has been visited many times throughout its history by extraterrestrial catastrophes. It was this point, more than his hypothesis about Ice Age causation that was lampooned and almost universally rejected in his own day and far into the next century. Only a few fringe theorists (Bellamy, Hoerbiger, and Velikovsky), disdained by establishment skeptics as crackpots, followed up on Donnelly's position, which he deduced largely through his examination of the consistency of mythic traditions in the Old and New Worlds.

It was not until the 1930s that Arizona's Meteor Crater was officially recognized by astronomers as the result of a major, meteoric impact. Forty years later, the sudden extinction of the dinosaurs was linked to an asteroid collision with Earth, a finding that has gained credence as new and supporting evidence has come to light. In the 1980s, some astronomers concluded that our moon was formed after a Mars-like planetoid smashed into the young Earth, gouging out great quantities of debris and hurling them into space, where they were caught in Earth's gravitational field, and over the course of eons coalesced into our one and only natural satellite.

With the advent of aerial photography literally hundreds of impact craters, some as large as forty miles across, have been identified around the globe. Donnelly's suspicion that an extraterrestrial event was somehow responsible for the destruction of Atlantis was given important assistance by one of Germany's pioneer space scientists, Otto Muck, a colleague of Wernher von Braun, employed as a research expert at the famous rocket testing center, Peenemunde, in the Baltic Sea. Inventor of the snorkel, a technological advance in the development of modern submarine warfare, Muck demonstrated that two deep-sea depressions off the South Carolina coast were major impact craters formed by a disintegrating asteroid that struck the ocean bottom and set off a chain reaction of seismic violence along the Mid-Atlantic Ridge, a geologically unstable gash in the sea floor on which Plato's doomed island once stood.

Muck's high scientific credentials together with the factual argument brought to bear in his book, *The Secret of Atlantis,* have not been debunked since its publication in 1965.[13] Donnelly began work on a book to be titled "God and the Sun," an examination of Atlantean religious beliefs, only three weeks after completing his book about a comet-instigated ice age. But the vituperative rejection of *Ragnarok,* so far ahead of its time in other respects, discouraged him and he returned to politics, leaving the manuscript incomplete.

Today opponents of arguments on behalf of Atlantis enjoy ripping his work from the comfortable vantage point of the late twentieth century, faulting his geology and ridiculing his interpretations of the evidence.

But even that unsympathetic critic, E. F. Bleiler, writes, "Surprisingly enough, Donnelly was pretty much abreast of the American archaeology of his day. In Middle and South America, too, Donnelly was reasonably up to date. Much the same holds true for Donnelly's Old World archaeology. As far as anthropology proper goes, here, too, Donnelly knew and utilized the important language books."[14]

It is, after all, his interpretation of comparative myth that has most successfully withstood the passage of time. Some of his geology has not fared well, but that should hardly be surprising in view of the huge strides made in the Earth sciences over the past ten or so decades. Donnelly employed state-of-the-art geology, and it is as unfair as it is ignorant to belittle the level of knowledge achieved by our predecessors. It is a remarkable tribute to Ignatius Donnelly that so much of his work has not only been verified by subsequent research, but at least some of his insights have proved absolutely prescient.

Nor is it meant here to suggest that his geology is entirely worthless. Some of his deductions in this field are no less ahead of their time than his explorations of Atlantean mythic traditions within New World cosmologies. While Atlantis was not a continent with land bridges connecting South America, his analysis of the Mid-Atlantic Ridge anticipated by eighty years the deep-water discoveries made by sonar. "Along a great line, a mighty fracture in the surface of the globe, stretching north and south through the Atlantic, we find a continuous series of active and extinct volcanoes."[15]

Sea-floor lava flows were not documented in photographs until the 1970s, yet Donnelly wrote in 1881 that "the great fires which destroyed Atlantis are still smoldering in the depths of the ocean."[16] Establishment academics did not hate Donnelly because some of his research is dated or his conclusions wrong. If that were the case they would have ample cause to despise Kepler, Newton, Darwin, and every research genius in history. Donnelly is officially condemned because he did not belong to the professional club of collegiate academics and holders of degrees.

Worse, he succeeded in popularizing science and history without the benefit of university training, but entirely through the power of his original and imaginative intellect. Previous to its release Donnelly worried in his diary that *The Antediluvian World* would be a failure, "because I am a provincial in location and a nobody in the scientific world; for mankind always looks to Jerusalem and thinks it impossible that any good thing can come out of Nazareth. It is difficult for a new man to get anyone to believe in him."[17]

But in the first chapter of his own book, he showed greater self-assurance: "The fact that the story of Atlantis was for thousands of years regarded as a fable proves nothing. There is an unbelief, which grows out of ignorance, as well as a skepticism, which is born of intelligence. The people nearest the past are not always those who are best informed concerning the past."[18]

This statement early on in his book wonderfully sets the even-handed tone for the argument that follows. A better appreciation of Donnelly is possible when the deplorable conditions of nineteenth-century American academics is understood. Science and history were stultifying in an elitism that was putting distance between the country's intelligentsia and its common people. In one stroke *The Antediluvian World* bridged that widening abyss and awakened the imagination of millions to consideration of life's higher, nobler questions.

The popular awakening generated by his book must have been particularly gratifying for a man who always believed his greatest achievement was creation of the National Bureau of Education, passed by the House in 1866, the birth of public education in the United States. Since its first publication in 1882 generations of readers have experienced *The Antediluvian World* as a mind-expanding adventure.

Lewis Spence, the great Scottish mythologist who followed Donnelly as the leading Atlantologist in the first half of the twentieth century, admitted that "any departure from his general method would be as vain as it would be unintelligent. The blueprints were there, and their impressive outlines must be followed." Spence affirmed that this method, "in its correctness, and integrity, remains unchanged."[19]

More than five thousand books and leading articles about Atlantis in more than twenty different languages around the globe over the years since 1882 are directly descended from *The Antediluvian World,* which is still among the best of its kind. What strikes the reader of this book, besides the awe and enthusiasm obviously felt by the writer, is Donnelly's rescue of the Atlantis question from the lifeless discussion of a dead past. He carried it into the contemporary spotlight and beyond, into future prospects, a visionary quality that permeates the whole work; one reason for its perennial relevance, and evident in the opening chapter: "Further investigations and discoveries will, I trust, confirm the correctness of the conclusions at which I have arrived."[20]

In both *The Antediluvian World* and *Ragnarok,* Atlantean research, newly born, had gone just about as far as it could within the technological limitations of the nineteenth century. Scientific archaeology was itself not much older. Although he continued to lecture widely about Atlantis, Donnelly was drawn back into the political arena with all its duplicity and disappointment. As he stated later, "one thing is certain—my books have lifted me out of the dirty cesspool of politics, nasty enough at all times, but absolutely foul to the man who does not win."[21]

Donnelly was not mired in contemplation of prehistory, for all his years of intense study. His mind operated freely over time with wonderful facility because he disregarded rigid conventional divisions of past, present, and future. History, modern life, and what was to come were all woven of the same cloth, to his way of thinking. Donnelly's political activities were far ahead of his own time, which accounts for their lack of success. Many of his reformist views were amazingly in line with some of today's hottest issues. He was the earliest American statesman to work for federal protection of the environment.

On July 15, 1868, he advocated, for the first time in Congressional history, the planting of forests on public lands by the government. He advocated universal public education for blacks, as well as whites, and was an outspoken champion of women's rights. In a typically Donnelly-style comparison, he declared, "Woman, it is urged, is physically weaker than man. That proves nothing. The right to vote is not a question of physical strength. If it were, the pugilist would have more votes than the philosopher."[22]

Ignatius Donnelly died of heart failure in St. Paul, as the hour struck midnight on January 1, 1901. The remarkable propriety of that moment implies some otherworldly significance precisely poised between two centuries. For a man who bestrode time with such deftness and facility, the instant of his passing could not have been more appropriate, nor better synchronized to characterize a life of historical consciousness and futuristic vision—a perfectly timed dramatic exit for a dramatic actor.

Like many idealists unable to realize their highest hopes, Donnelly considered himself a failure, an assessment seconded by his contemporaneous and future detractors. Indeed, his attempts to found a successful utopian community and lifelong struggles for national reform came to nothing. More than one hundred years after his death, his critics have vanished into oblivion, but *Atlantis, the Antediluvian World,* is still in print, enlightening and encouraging the search he inspired.

Altered States and the Afterlife

32
Snake Handlers
of the Gods

The performance begins as priests file out of the *kiva*—an underground chamber—circumambulating it four times to signify the cardinal directions. At the end of each circuit the men stamp with their feet on the wooden cover of the *sipapti,* the symbolic entrance to the Otherworld. The priests now work themselves up into a religious frenzy through chanting and the sound of rattles as they approach a brush shelter where the snakes are kept. They then pick up the snakes, place them in their mouths, and dance with them. The Hopi Indians of Utah still perform this ancient snake-handling ritual, the *Chu'tiva* dance.

In preparation, they gather wild bull snakes, whip snakes, and rattlers. The specimens are often very large, aggressive, and lethal. No effort is made to sedate or pacify them. Incredible as it may seem, the fat serpents drape themselves gently by head and tail from the priests' jaws for the duration of the performance, which entails dancing around the plaza four times. Participants in the Chu'tiva are virtually never bitten, and reports of fatalities are infrequent. At its conclusion, the snakes are released north, south, east, and west to bring rain for a parched earth.

The Hopi explain that the serpents do not bite them because the dancers, through altered states of consciousness achieved through long

Figure 32.1. Hopi snake dance.
Image from DeGolyer Library, Southern Methodist University.

ritual preparation and the trance-inducing qualities of the ceremony, raise their psychic energies to such high degrees of blessedness that the creatures resonate on the same spiritual level. At such moments both men and snakes become brothers; the animals recognize the bond and grow docile. The remarkable thing about the Hopi snake-handling ritual is that it is not at all unique.

Similar rites pervade all cultures and all time periods, from the Bacchanalian cults of ancient Greece and the brazen serpent of Moses to the religious ceremonies of modern Pentecostals in Florida. An article by Paolo Raspolli in the June 1998 issue of *FATE* described a feast day conducted by the residents of Cocullo, a small village located in a remote region in the midst of the mountainous interior of southern Italy. There, during the first Thursday of every May, townspeople round up hundreds of live snakes, entwine them about their arms, and festoon the statue of a local saint with garlands of writhing serpents.

Although the participants are devout Roman Catholics, their Cocullo festival is unlike anything else known in the Church. In the December 1996 *FATE,* Kathie Farnell told of other Christians, Pentecostals in the backwoods Appalachian Mountain congregations of North America, who also handle snakes as the central feature of their religious services. At first any apparent similarities between these otherwise radically disparate denominations seems coincidental. But on closer examination they do have something very fundamental in common. The theme linking these groups, despite the great geographic and cultural differences separating them, is the altered state of consciousness experienced by their followers, whether in Italy or in Appalachia.

But how can wholly unrelated sets of celebrants, even unaware of each other's existence, choose to manipulate serpents as a means to achieve spiritual rapture? Are they, in fact, the only snake handlers who aim at such catharsis? The Cocullo festival is the Catholic gloss of an ancient ceremony going back some 2,700 years. At that time the south of Italy was occupied by Greeks, who imported their snake cult from the Peloponnesus in the seventh century B.C.E. Raspolli recounts local tradition to the effect that the new settlers, plagued with venomous serpents, appealed to Apollo for help. He told them that if they captured as many snakes as possible and placed them in dedication on his statue every spring, they would no longer be troubled by the creatures.

The villagers obeyed these divine instructions to good effect, continuing their springtime festivities unmolested when Cocullo was Romanized by Caesar five hundred years later. In fact, their serpent ceremony was deemed so important that it later escaped the otherwise intolerant hostility of the popes toward all pagan rituals. They merely replaced the demonized Apollo with a tenth-century monk who had nothing to do with snakes, and substituted the original observance with a solemn High Mass on behalf of Saint Domenico. The Cocullo festival has been celebrated ever since in this Christianized disguise.

A seventh-century B.C.E. Greek seeing it now would find everything essentially unchanged, save for the statue of an unfamiliar deity. The origins and real function of the serpent festivals are far more profound than the mundane necessities of protection against snake bite.

The expressions of devout ecstasy gracing the faces of religious snake handlers betray a subtler, more powerful cause behind the worship. The modern Catholics of Cocullo evidence the same emotional transcendence as their ancient precursors, who brought the spiritual mysteries of Greece to Italy.

Incredibly, today's Festival of Saint Domenico preserves numerous important details identically used in prehistoric Europe as part of the ecstatic experience associated with ritual snake handling. Foremost among these is the serpentine bread baked for the occasion. So too, during celebrations for Apollo overlooking the Gulf of Corinth in southern Greece, snake-configured cakes were placed before his Delphic oracle. They were in honor of his defeat of Python, a monstrous serpent dwelling in a cleft of Mount Parnassus, a mythic tradition that easily lent itself to the god's protection against snakes in Italy.

The cakes were placed on the *cista magista,* or "sacred receptacle," a basket from which followers of Apollo desiring to personally connect with the god withdrew snakes, danced with them, and entered into spiritual frenzies. His ovoid cista magista was somehow identified with the similarly egg-shaped omphalos, or Navel Stone, signifying the sacred center of all creation. This most holy object of the ancient world reappears as a conical, bread-bedecked votive basket, the centerpiece of Saint Domenico's modern festival. The ecstatic quality of ancient Greek snake handlers was described by a hostile contemporary, Arnobius. He wrote of the *Feasts of Raw Flesh,* "in which with feigned frenzy and loss of a sane mind you twine snakes about you." This was supposedly done "to show yourselves full of the divinity and majesty of the god."[1]

The distaste Arnobius expressed for such rituals, which were rare (or, at any rate, underground to some degree) certainly prevailed throughout Greek civilization. Bacchus, the god of sacred inebriation, was originally worshiped in Asia Minor in ecstatic rites. His followers claimed that only in highly altered states of consciousness could mortals achieve complete union with divinity. The Bacchanalia were festivals of an ecstatic mystery cult that spread to Italy, where it was outlawed by the Senate in 138 B.C.E. because of the lascivious practices of its initially all-female devotees.

Even today the women worshippers of Dan in the West African land of Dahomey carry live snakes to honor this male-female deity in trance-state dances. Whether or not these frenzied serpent cults that spread to Greece and Italy from Asia Minor originated even farther east, in India, is not certain, although similar snake-handling practices were observed there from Indus Valley times (about 2800 B.C.E.). Although the invading Aryans of the eighth century B.C.E. purged these cults from the subcontinent, something of their influence still survives in the mythic tales of the Buddha.

One of the best known of these relates that he was once sunk in deep meditation on behalf of all suffering animals, when a great, ferocious cobra glided up behind him. Approaching closer, it recognized a kindred, compassionate spirit. The serpent rose up over the Buddha, who was totally oblivious to the circumstances of his physical surroundings, and spread out seven hoods to shade him from the heat of the sun.

This story is revealing of the core experience found in all snake cults, ancient and modern; namely, that even an instinctually driven serpent acknowledges a spiritually elevated human being. The cobra's seven hoods parallel the Buddha's seven major chakras shielded by the snake. Even today, various snake cults and rituals can still be found in India.

One example involves a woman who approaches the cave of an enormous cobra. She presents it with ceremonial cakes (another element in the Cocullo festival), then cautiously approaches the animal, smiling and praying in dancelike steps. Her job is to kiss the serpent three times on the back of its head. Rearing up in a strike mode, its hood flared in anger, the deadly snake sways back and forth, following the woman's movements. These priestesses are rarely bitten because, they insist, their souls have been elevated to resonate on the same spiritual frequency as that of the cobra, which realizes that it has become one with the human. Whenever they are bitten, the women believe the unfortunate person had not attained a proper level of sacredness, but she will none-theless attain nirvana in dying through the attempt.

The pre-Aryan snake handlers spread their influence beyond India, as the Gundestrup Cauldron proves. Discovered in a Danish bog, this richly crafted ritual vessel with embossed silver decoration depicts a man holding a serpent in his left hand. Although the cauldron is of Keltic manufacture and is dated as late as the first century B.C.E., archaeologists have identified the human figure as the so-called Master of Animals known throughout southern India. He is their master not because he dominates them but through his soul's sympathy and ecstatic harmony with all living things, which resonates with his high spiritual vibrations. As such, he is less a god than a shaman.

A far older portrayal of a religious snake handler appears on an Old Kingdom stone slate from the Third Dynasty city of Nekhen, about 4,600 years ago, in Upper Egypt. It depicts a young boy holding a ser-pent in each hand. This is *Heru-p-khart,* or Heru the Child, better remembered by his Greek name, Horus. His mystery cult, which flour-ished well into Rome's late imperial period, is a mystery still, but its fol-lowers were known to engage in frenetic ceremonies aimed at achieving spiritual catharsis as a means of personally uniting with *That Which Is Above.* A later, better known figure than Heru-p-khart is the famous statuette in faience and gold of a bare-breasted woman in an abun-dant, flounced skirt wielding two coiling snakes at arm's length. It was found over one hundred years ago in temple repositories at the Palace of Knossos, an ancient Minoan city on the island of Crete (see page 237).

The Minoans were a highly civilized people, the cultural precur-sors of the Greeks, who dominated the Eastern Mediterranean world for more than a thousand years. And while one of their scripts (known as Linear B) has been deciphered, surviving texts offer no descriptions of the figurine, which has been found duplicated at other Minoan sites, suggesting the importance of the image. The other, older written lan-guage, Linear A, may offer revealing information, but it still awaits translation.

Usually referred to as a goddess, the statuette more likely represents a Minoan priestess personifying the Earth Mother in a Bacchanalian-like cult. Her dramatic stance and wild eyes mirroring a mind in trance are typical of religious snake handlers from ancient initiates of the Macedonian mysteries to twentieth-century Pentecostals in Florida.

Actually, she may be depicted at the start or last moment of a frenzied dance, in which the priestess achieved an altered state of consciousness. The flouncing skirt may have been deliberately designed to dramatically rise and fall with her movements, like those worn by Turkey's whirling dervishes, who dance to attain the same kind of spiritual ecstasy.

Similar Cretan representations unquestionably portray serpent-handling women dancing themselves into rapture. Their identification with Earth Mother is found in the snake itself, a worldwide metaphor for telluric power. The animal was observed rising out of its hole in the bowels of our planet—a mysterious creature, often dangerous and powerful—then returning to its subterranean origins. More than symbolic, the snake was perceived as the actual sacred energy that adepts of the frenzied mysteries could tap in to from the ultimate source of power, Mother Earth.

This identification of the Minoan statuette is preserved in a much later Roman terra cotta bas-relief (second century B.C.E.) portraying Ceres, the Earth Goddess, similarly holding a serpent in each hand. Indeed, ecstatic snake handlers played equally prominent roles in several ancient American civilizations, such as the pre-Incan city of Tiahuanaco, high in the Bolivian Andes Mountains. Its best-known feature is the Gateway of the Sun, a colossal stone arch oriented to the western horizon.

At its top center appears the incised image of an anthropomorphic figure brandishing a serpent in each hand, while energy rays configured like snakes radiate from his head and attentive birds flank him on either side. Even here, in this remote highland of ancient South America, appear the same serpent-manipulator themes of ecstatic power

Figure 32.2. Minoan snake goddess from the palace of Knossos.
Heraklion Archaeological Museum, Crete.
Photograph by C. Messier.

and intimate harmony with other creatures. In North America too, ritual snake handling appeared during pre-Columbian times among the Mound Builders of northeastern Oklahoma. There they raised a large and important ceremonial center, today an archaeological park known as Spiro Mounds.

The site is outstanding for its many hundreds of mollusk shells engraved with mostly religious images, some of which depict dancers holding serpents in their outstretched hands, very similar to the Minoan statuette. Long, thin, copper plates dangle from one such Spiro Mound figure, who wears a flouncing girdle at his waist and a bobbing headdress—a costume to dramatically heighten his ecstatic performance. The same spiritual centering is evident among native snake handlers of Central America. Their ritual takes place on the vernal equinox, that annual moment where Nature is poised between the death of winter and the birth of spring.

The ceremony ends with a chief priest sprinkling water toward the four cardinal directions on the precinct where man and snake danced. This solemnized conclusion of the ritual and the day chosen for its performance emphasize the deep sense of centering the dancers aim to achieve. The Hopi claim that performing the Chu'tiva is a soul-elevating experience that terrifically empowers them, broadening and deepening their healing and psychic abilities as priests. They reach the Sacred Center where life and death meet. Remarkably, these are virtually the same words used by certain Christian fundamentalists in the rural U.S. South to describe their own spiritual interaction with serpents. They know nothing of the Hopi, the Minoans, or any of the rest of the religious snake handlers in the past and in other parts of the world.

Their cult began quite recently, after the beginning of the twentieth century, when a preacher was inspired with a new (to him) vision of the New Testament Book of Mark (16:17–18), which reads, "And these signs shall follow them that believe; In my name shall they cast out devils; they shall speak with new tongues; They shall take up serpents; and if they drink any deadly thing, it shall not hurt them; they shall lay hands on the sick, and they shall recover." These are some of the identical abilities Hopi priests claim to master after their dances with snakes.

True to the New Testament Book of Mark, Reverend Barefoot of Tallahassee, Florida, and his followers in the 1950s, while manipulating the snakes, claimed to have downed glasses of poison without lethal

*Figure 32.3. Snake handling at Pentecostal Church of God,
Lejunior, Harlan County, Kentucky.
Photograph by Russell Lee.*

consequences, performed the laying on of hands to successfully cure the sick, and to have spoken in tongues. (Once, a man who knew nothing of the language, began reciting perfect Cherokee during a service.)

Like their Hopi counterparts, the Christian snake handlers choose oversized, wild rattlers, refuse to sedate them in any way, and place the creatures in a serpent box. After an indefinite period of vociferous preaching, repetitive chanting, nonstop singing, excited gesticulating, and similar religious hysteria, celebrants waltz over to the snake pen, withdraw a serpent, and dance with it in their hands or drape it around their head and shoulders. Bites do occur and fatalities are not unknown, but both are surprisingly infrequent. After services all the snakes are released into the wild.

Kathie Farnell, in her penetrating *FATE* article on Christian snake handling, came closest to revealing what goes on in the mind and soul of these celebrants. She quotes one of them as saying, "I turned to face the congregation and lifted the rattlesnake up toward the light. It was moving like it wanted to get even higher, to climb out of that church and into the air. . . . I felt no fear. The snake seemed to be an extension of myself. And suddenly there seemed to be nothing in the room but me and the snake. Everything else had disappeared . . . all were gone, faded to white. And I could not hear the earsplitting music. The air was silent and still and filled with that strong, even light. And I realized that I, too, was fading into the white. I was losing myself by degrees, like the Incredible Shrinking Man. The snake would be the last to go, and all I could see was the way its scales shimmered one last time in the light, and the way its head moved from side to side, searching for a way out. I knew then why the handlers took up serpents."[2]

One wonders if the Cretan priestess portrayed by the Minoan statuette 3,700 years ago felt the same. The experience was in the nature of an epiphany, a sacred moment of sudden intuitive understanding; a flash of transforming insight; the manifestation of and transcending identification with divinity. Of course, these Pentecostals are not serpent worshippers. Nor are the Hopi. It is likewise doubtful that ophiolatry had much or even anything to do with the snake handlers of different civilizations in the past. None of them seem to have been interested in serpent symbolism, but focused entirely on the epiphany that snake handling brought about.

The remarkable similarity of that experience across time and the prodigious barriers of geography and time do not point to any lost or supposed cross-cultural connections in pre-Columbian centuries. The Pentecostals needed no help from ancient Greece. Rather, twentieth-century revivals of snake handling among ecstatic Christians and the far older Hopi Chu'tiva may be the surfacing of some spiritual instinct in collective human consciousness. Perhaps they represent a need to personally connect with the Creator by coming to loving terms with one of his most dangerous creatures.

33

The Miraculous
Maya Shamans

At dawn on December 21, 2012, the spiral arm of the Milky Way appeared to be lying upon the rim of the Earth, creating a great dark rift above it like a black silk fan spread open. In its very center, the sun rose. This was a unique astronomical event that has probably never happened before and may never occur again. What modern-day astrophysicists had to calculate on high-speed computers was predicted by Maya shamans millennia ago.

According to *The Maya Shamans,* the native peoples of Yucatán are self-appointed "timekeepers" for our planet.[1] They developed their own complex calendars using astronomy, trigonometry, and a binary system. Their secular calendar, the *Haab,* is based on a 365-day cycle, with eighteen months of twenty days followed by a five-day celebration cycle. It is within an incredible 0.00000001 degree of accuracy to the atomic clock, according to NASA space-age measurements.

Another Maya calendar, the sacred *T'zolk'in,* has a repeating rhythm of 13 x 20 (= 260) "sun faces." This expresses what present day helioastronomers have confirmed—that the sun rotates on a north-south axis as well, over a 260-day cycle. Why were ancient Maya so concerned with keeping accurate time so far into the future?

Author Alloa Patricia Mercier successfully answers this and other

*Figure 33.1. Although they flourished four centuries after the Maya,
the Aztecs not only continued to use the old calendar, but concretized
it in a monumental stone disc now at the National Museum of Anthropology
and History, Mexico City. Photography by Anagoria.*

related questions. An Englishwoman who traveled extensively throughout Central America to study Maya history, culture, and spiritual traditions, she visited their ancient cities, including Copán, Honduras;
Tikal, Guatemala; and Chichén Itzá, Mexico. She underwent intensive
training and initiations by Maya shamans themselves and learned about
the significance of the *T'zolk'in* calendar.

She was shown how it is intended to synchronize us with the
galactic pulse of time. It highlights fifty-two days (in the pattern of a
human's double-helix DNA) when the integration of two cycles merge
to create an accelerated energy pattern that opens portals or doorways

that intensify our reception of light emanations from Hunab K'u, the galactic God-mind. As out-of-body time travelers these ancient peoples observed and understood the rotation of heavenly bodies and our position in the Sagittarian arm of the Milky Way galaxy long before telescopes were invented.

They were sensitive to and recorded the varying energy patterns created by stellar and planetary movement and made practical use of them. Translations of Maya hieroglyphs tell the story of Hunab K'u, who is said to reside in a pyramid house in the constellation Orion. It is from there that all life emanates in the form of light and vibrations. The outward energy flow is so powerful near the source that it must be transduced, or stepped down, through lenses, including the sun, the moon, and the Earth, before we can receive it. It enters us through the top of our heads at the crown *chakra* (literally "wheel" in Sanskrit, for a human spiritual energy center) and travels down our spines as the fiery kundalini, symbolized by the serpent motif repeated throughout Maya hieroglyphics, architecture, and sacred ceremonies. In yoga, kundalini is a latent female energy coiled at the base of the spine.

When viewed through a prism the shortest wavelength, or fastest frequency of the rainbow spectrum, is the violet ray. Above that are ultraviolet rays, x-rays, and infrared rays, but the unaided eye cannot see them. Interestingly enough, modern astrophysicists have recently discovered a cosmologically rare source of ultraviolet rays emanating from the same area of Orion that the Maya claim to be the location of Hunab K'u, suggesting perhaps we are on the brink of a new age and that through increasing sensitivity to higher galactic frequencies we are all evolving toward our destiny as beings of light to spiritually enter the sacred home of Hunab K'u forever.

34
Voices of the Dead

Although familiar with Electronic Voice Phenomena (EVP), I never felt the need to test this simple ghost-hunting technique myself until a popular radio program transmitted several examples of words captured on audiotape, allegedly spoken by disembodied entities. The recordings seemed genuine enough, and the live experimenters explained their procedure in a credible manner. At the time of their broadcast interview I was working on a research assignment that, so far, seemed devoid of any potential for human interest.

My commission was to write the history of an old building in the historic Mississippi River town of Wabasha, Minnesota, some two hours' drive south of St. Paul. The late-nineteenth-century, two-story structure served over the decades as a harness shop, hardware store, and finally, a real estate office, where nothing apparently out of the norm ever took place. According to my investigation among the Wabasha Public Library's collection of moldy newspaper clippings and police files, no murderers, robbers, drunkards, demagogues, wife beaters, scalawags, roustabouts, or really interesting individuals of any stripe ever walked through the doors of that venerable edifice at the northeast corner of Main and Pembroke Streets.

There seemed to be nothing that could spice up my work-in-progress until it occurred to me, after hearing the ghost hunters explain themselves on the radio, that an EVP experiment inside the

125-year-old structure might find something spectral. It seemed a long shot, and I was not entirely convinced that recording statements from the dead was even possible. But I decided to give it a try and met with the current owner of the building to tell him what I had in mind. He proved surprisingly amenable to my proposal—roaming, tape recorder in hand, through his establishment after dark—and arranged for my wife, Laura, and I to go ghost hunting the following night. We arrived at the appointed hour, somewhat embarrassed by the unconventional nature of our self-styled mission in this mainstream Midwestern town, and descended a flight of wooden steps into the basement. We saw little and felt less as our handheld Panasonic did its job for about fifteen minutes, then we climbed a staircase through a hallway to the second-floor apartments. They were unlit and under reconstruction, with old furniture scattered about amid tools and stacked lumber.

The only illumination streamed through the front and side windows from street lamps on the sidewalks below. Although the disorderly apartment seemed vaguely spooky, nothing unusual occurred. Doubting that our first EVP attempt at an establishment not known for being haunted had captured anything more than (pardon the expression) dead air, Laura and I returned home to audition our hour-long recorded quest. The tape faithfully played back the sounds of our footfalls moving through the basement, then climbing creaking stairs to the second-story apartment, where we lingered in mostly silent expectation, but nothing more.

Then, about a third into the tape, just after I guessed aloud, "This must have been where the old rooms were," a woman's voice says above a whisper but clearly and distinctly, "Paul." About fifteen seconds later she repeats the name, only this time with stronger emphasis and greater clarity: "*Paul!*"

We subsequently learned that the second floor had been occupied by tenants for about twenty years after World War Two. Interestingly, a local car dealer who operates his business at the end of the same block occupied by the building we investigated, grew up during the early 1960s with his mother and grandmother in the apartment where our recorder picked up the woman's voice. His first name is Paul. Whether or not he is the man addressed by that unseen person, no one can say. But at least Laura and I are now quite sure that the EVP is real. Encouraged by this initial success, we pursued our personal research.

During daylight hours one midafternoon, Laura used a digital recorder around the back of our house, at the patio, to capture the distinct voice of an older woman who said simply, "I just love you."

Back in Wabasha I found a narrow space between two late-nineteenth-century buildings, on the exterior walls of which had been carved several dozen weathered names, by all appearances far more than one hundred years ago, before the later structure was made, compromising access to the other by its closeness. A distinct name deeply etched about five feet up into the old brick wall clearly read, "Arnold." I spoke aloud, asking him several questions about the afterlife. Returning home I reviewed the cassette tape, listening for any disembodied response to my questions, which went unanswered until I asked, "Are you happy?" A young voice, unheard at the moment of my experiment, spoke clearly through the recorder: "I'm happy!" with an inflection that suggested the self-evidence of his condition.

Sometime later unsettling incidents began to occur at home. Late at night musical instruments were played by invisible fingers, unfamiliar scents floated through the air, basement lights rapidly flashed on and off of their own accord, and peculiar sounds were heard, even a growl in our library. We swore off ever again experimenting with spirit communication, and the disquieting phenomena eventually ceased. Perhaps we had opened a door that should have remained closed.

35
Death, the Great Mystery of Life

The title of Herbie Brennan's book is not as facetious as its title may seem to some readers. In *Death: The Great Mystery of Life* the Irish author provides an insight as obvious as it is enlightening for those of us caught up in the daily distractions that prevent a true evaluation of life and the men and women with whom we share it. He cites the Toltecs, an eminently civilized people who followed the Maya and preceded the Aztecs in their rule of pre-Columbian Mexico. They believed that Death is the Great Teacher.[1]

What could they have possibly meant by this statement? They recognized the plain fact that everyone must eventually die. Persons in the Western world do not like to think about dying and prefer to imagine that our inescapable demise can be almost indefinitely put off through medical treatment, healthy diet, and exercise, but according to the Toltecs, this is the wrong way to look at death. Instead, they thought of death as not only inevitable, but imminent. We survive from heartbeat to heartbeat, from breath to breath.

You could be dead from a variety of causes before you finish reading this chapter. Rather than be depressed by such a consideration, there is a reversal of our fear of death, developing into a deep appreciation of existence. If our doctor informs us we have only one week of life left, we typically respond with a series of natural reactions. These usually include, in order of progression, shock, denial, sadness, anger, resignation. But the Toltecs knew an alternative. They did not wait for someone to tell them they were going to die. They already knew that. In assuming they could expire at any moment, they estimated their lives accordingly.

When faced with impending death we may choose to go through the standard routine. Or we might "embrace the horror" as an opportunity to concentrate on the things that mean the most to us, those personal values from which we have been distracted by the daily demands of trying to survive and prosper in modern society. If we knew we were about to pass away in a few days, our relationships with all those persons we love and with people in general would intensify and deepen. Time would suddenly become the most precious commodity, and we would use every moment of it to relish in the appreciation of life, especially nature's usually overlooked details.

Flowers and sunsets would take on a dramatically expanded significance. This is what the Toltecs meant when they claimed Death as the Great Teacher. The same recognition permeates Tibetan Buddhism, whose leader, the fourteenth Dalai Lama, has often been quoted to the effect that his whole life is spent in preparation for death. Far from any apparent morbidity, his attitude of compassion for all fellow beings is conditioned by coming death, which will someday sweep him from the world: "Gather ye rosebuds while ye may! Old Time is still a-flying, and this same flower that smiles today tomorrow will be dying."[2]

36

Reincarnation and the Dalai Lama

In spring 1992 five hundred people assembled at an auditorium in Madison, Wisconsin, to hear the fourteenth Dalai Lama speak. Smiling and bowing, he walked on stage in his traditional monk's robes, his hands clasped in prayer. He was greeted not by applause but laughter. Joy emanated from the man in a ripple effect until everyone present was merrily laughing along with him for no apparent reason. The crowd was simply delighted to see him. His fame and prestige as a Nobel Prize laureate had nothing to do with the audience reaction. Rather, the people were intuitively responding to "the presence of a purified mind," according to Yeyshe.

Yeyshe is the former John Samuelson, today a Tibetan-style Buddhist monk and teacher residing in Ridgeland, Wisconsin. Born and raised a Lutheran in the Midwest, he was a typical American save for outstanding skills as a carpenter and his developing atheism. The tragic accidental death of a close friend in 1985 brought him face to face with his own inevitable mortality for the first time. He sought answers to life's fundamental questions in conventional theology, but it left him

---

The information discussed in this chapter is based on an interview of John Samuelson by Frank Joseph, March 2000.

unsatisfied. His introduction to Tibetan Buddhism was through his former wife, who studied comparative religion at nearby Eau Claire.

She shared her enthusiasm with John. His interest grew, and he studied long and hard, finally concluding after several years of study and introspection that he should devote his life to the same spirituality embraced by the followers of the Dalai Lama. To exemplify the depth of his total commitment, John adopted the Tibetan name of Yeyshe. Although it is a complex religious ethic in the broad and ornate variety of its practices and ceremonies, Tibetan Buddhism can be summarized as a doctrine of karma (from the Sanskrit *kri,* "to act"), which holds that deeds performed in this life will produce appropriate consequences in forthcoming incarnations.

Tibetan Buddhists confront this moral law of the universe with rituals, visualizations, oracles, omens, astrology, esoteric psychology, and recognition of psychic phenomena. Colorful prayer flags snapping in the wind identify Yeyshe's quiet home in the country as a special place. Inside, golden images of Tibetan gods adorn mantels or reside in their own niches. Upstairs in a meditation room guests sit lotus-style on cushions before an altar of bells, smoking incense, and the sinuous figures of deities.

"The Dalai Lama, who describes himself as a 'simple monk,' has attained high levels of mental purity through a lifetime of self-discipline and spiritual dedication," Yeyshe explains. "Persons in the presence of such a purified mind intuitively respond with spontaneous joy, because it is a state to which people naturally aspire. They obviously recognize something fundamentally attractive in him with which their souls, not their conscious minds, resonate."

The general popularity of the most famous living Buddhist is undeniable, whatever the explanation. A poll of university seniors in Virginia asked students to name the five greatest human beings in the world today. They chose the Dalai Lama first, followed by Dr. Christian Barnard, Buzz Aldrin, Luciano Pavarotti, and Anthony Hopkins. The effect of such "a purified mind" on a crowd of people is no less endur-

Figure 36.1. The child Lhamo Thondup shortly after his "recognition" as the reincarnated fourteenth Dalai Lama

ing than the impression made by Padmasambhava, who introduced Buddhism to Tibet from India in the eighth century C.E.

While traveling through neighboring Nepal, Padmasambhava paused to meditate inside a cave near Kathmandu. After he left, local people entered the cave to honor the boulder upon which he sat. They were amazed to discover its surface had been impressed, like soft clay, with the holy man's palm prints. Skeptics dismiss the account as a religious fable, but are unable to account for the handprints still shown to visitors at the cave site. Since Padmasambhava's time other extraordinary missionaries have left similar impressions in stone as memorials to their spiritual power. Interestingly, a similar story was known among the Aztecs of pre-Columbian Mexico.

In their epic *The Flight of Quetzalcoatl,* it is asserted that Mesoamerica's founding father, "Feathered Serpent," was the greatest sorcerer to walk the land in ancient times.[1] During a moment of intense sorrow he sat down upon a large rock. When he arose the impressions of his hands were formed on the stone, as upon soft clay. The location of this miracle, like the Kathmandu cave, was revered as a sacred site, and known throughout the Aztec Empire as Tlamaqlaco.

While such stories are generally dismissed as superstitions by Westerners they are nevertheless supported by modern physics, which holds that there is no fundamental distinction between energy and matter—the latter is simply a denser organization of the former. The correct type of energy can interface with denser energy (or matter), explaining how Padmasambhava and Feathered Serpent were able to leave their palm prints in stone. The spiritual power of these men was of such a high order that in the midst of their concentration all energies began to merge, becoming pliable. Last year Yeyshe visited the Nepalese cave and saw the stone imprinted with its 1,200-year-old handprints.

"Padmasambhava attained a level of realization far beyond anything known to even most enlightened practitioners. But such miracles are not central to Buddhism, and can be distracting. Many Westerners are overly impressed about the palm prints in stone. They are anxious to become Buddhists so that they can perform the same wonders, and impress everyone with their supernatural abilities. These people completely miss the core message of Buddhism, which is the opposite of egotism. Many teachers will not even discuss miracles, because outsiders usually draw the wrong conclusions from them."

The circumstances of the fourteenth Dalai Lama's rise to prominence as the most famous Tibetan Buddhist of modern times concerns a phenomenon considered no less miraculous in the West—reincarnation. Although it has been a doctrinal part of Buddhism for many centuries, it has only begun to generate popular interest outside of Asia during the past fifty years. Reincarnation is "the appearance of the same entity over and over again in different lifetimes," observes researcher John Lash, "due to the capacity of the human soul to re-embody itself."[2] And karma is the force that drives that spiritual cycle.

The fourteenth Dalai Lama's reincarnation is remarkable because it features other psychic phenomena, such as scrying (the appearance of visions in a clear medium, such as water or crystal), prophetic dreaming, synchronicity, and omens. The story begins in 1933, when his predecessor—the thirteenth Dalai Lama—died. The body was embalmed at the Potala, the royal palace in Lhasa, the Tibetan capital.

There it was placed in state facing south. Sometime later, monks praying in front of the corpse were surprised to notice that the head had turned of its own accord to the northeast. This postmortem alteration was accepted as an omen for the general direction in which the next Dalai Lama would be found, but no search could be undertaken until the appearance of another, confirming portent, which occurred a year and a half later, when the regent of Tibet dreamed of finding the reincarnated Lama.

He led an expedition on a ten-day journey to a sacred lake, where the monks fasted and prayed for several days. They also scryed into the placid waters, where they saw the image of a three-storied temple with a golden roof. Nearby, to the east, they envisioned a simple peasant farmhouse with unusual blue eaves. The monks traveled in search of such a place. After several months they did indeed find the temple of their vision. To conceal their identity the monks dressed as beggars and went door to door in the village located east of the temple.

At a farmhouse with blue eaves a woman carrying her young son in her arms was visited by one of the disguised monks, who had been the thirteenth Dalai Lama's closest friend. When the little boy saw him, he reached out with his hand and grabbed the monk by the collar, asking, "Do you remember me?" Then, as he reached for the monk's prayer beads, the boy exclaimed, "This is mine! Why do you have it?"[3] Several weeks later the regent and his followers returned to the blue-eaved farmhouse and placed a rosary, walking stick, and drum that belonged to the thirteenth Dalai Lama on a low table. These were placed alongside better-made copies from which the child was asked to choose those items that were his. Unhesitatingly he picked out the originals, and the monks declared him the reincarnated Dalai Lama.

Today he remembers his past lives while dreaming but places little emphasis on reincarnation. "What is past, is past," he laughs.[4] Even so, all the Dalai Lamas from around 1400 C.E. to the present are regarded as physical rebirths of the compassionate Buddha-to-be, the divine bodhisattva Avalokiteshvara. Yeyshe explains that while reincarnation is interesting, valid, and important to appreciate, our conduct in this life is more vital. "What we do now will determine our future condition. The more compassionate our actions today, the more positively we develop as sentient beings, now and in times to come."

While his fame in the West continues to soar, the Dalai Lama is the most hated figure in Red China. The communist government there has demonized him as the worst Enemy of the People since Chiang Kai-shek. The Chinese overran Tibet—a free and independent country—in 1950. Conditions became so intolerable that the Dalai Lama was forced to flee at the risk of his life into India, where he resides today, the center of a refugee colony in Dharamsala. Yeyshe points out that the Dalai Lama is the most unique of all his predecessors because he alone has been forced by historical circumstances into world prominence. Earlier leaders were reclusive and remote, secluded behind the high walls of the Potala palace.

One of our time's great public figures, the Dalai Lama is also the most visible representative of Tibetan Buddhism. And among Buddhism's essential tenets is the concept of nonattachment. The term means letting go of everything that binds one to the physical world: All material is transient, only spirit is eternal. The Dalai Lama has been forced to walk his talk, because he is confronted with the greatest lesson in nonattachment—the loss of his country, the holy land of Tibet.

The Dalai Lama consistently refuses all calls for armed resistance, while his people continue to agonize and die. He presents himself as "a simple monk" who would prefer to be left alone to pursue the arcane practices of his religion.[5] While certainly true, such a portrayal masks the subtler energies of the ultimate weapon—spiritual power. Yeyshe recently returned from China and Tibet, where he witnessed firsthand the heavy-handed oppression inflicted on the inhabitants.

"Tibet might pass away, and its deliberate obliteration could be the ultimate exercise in nonattachment we might know. We believe there is a universal mind that pervades all sentient beings, and oversees the world with an infinite compassion. Our focus is not political but on that cosmic consciousness from which all enlightenment and peace derive."

Numinous Nature

37
The Secret Life of Water

To the astonishment of university-trained skeptics, experiments in Japan have revealed the mystical properties of water. Beginning in the last decade of the twentieth century, scientific investigations conducted under controlled conditions in a laboratory setting compared favorably with informal testing carried out by everyday people at home to demonstrate water's hitherto unsuspected sensitivity to human thought. The first investigator to suspect this subtle relationship was Masaru Emoto, born in Yokohama, Japan, in 1943. Two years before he was certified as a Doctor of Alternative Medicine by the Open International University in 1992, he established his own research offices specifically to investigate the potential healing qualities of water.

His IHM General Institute is a small, professionally staffed facility featuring state-of-the-art instruments, including an American-made magnetic resonance analyzer that accurately measures complementary magnetic fields between two or more objects and aids in establishing a harmonic balance of energy as a basis for healing. As part of his study of the therapeutic potential of magnetic resonance, Dr. Emoto was curious to learn if, like snowflakes, no two frozen drops of water were identical. Until he launched his inquiry, scientific studies of water crystals had never been undertaken.

But his research did not begin with instant success. Two months of intensive trial-and-error experiments revealed nothing of any significance until an expert in microscopic photography was engaged by the Institute. Kazuya Ishibashi helped establish a regimen by which images of crystal formation could be obtained and documented. Representative of what later came to typify the procedure, water was obtained from the base of Japan's most famous landmark, Mount Fuji. There, precipitation takes twenty years to travel through the great slopes of this active volcano, emerging as ground water in a spectacular display.

More than 100,000 tons of the world's purest water flows daily through Shiraito-no-Taki Falls. Samples are taken back to the Institute laboratory in sterilized containers, which are gently tapped to activate the water. Specimens 1 millimeter in size are withdrawn with a syringe and placed into fifty separate Petri dishes. Placed on a tray, they are stored in a deep freezer at -25 degrees centigrade. After three hours the tips of the samples are examined under a high-power, illuminated microscope in a laboratory with a constant setting of -5 degrees centigrade.

As the temperature of the frozen tip rises under the glare of the microscope lamp, a crystal forms, expands to its maximum extent, and melts. The formation process is irregular, and it requires a skilled operator/observer with an excellent sense of timing to properly bring into focus and photograph the process through all its stages of development with either a video or still camera. The task is made all the more difficult by the narrow field of view, confined as it is to a protrusion at the very tip. Water crystals grow three-dimensionally from the center of the core outward, making clear focusing a real challenge.

Patience is likewise required. Of the fifty samples examined, only a few crystallize. While these results may be interesting, if not unexpected, further research made some startling discoveries with potentially significant implications. As Dr. Emoto and his colleagues compared their burgeoning collection of frozen specimens, they learned that tap water mostly failed to produce crystals. In the very few instances where crystals did appear in tap water, they were invariably distorted, incomplete, or asymmetrical. Samples of tap water from Tokyo, Berlin, Rome, Paris, London, New York, San Francisco, and many other cities around the world all failed to crystallize, save in a very few corrupted examples.

Only natural fresh springs and distilled water produce crystals, although the stark simplicity of the latter contrasts greatly with the ornate designs of the former. The lack of crystallization in tap water, according to Dr. Emoto, "show[s] that the life forces in that area have been compromised in terms of energy. Anything in tune with Mother Nature manifests as a beautiful, hexagonal structure. Anything that is not, doesn't. I think that this is the message that water is trying to tell us by using itself as a medium. It's important for the water around us to produce nothing but beautiful, hexagonal crystals."[1]

Among the most outstanding crystal formations documented by Dr. Emoto is an example from Lourdes, a sacred site for millions of visitors from around the world, many of them suffering from incurable maladies. The Lourdes crystal is unlike the others, in that it is not hexagonal but unevenly circular, resembling a diamond necklace. What significance this configuration may or may not possess is unknown. In any case, its singular appearance at one of our planet's foremost places of pilgrimage suggests a profound connection. Revealingly, the hexagon has had its place in esoteric lore for thousands of years.

Hexagrams make up the sixty-four patterns in a widely respected Chinese system of divination known as the I Ching, which dates back more than three thousand years. According to author John Lash, the hexagram "has been correlated to the genetic code, which also consists of sixty-four unit systems of *codons,* or chemical units, which transcribed and direct the entire array of life processes."[2] The renowned Spanish metaphysician J. E. Cirlot was prescient in his definition of the hexagon: "it is a symbol of the human soul as a 'conjunction' of consciousness and the unconscious, signified by the intermingling of the triangle (denoting fire) and the inverted triangle (water)."[3]

In discovering the frozen hexagonal crystals, has Dr. Emoto stumbled upon a fundamentally spiritual "conjunction" between water and human DNA? There does seem to be at least some psychic relationship between human consciousness and water, as his experiments suggested.

Expanding his research, Dr. Emoto placed containers of distilled water between the loudspeakers of a CD player and exposed them to recorded performances. "Music is vibration," he observed. "If we expose water to music, its crystal structure should change."[4]

Distilled water, as mentioned, freezes into simple, unadorned hexagons. But in the presence of classical music the crystals blossomed into flowery shapes. More incredibly, their patterns seemed to suggest the very character of the individual pieces being played. For example, when favored with the strains of Mozart's "Eine Kleine Nachtmusik," the resulting crystals are appropriately delicate and exquisite. (Some of the Mozartian crystals even resemble the lacy attire fashionable during the period of composition in the late eighteenth century.)

Entirely different are the blunt, massive crystals formed by Beethoven's powerful Ninth Symphony, while patterns formed in close proximity to a traditional Japanese folk song look like the cherry blossoms depicted in "Sakura." Such intriguing correspondences have led some observers to conclude that the water is following the music, responding to the artistic intentions of its composer. What kind of crystals might be formed in response to acid rock or "gangsta" rap?

As Dr. Emoto states, "I think that music was created to bring our vibration back to its intrinsic state. For example, after World War Two, Japan went through a harsh period, experiencing suffering difficult for its people to bear. That's what spawned so many positive songs during that time. Each era, each community has a history of its own. It's human nature to create music that readjusts the vibrations distorted by history. That's why I'm certain that music was a form of healing before it became an art."[5]

Even more amazing were the results of an experiment documented at Dr. Emoto's Institute on October 5, 2002. Four sets of parents and their children held hands in a circle around two glass containers (A and B) filled with equal volumes of tap water from Tokyo. In unison, they spoke directly to A only: *Thank you, water! We love you.* Immediately following this declaration, they closed their eyes and attempted to send these words to the same container telepathically. The other vessel (B) was pointedly ignored. Both were subjected to the by now standard procedure followed in earlier experiments. Glass B, which received no attention from the group, was devoid of any crystal.

To the amazement of everyone in the group, the frozen specimen from glass A sprouted a multifaceted crystal, the first ever seen in tap water. Afterward, several participants admitted they began the test with more skepticism than expectation, and were therefore all the more surprised when the crystal formed before their very eyes. Apparently, their lack of belief in telepathy—to say nothing of its dubious influence on water—did not hinder the outcome of their experiment. Since that first telepathically induced specimen appeared sixteen years ago in 2002, the process that brought it about has been replicated numerous times in similar circumstances by investigators around the globe with the same results.

The implications of this discovery are profound, with ramifications for world health beyond imagining. If our tap water has been despoiled, could mass-telepathic engineering restore its original purity? The human body is composed of three-quarters water. The possibilities for change—both beneficial and harmful—that concentrated thought might have on our physical make-up seem limitless. The 2002 experiment suggests that the potential for noninvasive healing of a kind far more effective than today's most sophisticated surgical procedures could be the birthright of every man, woman, and child—a natural legacy forgotten or unrecognized until now. Inspired by Dr. Emoto's research, a Japanese mother and her son tried an experiment of their own.

They placed equal amounts of cooked rice in two separate glass containers. On one, they taped the Japanese word for "thanks," *ahrigato*. On the other they taped *baka*, or "fool." Every morning, mother and son spoke out loud to the jars, calling out "Thank you!" to one, and "Fool!" to the other. Photographs taken over the next thirty days showed a remarkable contrast. At month's end the glass container marked and regularly greeted with thanks was still a fluffy golden yellow and entirely edible. It produced a rich, pleasant aroma. The other jar, labeled and accosted as "fool," had rotted into a revolting mass of black matter that stank of decay.

News of the mother-son experiment quickly spread, and it was soon being repeated in households all over Japan. Hoping to duplicate its success, Dr. Emoto collected vials of distilled water, labeling them with various words and statements, such as "Love"; "I will kill you!"; "Harmony"; "You make me sick!"; "Please"; and so forth. They were written by hand in Japanese, English, French, Chinese, Greek, and Latin, together with several other languages, living and dead. The results were almost predictable—at once satisfying and disturbing. Containers bearing words of positive input grew crystal formations of intricate beauty, while the negatively labeled vials were either unaffected or contained

Figure 37.1. Shiraito Falls.
Photograph by InvictusOU812.

hideously distorted, grotesque images, sometimes of anthropomorphic forms twisted into nightmarish shapes.

Although Dr. Emoto passed away in 2014, his posthumous website says, "Dr. Emoto's International Hado Instructors will continue to spread the messages from water around the world with seminars, water ceremonies and the International Hado Instructor School in support of the Peace Project. The mission is to teach all people, especially children, the true power of our words, thoughts, emotions and prayer, through water, for peace within and around the world."[6] His numerous experiments have established a subtle organic relationship between water and man. As mentioned earlier, three-fourths of our body is water. Perhaps more than coincidentally, that is generally the same surface proportion of the planet on which we live. Dr. Emoto's work appears to have revealed something of a very fundamental link between our physical being and the world of Mother Earth.

38
The Soul of Matter

Can rocks be conscious? Do animals or plants have souls? Where and when did consciousness first appear? How are minds and bodies related? How does consciousness fit into the physical world? These are some of the big questions author Christian de Quincy attempts to answer in *Radical Nature.*[1] Professor of philosophy at John F. Kennedy University and managing editor of *IONS Review,* publication of the Institute of Noetic Sciences, he and his colleagues are engaged in the study of consciousness and human potential through scientific research.

Some of their recent conclusions and lines of investigation show that the dominant paradigm of scientific materialism, which views matter as "dead stuff" that mysteriously weaves mind and consciousness out of body and brain, is a comparatively short detour—an aberration—in the history of Western thought. In fact, many world views restore a sense of the sacred to modern life, where spirit and consciousness find a natural home in the cosmos.

Many of these views oppose the notion that matter and nature are dead, mindless, unfeeling, and disconnected from ourselves, conjuring an image that is hopeful and fulfilling, just as the scientific materialist view was empty and depressing. Based on philosophical traditions reaching back millennia, acknowledging the soul of matter calls for a radically different understanding of the living essence of matter.

The cosmos is a magnificent creation brimming with spirit and

Figure 38.1. The spirit of Nature interfacing with human creativity is dramatized in this anonymous Chicago mural.
Photograph by Frank Joseph.

consciousness. None of this is new, of course. During the mid-nineteenth century, the famous Native American Indian leader, Chief Seattle, tried in vain to explain the perennial philosophy to his Christian inquisitors by saying, "Even the rocks which seem to be dumb, as they swelter in the sun along the silent shore, thrill with memories of stirring events connected with the lives of my people."[2]

Millennia earlier, Hindu mystics taught that a compassionate intelligence interpenetrated every detail of the universe, from the spiral motion of a falling leaf to the similar movement of a galaxy. Individual human beings are not exempt from this interwoven process, but are no less intimately connected to it.

The "mind-body problem" recognizes the fundamental relationship among all aspects of nature. In refusing to recognize that basic relationship, modern man has cut himself off from his higher potential as a more highly developed being. The current concept of matter as inert and lifeless was really the exception in the long history of intellectual thought. Though it eventually came to be equated with a sort of self-evident truth in the contemporary mind, the universe is far more complex, vital, and alive than conventional scientists envisage.

39

The Fire from Heaven

At 7:17 on the morning of June 30, 1908, something exploded over Siberia with the force of a forty-megaton hydrogen bomb. The blast, two thousand times the power of the first atom bomb dropped on Hiroshima, Japan, thirty-seven years later, obliterated two thousand square kilometers of tundra and pine forests near the Tunguska River in Central Siberia. Had the incident taken place over New York, the city would have been utterly annihilated.

For nearly a month after the Siberian explosion, an additional ten thousand square kilometers were incinerated by resultant firestorms. Fortunately, due to the remote location of the occurrence no one was killed, but some nine hundred eyewitnesses reported seeing a fiery object coursing through the sky just prior to the blast. An interesting discussion of this event was written by Rupert Furneaux in *The Tungus Event*.[1] The oral accounts are part of UFO lore that includes the so-called Tunguska Event as a misguided attempt by extraterrestrials that tried to land on Earth in 1908. Most conventional astronomers believe the explosion was the result of a meteor collision with Siberia.

Strangely, it neither created a crater nor left any meteoric fragments. By way of comparison, Arizona's mile-wide Meteor Crater was caused by an object no larger than a semitrailer truck. An asteroid the size of a twenty-one-story building necessary to cause the Tunguska blast would have produced a much larger impact crater, called an astrobleme. Other

*Figure 39.1. Some of the several million trees blown over
by blast effects of the Tunguska Event*

theorists believe an antimatter particle was to blame, but such a particle would have detonated the moment it struck the upper atmosphere and destroyed the whole planet. Moreover, antimatter particles are invisible, and eyewitnesses to the event all reported a fiery object in the sky.

Their testimony also invalidates speculation that a mini black hole or a shot from Nikola Tesla's supersecret energy cannon was responsible. Like the antimatter particle, a mini black hole could not be seen, and its destruction would not have been confined to Siberia. A Tesla artillery piece strong enough to shoot through the center of the Earth would have blown away the ionosphere, resulting in global extinction. An even more extreme theory holds that the Siberian explosion was a blast from the future.

While anything is possible, there is no evidence for such speculation. Some astrophysicists believe the Tunguska incident resulted from a mountain of ice falling from a passing comet. They point out that such an object would not leave a crater because when atmospheric friction heated it to sufficient temperatures, the chunk would detonate in midair. Evidence for this possibility exists not only by the lack of an astrobleme but among the hundreds of thousands of trees that were knocked over in a radial pattern away from a central blast point. An icy cometary fragment would leave no rocky meteoric debris, either.

More persuasively, perhaps, the Tunguska Event took place just as the so-called Taurid meteor stream was passing our planet. These meteors comprise the debris, much of it ice, from the remains of a virtually spent comet that is named after its discoverer, Johann Franz Encke (1791–1865). Long before the onset of the twentieth century Comet Encke had become so diffuse that it was hardly noticeable to the naked eye, although its spawn of debris in the Taurid meteor stream still leaves bright streaks in the night skies of early June. Even so, a cometary explanation is not ironclad. An ice fragment of the size required to generate the early-twentieth-century explosion would have blown up much higher in the atmosphere than it did, a few kilometers above the surface of the Earth.

But the UFO theory is not without its holes, either. It seems difficult to believe that a civilization sophisticated enough to build an otherwise successfully operating spacecraft would have made it vulnerable, in event of a crash, to destruction on the scale of a forty-megaton hydrogen bomb explosion. Proponents of a UFO postulate that the alien space vehicle was atom powered and exploded in a nuclear blast after overheating in the Earth's atmosphere.

Astrophysicists tell us that such a propulsion system may push a vehicle almost to light speed, but that velocity is still far too slow to make interplanetary travel feasible, unless its occupants lived hundreds or even thousands of times longer than ourselves, and were willing to endure millennia-long voyages. Upholders of the UFO theory argue that the object seen by eyewitnesses must have made a controlled maneuver, because they said it deviated from its descent. But meteors have been observed and sometimes even photographed changing direction and veering off their lineal falls.

Such maneuvers are comparable to a hurled stone skipping over the surface of a pond. So too, meteors striking the thicker layers of our atmosphere occasionally change direction and skip back into space. An alteration of course for the Tunguska object does not necessarily imply it was controlled by some intelligence. Nor are the fused metallic pieces embedded in the trees and ground at the blast site necessarily fragments from a spaceship. Comets often contain abundant metals—so much so that NASA scientists envision mining operations on one in the future.

For several nights immediately before the Tunguska Event, meteorologists observed a marked increase in the intensity and frequency of the Northern Lights, auroras, and other strangely luminous celestial phenomena. The near miss of a giant comet like Encke—no matter how dissipated—would produce such effects through the sudden addition of meteoric material (mostly dust) into the upper atmosphere. Scientists of the time also noticed massive geomagnetic storms around the world just after the blast, which likewise impacted the Earth's magnetic field.

While these could be the effects of a large nuclear detonation, a sufficiently powerful meteoric or cometary collision would produce the same geomagnetic anomalies. Evidence for radiation at the site might be considered proof of an atomic-powered vehicle that exploded over Siberia. Indeed, tree rings in the vicinity show accelerated growth for 1908, radiation traces are still found at Tunguska, and some persons who witnessed the blast developed physical disabilities similar to radiation sickness. But every explosion of such an enormous magnitude, regardless of type, generates some amount of radioactivity.

All this has been argued back and forth for more than one hundred years. Recent disclosure of the Soviet authorities' reaction to the Siberian blast has only further muddled the controversy. After their first expedition to Tunguska to gather evidence, Russian scientists were the first to wonder if the explosion had been caused by a spacecraft from some extraterrestrial civilization. Their speculations tended toward certainty after the Americans destroyed Hiroshima with an atomic bomb. Its midair burst devastated the city in patterns remarkably similar to those found at Tunguska.

Accordingly, Stalin dispatched another scientific team to the area, this time under the direct control of his secret police (the NKVD), to find parts of the imagined crashed spaceship. Hoping to accumulate the wrecked extraterrestrial technology, he wanted to create a secret weapon superior to anything in the West. His henchmen did find some small, twisted metal fragments but apparently not much more. These specimens were classified Top Secret, and eyewitnesses who told the NKVD men everything they knew about the explosion were warned that if they spoke to anyone about it, they would be arrested and exiled to a prison camp.

In 1959, six years after Stalin's death, Russian scientists imagined that the effects of his despotism no longer held sway and publicly released their findings, which indicated that the 1908 blast was caused by the crash of a ship from outer space. Immediately thereafter the official Communist newspaper (ironically known as *Pravda,* or "The Truth") declared to the world that their scientists admitted they mistook meteoric material for the debris of an alien spaceship. Actually, the scientists were threatened with imprisonment if they did not embrace the party line.

Unknown to the hapless scientists, Soviet military men still believed that they might be able to reconstruct enough technology from the alleged crash site to build the ultimate weapon for use against America. Only with the collapse of communism in Russia did the truth about official suppression of the Tunguska evidence come out. Here, resemblances to its U.S. counterpart begin to emerge. The American military was likewise suspected of covering up a suspected crash site near Roswell, New Mexico, in the late 1940s.

There was the similar suppression of metallic evidence and the intimidation of eyewitnesses, together with official denials immediately following reports of a downed spacecraft—this one with physical remains of the occupants. The Siberian event seems to have been either a cometary fragment or an intelligently piloted vehicle whose approach to our perhaps unfamiliar thick atmosphere with its potential for high-temperature friction went disastrously wrong.

Both theories have their strong points and inconsistencies. If a colossal cometary fragment was responsible, then we must realize that the Earth is passing through an interplanetary shooting gallery and is sometimes the recipient of a bull's eye, perhaps more often than we care to admit. The celestial catastrophe that exterminated the dinosaurs and pushed all life to the brink of extinction 65 million years ago is now generally accepted. Less acceptable may be far more recent extraterrestrial collisions that imperil all mankind.

Had the Tunguska explosion (regardless of its cause) taken place over Moscow in 1968, it might very well have triggered a nuclear-missile exchange between the USSR and the U.S. And if such a terrific blast could have occurred 110 years ago, there is nothing to prevent us from concluding it can happen again any time. If, on the other hand, the detonation was indeed the result of a crashed spaceship, then the implications will bring a different kind of trauma.

40

Journey through
the Unexplained

America's most popular late-night radio personality, Art Bell, and our country's preeminent paranormal expert, Brad Steiger, teamed up to pool their knowledge and experiences in *The Source,* which covers a wide range of "unexplained" phenomena from human origins and lost civilizations to crop circles and out-of-body experiences. Unlike other generalized presentations of this kind, however, Bell and Steiger conclude that all these arcane phenomena share a common denominator, a generating source. "Each one of these seemingly disparate mysteries of the unexplained may be a manifestation of a single Source," they write.[1]

One in two Americans believe in extraterrestrial aliens from other worlds. Half of Americans polled believe in guardian angels. Increasing numbers of people are reporting various paranormal sightings and communication with the dead. Such reports prompt Bell and Steiger to wonder if human beings and their untypical experiences are the products of some high intelligence's imagination that produces energy creating the Unexplained.

Blame it on God, you might say. Another alternative identification of the Source is our own subconscious mind. University of California neuroscientists in November 1997 termed the "God module" in the human brain the result of developed mutations caused by numerous generations of fear-response situations with which our *Homo erectus* ancestors were forced to cope. This module is alleged to "hot wire" the human psyche for religious feelings, even experiences, as a kind of evolutionary residue from our deep genetic past.

Whatever the energies responsible for our perception of extranormal reality, Bell and Steiger ask that we embrace all possibilities.

41

Eyewitness in the Bermuda Triangle

Many investigators have written about the Bermuda Triangle from afar, but fewer descriptions of that infamous area of ocean can match the real-life accounts of people who have actually resided within its uncertain borders. One such person is Andrew Raymond, a Chicago contract engineer, who made the Bermuda Triangle his home from 1979 to 1982. During that time, he was project manager for the Island of Science, where professionally trained researchers experimented with solar power, the nutritional potential of seaweed, and an accelerated wind laboratory for alternative energy development.

Under his direction were forty native Bahamians and a dozen Haitians, who commuted daily from other nearby islands, while he resided on the Island of Science with occasional flights to Great Harbor Cay about thirty miles away. It was on one of these commutes that the Bermuda Triangle phenomenon would most often take place. Most of his flights from the Island of Science were strictly routine, but during a few of them his magnetic compass would spin crazily as though powered by its own electric motor.

For a no-nonsense man like Andrew Raymond, such occurrences had to be the result of presently unrecognized but ultimately explainable natural forces. He was familiar with most of the paranormal theories and stories about the Bermuda Triangle and dismissed them all out of hand as just plain malarkey. As a serious construction engineer Raymond had no room left for wacky speculations. But one flight in particular was to open his mind and shake any rational explanations for unusual happenings in the Devil's Triangle.

July 5, 1980, a date he cannot ever forget, began normally enough. It was one of those picture-perfect postcardlike days in south coastal Florida, with the early morning sun shining out of an unobstructed sky on a mirror-smooth sea unruffled by anything more than a slight breeze. He was hitching a ride back to the Island of Science with an old friend, Howard Smith, an experienced bush pilot, who was returning a repaired clutch plate for a small boat with motor problems in Grand Harbor, just seventy miles away. Smith's single-engine Cessna 172 was loaded with some of the most advanced instrumentation available to civilian airmen.

Among them was a costly DME (a sophisticated device for measuring the relationship between time and distance while in flight), the latest in radio direction finders, electric and magnetic compasses, and a transponder for receiving a radio signal and automatically transmitting a different signal as a navigational aid. They arrived at Bimini's Grand Harbor without incident by noon, had a leisurely lunch, then took off into the same pristine weather conditions for Little Stirrup Cay, northernmost of the Bahamas, and hardly more than an hour away. If he had piloted this itinerary once, Smith had flown it a hundred times, with never a hint of trouble.

Not long into the second leg of their flight, however, they ran into a thick cloud cover and the sky grew suddenly dark. The array of instruments appeared to function flawlessly. Both Smith and Raymond were surprised by the abrupt, unpredicted change in weather, but were not alarmed, despite flying blind through the unbroken overcast. When their DME informed them that they had reached their destination, Smith dropped beneath the cloud cover to initiate his landing approach. But the scene that spread out before them belonged to another world, or some alternate reality. Little Stirrup Cay was nowhere to be seen. Nor was there a sign of land anywhere in that otherwise island-bedecked part of the sea.

How could the otherwise infallible DME have misdirected them so far off course? No less bewildering was the eerie appearance of the water a few thousand feet beneath them. "It looked just like boiling copper," Raymond recalled. "I have seen every kind of light effect the sun can bounce off the surface, but never anything remotely approaching this."[1] Moreover, the sun was hiding behind the thick overcast, while the angry waves roiled as though heated by some impossible, submarine furnace, and glistened in a golden-red fire that seemed to be generated from within the sea.

Smith got on the horn to Fort Lauderdale for navigational assistance, but the radio was dead. Flying too low now, he initiated an ascent into the darkening cloud cover, trusting to his instruments. Now, both men remarked the strange tingling of electricity in the cabin air. Moments later, the little Cessna suddenly plummeted five hundred feet before Smith could regain control. It had been dropped by a microburst, a powerful downdraft associated with storm clouds. But they were not flying in that kind of weather.

Reaching for higher altitudes, the aircraft fell again, while Smith wrestled the controls. Twice more the Cessna dove into the microbursts, until Smith descended once more beneath the clouds. The evil-looking, boiling copper sea had reverted to a normal appearance, the sky suddenly cleared, and before them was another private aircraft. Their radio was still out, so they followed the other plane for a few minutes as it led them to a final approach to Grand Harbor, their point of origin. Incredibly, they were back where they started, even though they had flown, according to all their redundant instruments and their own visual observations, in a straight line in the opposite direction. With the exception of their radio, all instruments had operated perfectly. Later, Smith calculated the time aloft to the distance covered, and deduced that it would have been impossible to go out over open water as far as they did and round trip it back to Grand Harbor.

Figure 41.1. A Cessna 172

Afterward, Raymond learned of firsthand accounts from friends in the U.S. Navy and Coast Guard of numerous, inexplicable disappearances made yet more mysterious by the fact that the area defined as the Bermuda Triangle is among the most thoroughly monitored quadrants on the globe. It is constantly eavesdropped by the Bahama Air Service and Rescue, together with military and civilian radar and radio operators. Theoretically no serious trouble should occur without somebody taking notice. Raymond himself survived two separate shipwrecks in the Bermuda Triangle and was rescued before he had a chance to get wet.

In the fall of 1981 he was involved in a baffling tragedy that still haunts him. It concerned two physically fit, lifelong friends in their early sixties, who had grown up together in the Bahamas and were more familiar with those waters than almost anyone. Their sailing expertise was well known, so when they filed their float plan to West Palm Beach, no one doubted they could make the routine cruise in under six hours. Even so, they were in regular ship-to-shore radio contact with their wives back at Grand Harbor Cay. They broadcast their position every thirty minutes on a high-powered global transmitter. The two old sea hands cast off at 9:00 a.m. under a windless, cloudless sky, across a glass-smooth sea.

As promised they radioed their precise location on the half hour, describing the ideal conditions through which they sailed. But when they failed to make their 1:00 p.m. transmission, their wives alerted the authorities. Within minutes, an armada of Coast Guard, B.A.S.R., and private boaters, including Andrew Raymond, plus a squadron of search aircraft, swept the placid waters in all directions, in a 200-mile radius of the fifty-eight-foot *Hattaris*'s last-known position. The intensive search went on after nightfall and all the next day. Efforts continued for another week before being called off. During all that time the sea remained innocently calm. But it bore not a single trace of the vanished yacht or its two accomplished mariners. No oil slick, not so much as a single seat cushion—absolutely nothing was left behind.

"I have seen all kinds of vessels, large and small, go down," Raymond said. "Without exception, they all leave huge amounts of debris, which survive on the surface for days later. You would not believe the masses of material that cover the sea left by a wreck. Even the smallest motorboat belches clouds of oil long after sinking. For a boat as large as the craft they sailed to go down and leave neither a big telltale oil slick nor a carpet of floating junk is impossible, especially considering the ocean's calm condition at the time the *Hattaris* went missing."[2]

Some days after the unsolved disappearance Raymond saw what might have been a clue to the deadly mystery of the Bermuda Triangle. While walking along the beach in water up to his knees, he came upon one of the Bahamas' famous blue holes. These are large marine caverns, or sinkholes, that are open to the surface and have developed in a bank or island composed of a carbonate limestone or coral reef bedrock. They vary in diameter from a few feet to one hundred yards and go down straight as a shaft.

For decades, Dean's Blue Hole, in a bay west of Clarence Town on

Figure 41.2. The location of the Bermuda Triangle

Long Island in the Bahamas, was the world's deepest known example of its kind. The 663-foot shaft was finally eclipsed in 2016 with the discovery of Longdong, or "Dragon Hole," located among the Paracel Islands near Discovery Reef, going down 987.2 feet into the bottom of the South China Sea.[3]

Exploring another blue hole during the early 1970s Jacques Cousteau photographed a perfectly preserved, late-nineteenth-century rowboat sitting on a shelf about eighty feet beneath the surface, as though carefully placed there by some mermaid who collected antique vessels. Raymond speculates some of these blue holes may go down to the very floor of the sea, where submarine earthquakes surge water pressures through them to generate violent oceanic and atmospheric effects. Appearing without warning for brief episodes, they resemble

Figure 41.3. Dean's Blue Hole, noticeable as the darker water in this image. Photograph by Ton Engwirda.

whirlpools like those created when plugs are pulled from bathtubs of water.

The force they exert on the surface of the sea is so powerful that anything within its immediate vicinity is sucked without a trace to the bottom, including aircraft, which are pulled into the vortex by downdrafts similar to the microbursts Andrew Raymond and Howard Smith experienced in 1980. The atmospheric disturbances caused by such a vortex could account for the electromagnetic anomalies encountered in the area of these unusual phenomena.

Whatever the source of these disappearances, Andrew Raymond will never forget his years in the Bermuda Triangle. He needs no one to convince him of its terrible mystery, because he knows it is real.

42

Communication with Elemental Beings

With the fall of Eastern European communism, the long-suppressed spiritual life of people living in the Balkans was reborn. An important spokesman of that rebirth is Slovenian author Marko Pogacnik. With his country's successful struggle for independence from Serb domina tion in the early 1990s, he became one of the continent's best-known geomancers—an expert in defining the Earth energies inherent in natu- ral landscapes.

Nature Spirits & Elemental Beings is a result of Pogacnik's effort to restore a fundamental harmony between the spiritual forces of the environment and human beings.[1] One technique used to do this is lithopuncture—from the Greek *lithos* (stone) and the Latin *pungere* (to pierce). To lithopuncture a place involves positioning stone slabs— with sculpted signs that Pogacnik calls cosmograms—on points of the Earth's geomagnetic organism, which are equivalent to acupuncture points of the human body.

Stone slabs are positioned in such a way that they provoke a reso- nance on the energy level, while the cosmogram operates on the level of consciousness. It was during a lithopuncture operation for the City Council of Derry, in Ireland's politically troubled Londonderry during September 1992, that Pogacnik experienced more than the balancing

Figure 42.1. The Beaghmore Stone Circles.
Photograph by Alun Salt.

of telluric or planetary energies to which he had become accustomed. Setting up his lithopuncture operation among the nearby Beaghmore Stone Circles, an intelligent, unseen force assumed control of his arm movements.

The Beaghmore, a megalithic site dating to the New Stone Age five thousand years ago, doubtless amplified the energies Pogacnik encountered. Mystified by the invisible power that temporarily dominated his body, he soon learned from his daughter, Ajra, that the lithopuncture had tapped into an elemental being confined to the Beaghmore area. A trusted channeler, Ajra defined the entity as a conscious energy form and an expression of the local landscape—something the ancient Greeks called a *genius loci,* or "spirit of the place." Surprised but intrigued, Pogacnik was determined to contact the resident entity himself through meditation.

He claims to have easily established contact, and worked with the Irish elemental to successfully complete his lithopuncture operation originally envisioned for Beaghmore. That experience convinced Pogacnik to consult each genius loci before undertaking his geomancy wherever he was called upon to heal a particular landscape or site. In the course of his meditations and communications with the underworld spirits he was introduced to various species and hierarchies of unseen beings he knew only from fairy tales.

Despite their vast differences of function and character they are all inflections of Earth energy, different from one another primarily because of the special demands of the local sites they inhabit. Methods by which we, too, may enter into the fairy kingdom have yet to be clearly defined, save in the power of imagination. There seems to be an indefinite boundary between the visible and invisible worlds.

No less than world-renowned scientist James Lovelock speaks confidently of the Gaia Principle, wherein the Earth is regarded as a living entity itself. If the Earth is a living entity, who is to say that Earth entities are not also present? When one sees the unicursal drawings made by Pogacnik after his encounters with the various kinds of Earth entities he witnessed during his lithopuncture and meditations, one may wonder if visions of this kind are not quite so unbelievable after all.

Powerful Parallels

Collecting thirty-one of the world's outstanding "power places" in this single volume not only discovers new insights into these proverbial "sacred sites" but more surprisingly discloses hitherto unseen patterns and unsuspected themes connecting one to another. Such revelations are all the more astonishing in light of the often immense time discrepancies and oceanic barriers separating so many curious locations.

These seemingly inexplicable, certainly unexpected commonalities appear less circumstantial than comprehensible within the context of immemorial human nature as it strives to touch the subtler spiritual dynamics underpinning and driving the world of external appearances. How else, for example, can we explain the similarly mystical phenomena associated with the Nile Delta's Great Pyramid—the supreme masterpiece of a lost race that flourished fifty centuries ago—and James Onan's downsized replica outside Chicago, Illinois, erected less than half a century ago?

This question was convincingly answered by Edward Leedskalnin, when he described how, as the architect of Coral Castle, he assembled Florida's strangest complex after discovering paranormal construction techniques employed by pharaoh's architects, who anciently accessed the same arcane energies that inspired both himself and Onan.

That monumental pyramids independently came into being throughout the premodern world and among disparate peoples unknown to each other is alone remarkable in the extreme. How was it possible such a singular, geometrically challenging design was not only repeated among cultures as wildly differing from one another as Asian, Mesoamerican, and Near Eastern civilizations but that their geographically separated, though often contemporaneous pyramids shared identical features and functions? Is it merely coincidental, as chapters 1 and 2 point out, that the prehistoric ground plan of the Ohio Valley's Mound City precisely matches the base dimensions of the Nile Valley's Great Pyramid, which itself shares the same construction date with the Mississippi Valley's pyramidal Monks Mound?

Then there are the Great Serpent Mounds of Scotland, Kansas, and yet again, Ohio, together with the anthropomorphic effigy earthworks of giants on identically oriented hillsides in southern Wisconsin and southern England. What are we to make of these intriguing comparisons?

Pre-Columbian contacts, as much as archetypal human response to spiritual and/or telluric energies, are no less discounted by mainstream scholars, who can, however, offer no plausible explanations. But just such unconventional possibilities suggest themselves in power places like the Classical World's foremost oracle at Delphi near the south coast of Greece, and its modern world counterpart at Medugorje in Croatia, where deification of the Eternal Feminine was similarly personified by a sibylline Queen of Heaven. At the much older sacred site she spoke through the Pythia, a psychically sensitive woman intuitive, whose late-fifteenth-century C.E. British compeer was chapter 27's Mother Shipton.

All these and many more compelling analogies begin, perhaps for the first time, to clearly inflect and reflect on each other in the foregoing pages. Our parallels expose themselves as related phenomena, either by way of self-evident, pre-Columbian cultural contacts—however much decried by blinkered archaeologists—or through the impetus of human nature.

As such, the extraordinary locations cited here, together with their no less extraordinary men and women—Power Places and the Master Builders of Antiquity—continue to live in the perennial gift of their eternal legacy. It connects us still with the world's numinous energies and those within ourselves, so long as we continue to recognize and access them. Therein lies the higher purpose of this book.

Notes

INTRODUCTION

1. Carl Llewellyn-Weschke, Editorial: "An Enduring Legacy," *FATE,* vol. 51, no. 8 (August 1998): 5.

CHAPTER 1.
OLD WORLD CONNECTIONS WITH
NEW WORLD SACRED CENTERS

1. Ernest Hemingway, *Ernest Hemingway on Writing,* ed. Larry W. Phillips (N.Y.: Touchstone, 1999), 133.
2. Herbert E. Bolton, *Coronado: Knight of Pueblos and Plains* (Albuquerque: University of New Mexico Press, 1990), 44.
3. William E. Unrau and H. Craig Miner, *The Kansa Indians: A History of the Wind People, 1673–1873* (Norman: University of Oklahoma Press, 1986).
4. R. Clark Mallam, *The Iowa Effigy Mound Manifestation: An Interpretive Model* (Iowa City: University of Iowa, 1976), 76.
5. Mallam, *The Iowa Effigy Mound Manifestation,* 79.
6. Patty Loew, *Indian Nations of Wisconsin* (Madison: Wisconsin Historical Society Press, 2001).

CHAPTER 3.
RIDDLES OF THE PACIFIC

1. David Hatcher Childress, *Ancient Micronesia & the Lost City of Nan Madol* (Kempton, Ill.: Adventures Unlimited Press, 1998), 193.

CHAPTER 4. THE GREAT PYRAMID
OF CHINA

1. Wilson V. Z. Faung, *Chin Shih Huang: The First Emperor of the Chin Dynasty* (Taiwan: China Printing, 1971), 39.
2. Arthur Waldron, *The Great Wall of China: From History to Myth* (Cambridge University Press, 1992), 62.
3. Laura Lee, "China's Lost Pyramid," *Atlantis Rising*, no. 11 (April/May 1997): 33.
4. Hartwig Hausdorf, *Die Weisse Pyramide: Ausserirdische Spuren in Ostasien* (Munich: Langen/Müller, 2002), 178.

CHAPTER 5. CONSTRUCTION WONDERS
OF THE ANCIENTS

1. William Corliss, *Ancient Infrastructure: Remarkable Roads, Mines, Walls, Mounds, Stone Circles* (Glen Arm, Md: Sourcebook Project, 2006).

CHAPTER 6. ANCIENT ACOUSTICS

1. Paul Devereux, *Stone Age Soundtracks: The Acoustic Archaeology of Ancient Sites* (London: Vega, 2002).

CHAPTER 7. IS A TEMPLAR TREASURE
AT THE BOTTOM OF THE MONEY PIT?

1. Michael Kaulback, "Knights Templar in the New World," in *Discovering the Mysteries of Ancient America* (Wayne, N.J.: New Page Books, 2006), 88.
2. Steven Sora, *The Lost Treasure of the Knights Templar* (Rochester, Vt.: Destiny Books, 1999), 142.
3. Sora, *The Lost Treasure of the Knights Templar*, 262.
4. Kaulback, "Knights Templar in the New World," 85.
5. Kaulback, "Knights Templar in the New World," 86.
6. Gerard Leduc, "Templars of Quebec," *Ancient American* 12, no. 6 (1996): 29.
7. Leduc, "Templars of Quebec," 29.
8. Leduc, "Templars of Quebec," 28.
9. Nelson Jecas, "Templar Cross on East Coast," *Ancient American* 10, no. 4 (1995).

CHAPTER 8.
THE NAVEL OF THE WORLD

1. Richard Hastings, *Encyclopedia of Religion and Ethics,* vol. 9, *Mundas–Phrygians* (London: T&T Clark International, 2000), 216.
2. Joseph Campbell, *Occidental Mythology* (N.Y.: Penguin Books, 1991), 112.

CHAPTER 9.
THE ATLANTIS BLUEPRINT

1. Colin Wilson and Rand Flem-Ath, *The Atlantis Blueprint: Unlocking the Ancient Mysteries of a Long-Lost Civilization* (N.Y.: Delacorte Press, 2001).

CHAPTER 10.
CLOSING IN ON THE ARK
OF THE COVENANT

1. Graham Phillips, *The Templars and the Ark of the Covenant: The Discovery of the Treasure of Solomon* (Rochester, Vt.: Bear & Company, 2004), 148.

CHAPTER 11.
THE MYSTERY OF THE CATHARS

1. Jean Markale, *Montségur and the Mystery of the Cathars* (Rochester, Vt.: Inner Traditions, 2003).

CHAPTER 12.
TODAY'S MEGALITH BUILDERS

1. Rob Roy, *Stone Circles: A Modern Builders Guide to the Megalithic Revival* (London: Chelsea Green, 1999).

CHAPTER 13.
THE TUTANKHAMUN PROPHECIES

1. Maurice Cotterell, *The Tutankhamun Prophecies: The Sacred Secret of the Maya, Egyptians, and Freemasons* (Rochester, Vt.: Bear & Company, 2001).

CHAPTER 14.
REMOTE VIEWING THE GREAT SPHINX

1. Paul H. Smith, *Reading the Enemy's Mind: Inside Star Gate; America's Psychic Espionage Program* (N.Y.: Forge Books, 2005), 111.

2. Joseph McMoneagle, *Mind Trek: Exploring Consciousness, Time, and Space Through Remote Viewing* (Newburyport, Mass.: Hampton Roads Publishing, 1993), 109.

3. McMoneagle, *Mind Trek,* 110.

4. Ingo Swann, *Natural ESP: The ESP Core and Its Raw Characteristics* (N.Y.: Bantam Books, 1987), 262.

5. Angela Thompson Smith, *Remote Perceptions: Out-of-Body Experiences, Remote Viewing, and Other Normal Abilities* (Newburyport, Mass.: Hampton Roads Publishing, 1998), 98.

6. Lyn Buchanan, *The Seventh Sense: The Secrets of Remote Viewing as Told by a "Psychic Spy" for the U.S. Military* (N.Y.: Gallery Books, 2003), 151.

7. Thompson Smith, *Remote Perceptions*, 49.

8. Kevin J. Todeschi, *Edgar Cayce on the Akashic Records* (Virginia Beach, Va.: A.R.E. Press, 1998), 190.

9. Smith, *Reading the Enemy's Mind,* 135.

10. Thompson Smith, *Remote Perceptions,* 134.

11. John Anthony West, *The Traveler's Key to Ancient Egypt: A Guide to Sacred Places* (Wheaton, Ill.: Quest Books, 1996), 152.

CHAPTER 15. THE BOOK OF LIVING AND DYING

1. Joann Fletcher, *The Egyptian Book of Living and Dying* (N.Y.: Chartwell Books, 2012).

CHAPTER 16. GODS OF EDEN

1. Andrew Collins, *Gods of Eden: Egypt's Lost Legacy and the Genesis of Civilization* (Rochester, Vt.: Bear & Company, 2002).

CHAPTER 17. THE VALLEY OF THE UFOS

1. Rogers Worthington, "UFOs Light Up Skies, But Only Questions Are Left Hovering," *Chicago Tribune,* July 9, 1987.

2. James M. Barlow, "UFOs: Seeing Is Believing for Local Resident," *Melrose Chronicle,* February 24, 1988.

3. Howard Blum, *Out There* (N.Y.: Pocket Star Books, 1991).

CHAPTER 19. ILLINOIS SACRED SITES

1. Charles Neely, *Tales & Songs of Southern Illinois: Timeless Folklore in Story & Verse* (Herrin, Ill: Crossfire Press, 1989).
2. Roger Biles, *Illinois: A History of the Land and Its People* (DeKalb: Northern Illinois University Press, 2005), 59.

CHAPTER 20. THE FORGOTTEN ENIGMAS OF KANSAS

1. Dennis Graf, "Rock City Still Baffles Experts," *Kansas City Star,* November 9, 1998.
2. Jim Brandon, *Weird America* (N.Y.: Plume, 1978).
3. David Hatcher Childress, *Lost Cities of North & Central America* (Kempton, Ill.: Adventures Unlimited Press, 1992), 231.

CHAPTER 21. THE SACRED AND PROFANE IN SOUTHERN WISCONSIN

1. August Derleth, *The Cthulhu Mythos* (1929; repr., N.Y.: Barnes & Noble, 1997).

CHAPTER 22. PREHISTORIC LANDSCAPE SCULPTURE OF THE MIDDLE WEST

1. George Constable, ed., *Mystic Places* (N.Y.: Time-life Books, 1987).

CHAPTER 23. ILLINOIS'S GOLD PYRAMID, IOWA'S GROTTO OF GEMS, AND TENNESSEE'S GREEK TEMPLE

1. Lori Erickson, *Iowa off the Beaten Path: A Guide to Unique Places* (Guilford, Conn.: Globe Pequot Press, 2010), 23. Quote is that of Father Louis Greving.

CHAPTER 24. THE INSCRUTABLE MYSTERIES OF CORAL CASTLE

1. Rusty McClure, *Coral Castle: The Mystery of Ed Leedskalnin and His American Stonehenge* (Dublin, Ohio: Ternary Publishing, 2009), 152.
2. McClure, *Coral Castle,* 150.
3. McClure, *Coral Castle,* 155.

4. McClure, *Coral Castle,* 155.

5. Vincent Gaddis, *Invisible Horizons* (N.Y.: Ace Books, 1965), 86.

6. Ray Stoner, *The Enigma of Coral Castle* (St. Petersburg, Fla.: Bradford Institute of Ultra Science, 1983).

7. Bruce Cathe, *The Energy Grid* (Kempton, Ill.: Adventures Unlimited Press, 1997), 112.

8. Stoner, *The Enigma of Coral Castle,* 43.

9. James Wyckoff, *Using Pyramid Power* (N.Y.: Kensington Pub., 1977), 79.

10. Cathe, *The Energy Grid,* 100.

CHAPTER 25. FOUR THOUSAND YEARS OF PROPHETS

1. Tony Allan, *Prophecies: Four Thousand Years of Prophets, Visionaries and Predictions* (San Francisco, Calif.: Thorsons, 2002).

CHAPTER 26. JULES VERNE, THE CLAIRVOYANT AUTHOR

1. Jules Verne, *Paris in the Twentieth Century* (Oakland, Calif.: Del Rey, 1997).

2. Verne, *Paris in the Twentieth Century,* 54.

3. Verne, *Paris in the Twentieth Century.*

4. Verne, *Paris in the Twentieth Century,* 134.

5. Verne, *Paris in the Twentieth Century,* 137.

6. Verne, *Paris in the Twentieth Century,* 139.

7. Verne, *Paris in the Twentieth Century,* 139.

8. Verne, *Paris in the Twentieth Century,* 141.

9. Verne, *Paris in the Twentieth Century,* 141.

10. Verne, *Paris in the Twentieth Century,* 144.

CHAPTER 27. AMAZING MOTHER SHIPTON

1. Diana Windsor, *Mother Shipton's Prophecy Book: The Story of Her Life and Her Most Famous Prophecies* (London: Ilex Leisure, 1996), 49.

2. Pauline Gregg, *King Charles I* (Oakland: University of California Press, 1984).

3. Windsor, *Mother Shipton's Prophecy Book,* 56.

4. Windsor, *Mother Shipton's Prophecy Book,* 61.

5. Windsor, *Mother Shipton's Prophecy Book*, 44.

6. Windsor, *Mother Shipton's Prophecy Book*, 50.

7. Windsor, *Mother Shipton's Prophecy Book*, 61.

CHAPTER 29. THE WORLD-SHATTERING SECRET OF SIR FRANCIS BACON

1. Tedi Trindle, "Return of the Vault People," *Piker Press*, April 4, 2014. www .pikerpress.com/article.php?aID=390.

2. Francis Bacon, *The Works of Francis Bacon: Lord Chancellor of England* (University of Michigan Library, 1825), 390.

3. Manly P. Hall, *The Secret Teachings of All Ages* (N.Y.: Tarcher-Perigee, 2003), 87.

CHAPTER 30. THE MAD COUNT OF ALTERNATIVE ARCHAEOLOGY

1. Byron Khun de Prorok, *In Quest of Lost Worlds* (Kempton, Ill.: Adventures Unlimited Press, 2002), 138.

CHAPTER 31. THE VISIONARY OF ATLANTIS

1. Ignatius Donnelly, diary entry, November 3, 1880. Ignatius Donnelly and Family Papers, Minnesota Historical Society, St. Paul.

2. Donnelly, diary entry, July 22, 1881.

3. Donnelly, diary entry, November 12, 1882.

4. Ignatius Donnelly, *Atlantis, the Antediluvian World* (N.Y.: Harper & Brothers, 1882).

5. J. Gerber, *Rome's Historian* (N.Y.: Pantheon Press, 1948), 222.

6. Plato, *Timaeus and Critias*, trans. Thomas Telford (N.Y.: Macmillan, 1880).

7. David Anderson, *Ignatius Donnelly* (Boston: Twayne Publishers, 1980), 133.

8. Abraham Lincoln, *Speeches and Writings, 1859–1865* (Washington, D.C.: Library of America, 1989), 126.

9. "Ignatius Donnelly, the Sage of Nininger," *St. Paul Dispatch,* February 27, 1882.

10. Leslie Guelcher, *A History of Nininger* (Stillwater, Minn.: Croixside Press, 1982), 67.

11. Larry Richard Peterson, *Ignatius Donnelly* (N.Y.: Arno Press, 1982), 71.

12. Ignatius Donnelly, *Ragnarok* (N.Y.: D. Appleton & Company, 1883).

13. Otto Muck, *The Secret of Atlantis* (N.Y.: Times Books, 1978).

14. E. F. Bleiler, introduction to *Atlantis, the Antediluvian World* (N.Y.: Dover Publications, 1976), 8.

15. Ignatius Donnelly, *Atlantis, the Antediluvian World* (N.Y.: Harper & Brothers, 1882), 68.

16. Donnelly, *Atlantis, the Antediluvian World,* 193.

17. Donnelly, diary entry, July 25, 1883.

18. Donnelly, *Atlantis, the Antediluvian World,* 241.

19. Lewis Spence, *The History of Atlantis* (1927; repr., N.Y.: University Books, 1968), 236.

20. Donnelly, *Atlantis, the Antediluvian World,* 144.

21. Donnelly, diary entry, August 5, 1889.

22. Donnelly, diary entry, February 3, 1884.

CHAPTER 32. SNAKE HANDLERS OF THE GODS

1. Arnobius, "Feasts of Raw Flesh," in *Seven Books Against the Heathens,* trans. Christian Classics Ethereal Library (Intra-Text Digital Library, 2003, Number 7). www.intratext.com/IXT/ENG1008.

2. Kathie Farnell, "Snakes and Salvation," *FATE,* vol. 49, no. 12, (Issue 560. December 1996): 28.

CHAPTER 33. THE MIRACULOUS MAYA SHAMANS

1. Alloa Patricia Mercier, *The Maya Shamans: Traveling in Time* (London: Vega, 2002).

CHAPTER 35. DEATH, THE GREAT MYSTERY OF LIFE

1. Herbie Brennan, *Death: The Great Mystery of Life* (N.Y.: Carroll & Graf Publishers, 2002).

2. Robert Herrick, "To the Virgins, to Make Much of Time," in *Complete Poetry of Robert Herrick* (N.Y.: W. W. Norton & Company, 1968).

CHAPTER 36. REINCARNATION AND THE DALAI LAMA

1. Enrique Florescano, *The Myth of Quetzalcoatl* (Baltimore, Md.: Johns Hopkins University Press, 1999).

2. John Lash, *The Seeker's Handbook* (N.Y.: Harmony Books, 1990), 211.
3. The Dalai Lama, *My Land and My People: The Original Autobiography of His Holiness the Dalai Lama of Tibet* (N.Y.: Grand Central Publishing, 1997), 174.
4. The Dalai Lama, *My Land and My People,* 174.
5. The Dalai Lama, *My Land and My People,* 209.

CHAPTER 37.
THE SECRET LIFE OF WATER

1. Masaru Emoto, *The Hidden Messages in Water* (N.Y.: Atria Books, 2005), 39.
2. John Lash, *The Seeker's Handbook* (N.Y.: Harmony Books, 1990), 162.
3. J. E. Cirlot, *Dictionary of Symbols* (N.Y.: Philosophical Library, 1962), 97.
4. Emoto, *The Hidden Messages in Water,* 107.
5. Emoto, *The Hidden Messages in Water,* 108.
6. "Masaru Emoto Events," Accessed November 30, 2017, www.emotoevents .com/events.

CHAPTER 38.
THE SOUL OF MATTER

1. Christian de Quincey, *Radical Nature: The Soul of Matter* (Rochester, Vt.: Park Street Press, 2010).
2. Bob Blaisdell, *Great Speeches by Native Americans* (N.Y.: Dover, 2000), 61.

CHAPTER 39.
THE FIRE FROM HEAVEN

1. Rupert Furneaux, *The Tungus Event* (San Francisco, Calif.: HarperCollins, 1977).

CHAPTER 40. JOURNEY
THROUGH THE UNEXPLAINED

1. Brad Steiger and Art Bell, *The Source: Journey through the Unexplained* (N.Y.: New American Library Trade, 2002), 159.

CHAPTER 41. EYEWITNESS
IN THE BERMUDA TRIANGLE

1. Andrew Raymond, interview by Frank Joseph, November 1990.
2. Andrew Raymond, interview by Frank Joseph, November 1990.

3. Stephanie Pappas, "World's Deepest Blue Hole Is in South China Sea," *LiveScience,* July 27, 2016, www.livescience.com/55568-deepest-blue-hole -in-south-china-sea.html.

CHAPTER 42.
COMMUNICATION WITH ELEMENTAL BEINGS

1. Marko Pogacnik, *Nature Spirits & Elemental Beings: Working with the Intelligence in Nature* (Moray, Scotland.: Findhorn Press, 2010).

Index

BOOKS OF RELATED INTEREST

Advanced Civilizations of Prehistoric America
The Lost Kingdoms of the Adena, Hopewell, Mississippians, and Anasazi
by Frank Joseph

The Lost Civilization of Lemuria
The Rise and Fall of the World's Oldest Culture
by Frank Joseph

Military Encounters with Extraterrestrials
The Real War of the Worlds
by Frank Joseph

Before Atlantis
20 Million Years of Human and Pre-Human Cultures
by Frank Joseph

Atlantis and the Coming Ice Age
The Lost Civilization—A Mirror of Our World
by Frank Joseph

Our Dolphin Ancestors
Keepers of Lost Knowledge and Healing Wisdom
by Frank Joseph

Lost Knowledge of the Ancients
A Graham Hancock Reader
Edited by Glenn Kreisberg

Forbidden History
Prehistoric Technologies, Extraterrestrial Intervention, and
the Suppressed Origins of Civilization
Edited by J. Douglas Kenyon

INNER TRADITIONS • BEAR & COMPANY
P.O. Box 388
Rochester, VT 05767
1-800-246-8648
www.InnerTraditions.com

Or contact your local bookseller